Aforethought

Since the late 1980's I've written about my family life and times in humorous columns for various newspapers and magazines, including the grand old Scottish morning newspaper The Press & Journal. To my amazement the columns proved quite popular and they were first published in book form in 2009 under the title, 'The Familiar' by the Edinburgh publisher Black & White.

Like all the best career moves the idea of writing a 'living autobiography' happened by accident. The first column was written to fill an unexpected hole in a newspaper. The deadline was tight so I used what was to hand, namely my family's move to the country, an event we are still recovering from. Before I knew it one column had turned into a thousand.

Most writers would have something better to do, but the truth is, when you get paid to air your dirty linen in public, it becomes addictive. The selection in this volume dates from 2011 to 2018 and marks my family's move from rural Scotland to the sunny south east coast of England.

Happily I've never stopped doing stupid things so I've always had plenty of material to work with. No barrel was ever scraped during the writing of these columns.

Roddy Phillips

Published by Bourne to Write
January 2019

First Edition
Text copyright © 2019
Roddy Phillips
All Rights Reserved
bournetowrite.co.uk

Front cover painting 'Miranda' by Catriona Millar

catrionamillar.com

**Bourne
toWrite…**
creative writing
workshops

To Lang
best wishes

Deedy Phillips
+.

Always for Catriona

Big Head

I've always had a big head. Nothing out of the ordinary that you could point at in the street or make a career out of but big enough to make hat wearing a consideration.

Photographic evidence shows a relatively hat free childhood apart from a school cap which was only really worn so that other boys could whip it off and throw it over garden walls.

My wife says I have a face for hats, just not the right sort of head. By 'sort' I assume she means 'size'.

Modern shaped hats are a particular fashion disaster. Anything tight and trendy transforms me into a scary monk-like figure. Even an ordinary hat with a brim is guaranteed to raise a laugh.

Last year in Spain however, I bought a straw cowboy hat. For some reason, possibly because my brain had been turned into a smoothie by the heat I thought I would be able to wear this hat without my family laughing hysterically.

I tried it on in the beach front shop and my wife gave it the thumbs up, although later she admitted the sun was in her eyes at the time and she hadn't really appreciated the full impact of what was happening.

I strolled around convinced I was in a Spaghetti western. Catching blurred reflections of myself in the pool or in windows I was relieved at how human I looked. Maybe my head was shrinking as I got older, I thought, or perhaps it was the intense heat.

Then I saw a photograph of myself and realised that because the hat was so big and the brim so wide I looked as if my face had grown a balcony.

When my wife tried on the hat it covered her head completely. In fact everyone who tried on the hat vanished. Eventually when trying on the hat for a laugh became a regular party routine I accidentally left it in a café and the following week had to lie down in a darkened room with sunstroke.

I should have guessed all of this because at one point I wore the cowboy hat while cycling and when I stopped next to a bus queue two old ladies stood underneath it to hide from the sun.

All of this came back to haunt me earlier this week in a bike shop. We'd bought a pair of folding bikes and my wife was telling the assistant about the cowboy hat. The whip thin boy laughed and reminded us that from a safety angle this wasn't a great idea.

"It kept the bike cool though, it was so big!" replied my wife and we all laughed, "so he'll need an extra extra large helmet," she added smartly.

The thin boy shook his head, apparently the biggest helmets in stock were large, anything bigger had to be ordered from a specialist supplier.

To some degree this sounded like good news. If I couldn't wear a helmet then I wouldn't be able to ride a bike, particularly a bike I'd have to continually fold and unfold and heave into the car boot.

"I don't remember wearing a crash helmet when I was young," I remarked.

"That's because your head was so big you probably couldn't get one to fit," replied my wife, then turning back to the assistant continued, "so how big are the large helmets?"

The boy looked at my head and I gave him a twirl.

"Well, your husband's head would have to be very big for a large helmet not to fit, I mean, they are quite generously accommodating," he said earnestly pulling one out from the display stand.

I tried it on and it perched on the top of my head like a huge bright red growth. My wife had to turn away so she could control herself, the boy meanwhile stared at me quizzically as if I was something he could fix given enough time and money.

The boy stroked his beard. Up until then I hadn't noticed he had a beard and now I saw him in a new more intellectual light.

"Would you mind if I measured your head?" he asked.

"Is it for research purposes?" I asked as he pulled a special paper measuring tape from the display stand.

I bent down and the tape was stretched round my head.

"Wow 61 centimetres!" declared the boy, "that is a big head, lots of brains though."

"Wow 61 centimetres!" echoed my wife, turning to an older couple who were both equally amazed.

Just to get our findings into perspective we then measured my wife's head and the skinny boy's. Both were around the 52 centimetre mark. So finally it was official – I have a big head.

After much deliberation I bought a large helmet that was adjustable, but when I speak it pops up and down on my head so it looks as if I'm suspended on a bungee rope. If my wife's riding behind me I can hear her laughing. Still as the assistant said, 'lots of brains though'.

Ye Dancin?

There had been some wild talk about going dancing and the 'C' word had been already been mentioned several times much to my alarm. Somehow I can't see myself in a Club unless it has plump leather armchairs that are smoother than a baby's cheek and silver service.

Of course I can't actually say I'm too old to go clubbing because then by implication my wife would be thrown into the same leaky boat. All I can do is plead injury, the latest being a very handy torn ligament in the sole of my right foot.

"Well you can just sit like some poor old soul and watch," said my wife.

While I shy away from causing a public disturbance with my 'old uncle at a wedding' dance routine my wife seems permanently on the verge of strutting her funky stuff. Apparently she still has her mojo and its in full working order, although I can't say I've ever seen it.

We had just passed a dance class and stopped to watch. Amnesty International need to know about the widespread abuse perpetrated by Strictly Come Dancing. The length and breadth of the country innocent people are building up a sweat while being subjected to old Joe Loss hits.

Suddenly the idea of going clubbing seemed very attractive, but up ahead there was obviously some street dancing in full swing. This is another curious development. Not content with dancing indoors people are now compelled to air their moves al fresco.

"Doesn't look very interesting to me," I said staring up the street at the jiggling figures, silhouetted in the dusky evening light.

"Come on!" shouted my wife, "it looks like fun, maybe we can join in."

You can imagine my delight at hearing this. But as we drew closer we began to wonder what exactly was going on. Three or four people were certainly moving in an agitated state, but there also appeared to be something on the ground, something large, black and immobile.

"Oh my God it's a man!" shouted my wife.

In fact his name was George and he was dressed in a black dinner suit and bowtie. He was lying perfectly still face upwards on the pavement while around him two women and two men performed a distressed two-step.

George looked about 75, in fact he was 91. His wife who was the calmer of the two ladies said he'd always had young looking skin and a thick head of hair, although it was now white.

He hadn't particularly looked after himself, he hadn't used moisturiser or any beauty products it was just a genetic fluke. That and the dancing of course, that was the real secret of his youthful appearance.

We were taking all of this in while I phoned an ambulance and my wife went into emergency first-aider mode. Under the streetlight George was starting to look very pale and he still hadn't responded to my wife's questions.

"Have you been out dancing George?" she asked.

"Yes we have," replied his wife, an elegant lady of indeterminate age with a Yorkshire accent, "just round the corner, it was a competition night," she continued.

The other couple and their friend were passersby who had seen George fall.

"One moment he was walking in front of us and the next he just crumpled." Said one of the women.

"We got the fright of our lives," said her partner, "we thought he'd cracked his head open, but there's no blood."

My wife hadn't moved George but she had gingerly undone his bowtie and his top button. Meanwhile I was going through the twenty-question triage routine on the phone.

Suddenly my wife interrupted. George was breathing but his pulse was weak and my wife recommended we undo his clothing, particularly his trousers and his cumberbund, which were very tight and restricting his blood flow.

I decided I would break the news to his wife.

"George seems to be fine but we'll have to take his trousers off," I said gently.

"His trousers!" she declared, "I haven't had his trousers off for thirty years!" then turning to the other woman she said, "they want to take his trousers off in the street, do you think that's a good idea, I don't think George would like it."

My wife stepped in and complemented me on my negotiating skills and then ensured everyone that she was only going loosen George's trousers and remove his cumberbund so he could breath more easily.

There was a brief discussion and then my wife went to work, struggling first with George's belt and then his waistband fastener. I stood back deciding I was more effective in an ancillary role.

"Right," said my wife, "I'm just going to undo your trousers George."

Suddenly George sat bolt upright, stared at my wife with a slightly wicked smile and said very slowly, "help yourself love."

My wife jumped with fright and George looked up and round at the concerned faces gazing down at him.

"Did we win?" he asked.

In fact they came third. But I'm happy to report that in the end George was a winner.

Mule Train

I never really understood the nursery rhyme about the Grand Old Duke of York and his ten thousand men being neither up nor down until a few days ago when we arrived at our holiday cottage in Ambleside.

On the holiday cottage website it mentioned the house was a short walk up a lane, but the word 'up' is obviously more subjective than I thought. In my mind there isn't really much 'up' involved in going up a lane. Likewise going down a lane wouldn't necessarily involve falling flat on your face.

In the Lake District the word 'up' has a more literal meaning, which you would think we would have the hang of by now.

But when we stopped at the bottom of the characterful lane my first thought was how I was going to squeeze the car up such a narrow road.

"I don't think that's a road," said my wife, "I think that's the lane to the house."

"Not a lane to a mountain?" I suggested.

This lane branched off from a wider lane that runs between a bank and a Thai restaurant and leads to a popular wooded waterfall walk, which is also basically vertical. A lot of stuff in the Lake District is vertical, it should really indicate that somewhere in the name.

My wife was reading the directions but I still didn't believe her. Obviously we had taken a wrong turn. So we drove all the way round Ambleside's charming one-way system again and five minutes later we were staring up at the same lane and heaving a unified sigh.

"But it's sheer," I croaked.

"Indeed," said my wife as we sat there sharing a vision of us driving a pack of mules loaded with our belongings up the vertiginous lane. There was a branch of the St John Ambulance at the bottom of the lane, which was looking handier by the second.

"In other parts of the world they have an ingenious system called steps," I mused, then added, "actually it doesn't look that bad you know."

If I was trying to convince myself I was failing miserably, although I could see why hillwalkers would hire the place. They would get a warm up every time they went out for a pint of milk.

"So where's the parking space?" asked my wife.

Having been faced with the prospect of roping up and getting the pitons out I'd completely forgotten about the parking space, which in cramped Ambleside was probably worth its weight in anoraks.

We found the space an unhelpful 800 yards from the bottom of the vertical lane and unless I had a bendy circus car it was inaccessible thanks to a permanently parked white van and an even more permanent wall of Cumbrian slate.

That was when I had my Grand Old Duke of York moment.

'Neither up nor down..." I announced.

On the second or maybe it was the third trip round the one way system I'd spotted a house called 'On't Top, In't Middle' and I thought 'that's how we get to it – from the top down.

The holiday house may have been on't top but it was also in't middle of a preposterously steep lane that snaked further up before disappearing behind some bushes.

I had to climb the vertical lane to prove my theory but five minutes later and almost on my hands and knees I emerged out onto a perfectly flat road lined with guesthouses boasting commanding views of the village and the surrounding vertical landscape. It was almost worth the crawl.

I had to ask a lady walking her dog what the road was called and how to get to it but I was elated. In fact I think I now know how mountaineers feel when they've taken a fresh summit. If only I'd had a flag.

I ran back down to my wife with the news - I had to run basically because of the gravitational pull.

So we drove round Ambleside again, in fact twice again because I missed the opening the first time but eventually we were on't top and wheeling our luggage gingerly down the lane.

Getting back up to the car was the knackering bit but after the twentieth time my legs went numb and they seemed to move of their own volition.

All that work must have dulled our senses because it was at least half an hour before we realised the house smelled of fish, which wasn't really what we were hoping for.

The fridge and the freezer hadn't been cleaned but then there were no towels, soap or toilet paper, but one thing was for sure, after abseiling the contents of our car down into the place we weren't moving in a hurry. Like the Grand Old Duke of York's men we were neither up nor down.

A large Viking lady from the holiday home company turned up with a tiny cleaner I think she'd caught trying to escape.

"I can't smell fish, can you?" she shrieked at the cleaner who shook her head nervously, "no, not fish!"

"Must have been our imagination," replied my wife.

Apparently there were no pack mules to be hired either.

The Bike Shaped Hole

I could tell something was wrong the moment I stepped out of the door. Which was strange because I couldn't see anything untoward, it was more of an atmosphere, or to be precise a change in atmosphere.

When our boys were young I would sometimes walk into their room and I would know something had just happened. The boys would appear to be playing happily but a few seconds earlier a banana might have been shoved into the video recorder or a flurry of punches and nips exchanged.

Freud would have said I'd heard something almost imperceptible and that's why I went into the room in the first place and he would probably have been right, cigar or no cigar.

Standing at our front door on Monday morning all I could see was the usual view, but maybe I'd glimpsed something out of the corner of my eye.

My wife appeared beside me and for no particular reason asked if everything was OK.

"I don't think so," I replied ominously, "but I'm not sure why."

At first I wondered if it was the car, but I could see it was still there and it appeared to be intact, but I was getting warm. Walking round the front of the car I spotted one of our new bike chains lying on the ground. Unfortunately there wasn't a bike attached to it. The other bike stood proud and unsullied.

"Oh no, your bike's been stolen!" shouted my wife when she joined me.

Baffled I stared at the lonely bike chain.

"What makes you think it was my bike that was stolen, they' are literally identical after all?" I asked.

"Fairly obvious isn't it?" replied my wife enigmatically waving her hand at the scene, "luck of the draw I suppose, anyway no use crying over spilled milk."

When something extraordinary happens like getting your bike nicked from outside your own front door it takes a little time for your brain to catch up because it's set so firmly in trust mode.

But once it's got the idea that a barrier has been broken anything seems possible. Maybe the house will get nicked, most definitely the car because it can be driven away, in fact anything that can be moved will now be stolen in the middle of the night or while we're out.
My wife said this was a normal reaction. I was in shock, soon it would turn to dark terrible thoughts of revenge which would eventually condense into a single small grey cloud of grief from which there would be no escape.

I'd only had my fold-up bike for a week but we had bonded and I'd learned to love it. I'd even forgiven it for allowing me to fall off when I scratched my nose and lost my balance.

For a full week we had diligently folded our bikes and taken them into the house for safekeeping but we got lazy after a particularly long cycle and thought we'd try out the sturdy locks we'd bought.

We spent half an hour putting them on and taking them off, wrapping them around the fence post and up and round various parts of the bikes. It's tricky making a folding a bike secure because it breaks into various sections through which a chain can easily be pulled.

In the end we were satisfied that nothing human would be capable of freeing the bikes, not without the aid of heavy duty equipment. Although removing the fence post was an option.

Since they survived the first night and it was dry we left them out the following night and hey presto we managed to lose one of them.

My wife was all for sorting out the mess that had been left – my chain was in bits on the ground but I didn't think it was a good idea.

"Better not touch anything," I declared holding my arms out, "this is a crime scene!"

My wife laughed but I was on the phone and about to make an official report.

"They'll want to take fingerprints," I continued.

In fact the police resisted it, although I'm sure they were tempted, particularly when I told them how new the bike was.

Still they did advise me to keep an eye out for it, which I've been doing with growing enthusiasm. In fact anyone found riding a navy blue Raleigh Swift better have their receipt at the ready.

Amazingly this is the first thing I've ever had stolen and I'm finding it hard to come to terms with. My wife is in a similar position although she did remember that once she had a Milky Way stolen and she was upset right through double geography.

Anyway I've bought another bike, which I'm now sleeping with but it will never be the same. I have a bike shaped hole in my life, which I'd love to transfer to the person who created it.

Lobster Man

I think I might be going through what my mother would have referred to in hushed reverential tones as 'the change'. Although it might not be the change she had in mind. It's more likely to be something more on the comic book side.

"So what is it you think your changing into?" asked my wife with a pinch of interest, "some kind of big scaly reptile type thing, Lizard Man perhaps or just the plain old Thing?"

I was looking at the soles of my feet, which had metamorphosed over night from my reasonably ordinary feet to those of a red, scaly amphibious being, possibly from another planet.

On this distant planet there would be no need for shoes, the inhabitants would roam barefoot over the boiling surface, diving occasionally into steaming pools for food.

"Maybe it's a genetic race memory," suggested my wife, "I would ask the pharmacist, see what they say."

The previous day I'd noticed a slight rash on my right wrist. The sort you might get if you brushed against a stinging plant. I thought nothing of it until a few hours later it when I spotted it on both wrists.

Obviously something had irritated me yet the rash seemed inert and for two days it enjoyed the confined space of my wrists, imperceptibly changing shape and direction so that in the morning it was like a bangle and by lunchtime it was a tight little oval of a constellation that in the evening on my right wrist, seemed to spell the word 'YOU'.

My wife peered at it disbelievingly then jumped back letting my hand go. In the mirror it read UOY.

"Maybe it's an acronym," I pondered, "I wonder what it stands for?"

"Hopefully it's not a prophecy forewarning me of the shape of things to come," said my wife who now thought it read YEN.

Just as well I photographed it with my phone because by bedtime it had changed again into an elongated vortex, which I've heard is the natural order of all things, even mysterious rashes.

The central theory that it was a sweat rash never really took root with me. I've had rashes similar to this in the past and they were a result of antibiotics or washing powder, neither of which applied on this occasion. But then I've never had a rash that could spell.

At one point I put my wrists together and the red dots appeared to make the shape of numbers, possibly it was some kind of countdown.

The pharmacist peered hard at it and agreed.

"Is that a nine?" she asked.

"Maybe it's a phone number," I ventured, "or the number to a safety deposit box?"

"Probably just an allergic reaction of some sort," replied the pharmacist smartly, obviously remembering she had better things to do than stand and discuss my numerically inclined rash.

"Been weeding recently?" she added.

Actually I had. But then I'd also handled a number of exotic rugs and when moving them my wrists had rubbed against them.

We settled on the rugs with a hint of weed thrown in just to be on the safe side.

The diagnosis was to leave the rash to its own devices while keeping a casual but not too obsessed eye on it. Advice several people chorused. One person told me to relax and not to think about it because that would make it worse.

"So if I had a broken leg and thought about it, you reckon it would get worse?" I asked, just trying to clarify the point.

"Absolutely!" they replied, "don't do anything rash."

I went away thinking about that, rather than the rash, which was probably what they meant.

Driving home the steering wheel suddenly felt different, possibly slightly distant, it was difficult to put my finger on it, literally. At a set of traffic lights the palms of my hands appeared to glow red in sympathy and my fingers looked swollen.

The rash had marshalled its forces and was on the move, rapidly invading my palms and fingers before my very eyes. By the time I reached home it had pitched camp on my lower arms in preparation I imagined for the main assault on my shoulders and chest.

"Weird!" intoned my wife as she examined it, "strange how its spreading up both sides of your arms simultaneously, you'd almost think it had a plan."

I tried not to think about the plan. Just as well because by the following morning the plan had been thrown out and a new strategy was underway involving the soles of my feet. Basically I was being invaded from two ends, it was a classic pincer action.

There was also the scaly dimension to deal with which was threatening to turn me into Lobster Man.

Pharmacist number two also came up with weeds and I volunteered the rugs. Dr Google recommended an anti-histamine.

I'm going to give the rash a chance to clear off before resorting to the GP. Having said that I might be tearing up bridges and devastating major cities by then.

Unappealing

I was waiting for my wife outside a shop, casually unpeeling the palm of my left hand when I realised I was being watched. Two small boys and a smaller dog stared up at me with a blank yet focused interest.

Their grandfather meanwhile sucked on his Vape unconcerned. Strawberry I think it was. A man shedding his skin in public was obviously nothing compared to the stuff he had seen and judging from his face he had seen quite a lot of it.

One of the little boys started to say something but his brother nudged him into silence and the dog barked. I'd found a particularly compliant section of skin on the heel of my hand and was steadily unpeeling it like a price sticker from a book.

It had to be teased out of itself and convinced that leaving the home it had grown up into was a good idea. For the moment it was playing hard to get, but that would change and eventually it hit the deck with the rest of its pals.

"Is that painful?" asked one of the little boys, unable to keep it in any longer.

"Of course its painful," said his brother with that 'don't ask stupid questions' edge in his voice.

"Actually its not," I said.

"Why is it not?" asked the first little boy.

"Is it skin?" asked his brother.

"It sure is," I said, tugging at another strip, which also wasn't ready to let go. Sometimes it's like that. I think - here's a really great bit that's going to come off a treat, like a strip of wallpaper - but I get so far and then it won't budge.

"Is it glue?" asked boy number one and the dog barked again.

"I'm afraid it's definitely skin," I replied.

The grandfather looked over for a moment and checked his watch.

"Why are you taking it off?" asked the older brother.

It was a question I had asked myself many times over the past few days.

"Because my wife won't let me do it in the house," I said, unpeeling a sizeable strip from the side of my right thumb.

"He's like a snake," growled the grandfather suddenly between puffs, making us all turn and look at him, "he's a snake man changing his old skin for a new one."

The little boys looked back at me for confirmation.

"It's more of a Dr Who kind of thing," I said, "you know, like when Dr Who regenerates and turns into a younger actor you've never heard of so you stop watching it for a while."

The boy's mother appeared from the shop, glanced at my paper birch hands and silently led her sons to a place of greater safety. They both looked back at me and the dog barked.

I hadn't intended to turn into a sideshow but it's hard when your hands are constantly unappealing. Shop assistants for instance don't like it. In one department store the girl who served me glanced at my flaky mitts and dangled my receipt at arm's length while managing to look simultaneously repelled and sympathetic.

In another shop an over chatty assistant informed me her sister was also an excema sufferer.

"Oh its not excema!" I snapped, "it's an allergic reaction, I've actually never had excema."

She must have thought the allergic reaction had also affected my mind. She probably wasn't the only one. At an important meeting I decided to wear surgical gloves to avoid shedding skin across someone else's boardroom table.

It's funny how bright blue surgical gloves clash with a business suit. Suddenly I looked like a doctor about to give everyone in the room a very private examination. For some reason no one wanted to shake my hand.

"It just started with a few red spots on each wrist," I explained making everyone spread themselves further round the table, "at one point it started to spell words and numbers."

"Is it contagious?" someone asked.

"I don't think so," I said, "I just hope this blue colour isn't permanent."

Everyone laughed and moved to a safe distance.

My wife was more concerned about the mess.

"Look at all this skin!" she declared pointing at the kitchen floor, "is this yours?"

What could I say? As far as I was aware there was no one else in the house in the throes of a dramatic skin change.

"Honestly!" continued my wife, "you need to man up, women do this all the time, it's called exfoliating."

"This is not a beauty treatment!" I replied.

My wife grabbed one of my flaking hands and stared at it.

"No kidding," she said.

I'm assuming the peeling will stop once the top layer's completely gone. Until then I'm sticking with the surgical gloves. If nothing else they guaranteed me plenty of space on the train. .

The Hatch

Tradesmen we have decided are like buses, you can wait for hours, sometimes days, even weeks for one to come and then ten of them come all at once. Maybe it is some kind of herding instinct, certainly earlier this week they were all herding in our house.

At one point we had every trade covered apart from an electrician and then as if by magic one turned up with spotlights we had ordered. Suddenly we had a full set, or rather a full house, then ten minutes later we had a full loft.

It was like a version of the old joke about how many tradesmen does it take to change a light bulb or in our case, find an escape hatch in our loft.

Just two days earlier it started with a rather interesting shadow on our bedroom wall. The fact that the shadow had been in the same position since we moved our bed for the decorators didn't bother us. Perhaps we were in denial, but more likely just plain stupid.

Dougie the painter however, was bothered by the shadow. He kept switching on and off the light and standing in front of the window.

"Look!" he announced at one point, holding his arms out and flapping them as we stared at the wall, "now that's a shadow!"

His partner Paul nodded in agreement and echoed Dougie's movements so they looked like shadowy song and dance men.

We like double acts, it facilitates banter and if you're lucky, sometimes you get two for the price of one.

Then it rained heavily overnight and the shadow turned into the dampest shadow we've ever touched. We had a leaky roof.

Just to balance things out we also had leaky radiators so a 'Dougie recommended plumber' was phoned along with 'Dougie recommended roofers'.

Curiously we had already phoned a 'Dougie recommended joiner' to install a Ramsay ladder so we could have easy access to our loft, and even more curiously it was screwed in place just minutes before the 'Dougie recommended roofers' arrived.

"You'd almost think the whole thing had been planned!" beamed my wife.

"Absolutely!" I agreed almost bouncing with joy as the house filled up with tradesmen. Only later did I begin to think how neatly the whole thing had fitted together.

At the time, we were in full 'fix it' mode. We had a leaky roof and we would need a scaffold tower to inspect it properly.

"No problem!" we shouted "bring one in!"

"It'll be three hundred quid," intoned Dale the head roofer, "a day."

"Bring one in..." we moaned through gritted teeth.

But then there was some tense stubble stroking and exciting talk about an escape hatch in the loft, which might lead to the roof. If we could find it there would be no need for the three hundred quid tower.

"Hurrah!" we chorused, even though I had never seen an escape hatch in the loft. Still sometimes you just get carried along with a crowd and you have to go with it.

Dale led the way up our new Ramsay ladder followed by his partner Tommy and then myself making excuses for the department store of stuff they were about to encounter.

Dougie, Paul and to my surprise and delight Gary the electrician followed. Sam the plumber was last up.

There's a single lightbulb in the loft so most of it was in spooky darkness. As we moved around bumping into one another and making our apologies we had to bob and weave under the beams and up and over the clutter.

This, I thought, is what it must have been like below decks on a ship of the fleet at Trafalgar. Except of course we would have been well aware of the gun hatch's location. Eventually we all collected in the centre of the loft at the top of the Ramsay ladder with nothing to report.

"Do you think it's safe having seven blokes in a loft?" I asked as the timbers creaked worryingly around us.

There was a silence while everyone visualised themselves crashing through the ceiling in an avalanche of breaking bones. Dougie was first down, swiftly followed by his partner Paul and then Gary the electrician.

Just as I was about to step onto the ladder I spotted a break in the roof timbers and some dangling rope. It was the hatch. We'd been looking for something mansize but in fact it had been cut in the roof so that a time-served monkey could nip out and do any necessary repairs.

The roofers stared at it until Dale sighed and got down on his knees and began opening it. Like a potholer he went through it leading with an outstretched arm. Five minutes later we were back down in the hallway, loft sealed up again and discussing the repairs. Everything now seemed to be going to plan.

Then my phone rang.

"That's the valve fixed," announced Sam, "should I just stay up here in case anything else leaks?"

I looked at my wife.

"It would be handy, keeping a plumber in the loft," she admitted.

The house emptied surprisingly quickly after that.

Facercises

You would think that after all this time my wife would know whether or not I brushed myself down before having a shower. But then as she often tells me, you need an element of mystery in a marriage.

What you don't need is a big brush scudding across your birthday suit of a morning, not unless you've specifically requested it.

"But it's so good for you," insisted my wife enthusiastically, "so energising and reviving."

The 'but', tells you how concerned I must have looked. Although I don't know what was alarming me the most, the fact that my wife wasn't sure if I was a pre-shower brushing kind of guy, or that she had obviously tried it herself and found it a rewarding experience.

After giving it a few seconds thought I wondered if it was something you could do in pairs, like mid-sauna birching. But apparently I was never going to find out.

I forgot all about it until I discovered a rather luxurious brush in the shower, the sort of thing a gentleman would use to put a mirror finish on his shoes. Aha, I thought, this explains why my wife always has such an enviable youthful glow.

It also explained why after giving myself a vigorous brushing I was beaming like a human torch. However, I was so pleased with the result I forgot to have a shower, but I do remember thinking it seemed unlikely that my father would ever have buffed himself with a big shoe brush. I also wondered if I should have worked down from my shoulders and missed out my face.

We were in the car when my wife was struck suddenly by the high sheen of my profile and for a moment considered using me as a mirror to retouch her make-up.

"Flipping heck!" she exclaimed, "we are a shiny new person today."

I took this as a compliment and smugly confessed that I had made friends with the shower brush.

I was expecting noisy approval but my wife just stared at me like a lipless goldfish. I was mesmerised, but thankfully she returned to normal in time to warn me that I was hurtling towards a red light.

"I hope your not going to make a habit of that," I said, twitching in my seat.

"Just three times a day," she replied, then pursed her lips tightly together like a disapproving old spinster.

A car pulled up in the inside lane and the driver was just getting interested when my wife relaxed and declared that she felt much better.

I was greatly relieved to hear this, but even more relieved when she told me that I didn't have to brush my face anymore to achieve that youthful healthy glow.

"Facercises," she announced, "that's what you need to do."

I gave her my version of the disapproving old spinster and she congratulated me for making such an admirable first attempt.

"Well done," she said, "now purse your lips even tighter together and imagine you're crushing a pencil in the middle of them."

I did as I was told, but had to be reminded to keep breathing. Then I had to count to thirty-five until I felt a burning sensation in my upper lip. Which I did, and although it was not entirely pleasant it was certainly preferable to a close-up confrontation with the shower brush.

When I glanced in my rear view mirror I was amazed to find I was wearing someone else's mouth, my lips had literally changed shape and now appeared fuller and more defined.

That was because, my wife explained, I had just performed my first lip shaper exercise, just one of the many natural facelift techniques devised by the American Facercise guru Carole Maggio – 'So easy you can do them in the car'.

Apparently if I continued my Facercise routine for just six weeks I could end up looking like Mick Jagger.

This was too good an offer to turn down, so that evening I sneaked off with my wife's copy of the 'Facercise' book and got down to some serious training in front of the bathroom mirror.

I thought I'd better do a warm up first because I didn't want to wake up in the morning with a permanently pulled face. Carole herself demonstrates some of her easier Facercises on the cover of the book as a teaser, so I copied these.

Pulling a set of faces with her fingers massaging the appropriate muscles, Carole looks as if she's doing a strange version of deaf sign language. If I could have deciphered it I was fairly certain she was saying something like, 'Thankyou for paying £7.99 for this book you wally."

But I decided it was worth it if I was going to be mistaken for Mick Jagger – in his prime of course. Plus, if it worked it was going to be a lot cheaper than a facelift.

I had already mastered the Lip Shaper and was well on the way to developing a nice juicy pout, so next on my list was the Face Slimmer, or the Grampa Broon with his falsers out. All I had to do was open my mouth and forcefully roll my lips over my teeth and then pull the corners of my mouth backwards to my back teeth and roll them in tightly.

This is a lot scarier than it sounds and after frightening myself in the mirror for the allotted thirty-five seconds I decided it would be better if I didn't see what I was doing. But to be honest I didn't mind anyone else seeing me and since Carole has thoughtfully designed many of her Facercises to be done in the car I've now been driving around for the past week looking like a complete lunatic.

You've got to pick your moments though. Particularly if you're practising a Facercise like the Nose Shortener, which involves doing press-ups with the tip of your nose against your forefinger.

After a few days I found I had all the satisfaction of doing a rigorous workout, but with none of the pain. At last I had found the perfect keep-fit regime that would roll back the years, if only from the neck up.

As usual I spoke too soon, or I would have done if I could have moved my jaw because one afternoon I suddenly felt as if my face had gone to the gym for a month and my body had stayed at home with its feet up.

When my wife saw me she jumped and shouted, "blimey for a moment I thought it was Mick Jagger!"

The trouble is, I'm now hooked on Facercises, probably because the adrenaline rush is literally going straight to me head. Nothing to do with vanity of course.

The Crooning Canine

Of all the things my wife and I have discussed at four in the morning the singing dog is probably one of the most unusual. It didn't exactly wake me up last Friday night, I was on a bladder run, but it certainly kept me awake.

I thought it was howling, but my wife decided it was singing.

"Listen!" she said, grabbing my arm, "it's singing Somewhere over the rainbow, skies are blue..."

I was more interested in where the dog was singing rather than its repertoire.

There are several small dogs in our vicinity, namely a cocky Jack Russell a couple of pampered poodles and a one-eyed Collie, but so far none of them have shown any talent in the X Factor department. This crooning canine however, had a genuine gift for holding a tune between its teeth and worrying it half to death.

"Why doesn't the owner tell it to be quiet?" I muttered into the dark.

"Maybe they like it," muttered my wife back, "maybe they've had it specially trained."

"I wonder if it does requests?" I said.

But my wife was asleep. Which was a pity because the howling hound had dropped an octave and turned into a light baritone. I was expecting great things, a medley perhaps from Tails of Hoffman.

I tried reading but my mind was continually drawn into making musical sense of the wailing dog's performance. At one point I would have sworn it started strangling the Beetles song, 'Its Been a Hard Day's Night'

It was then I began to wonder if it was some kind of recording. We once lived next door to a bloke who surprised us with a spontaneous dog. Ronnie had a home office through the wall from my study and one morning a dog arrived to keep him company, a loud yapping dog that was so persistent I went round to speak to Ronnie but he was out.

It turned out to be his computer screen saver, which he had accidentally left on with the volume full up. He presented it to me it with a certain amount of pride when I went round that evening.

"What do you think?" he asked, beaming at a cartoon puppy romping and barking all over his screen, "amazing eh?"

It was amazing all right, amazing that I hadn't dug my way through the wall and deleted the digital pest.

I was lying thinking about this while the pining pooch went into a rendition of what sounded like 'Tie a Yellow Ribbon round the old oak tree.' I'll be tying a yellow ribbon round your neck if I find you.' I thought, through gritted teeth.

The following morning it all seemed like some strange dream, but unfortunately it wasn't.

"I thought it was very plaintive," said my wife, nodding over her coffee, "haunting but very plaintive."

I don't have any singing dog CDs in my collection so I had nothing to compare it with. It certainly haunted me, but when it started up again around 2am the following morning I was ready for it.

A quick sortie round the house revealed that the dog was located directly below our bedroom window, which didn't make sense because we have no neighbours at the front of the house.

Obviously the sound was being carried on the wind. It was a very windy night and even through my earplugs I could still faintly hear the dog whining away like some madman playing the saw.

After a weekend of the canine serenader I made enquiries at the local post office where a customer informed me they had a dog that sang in the middle of night. Mystery solved I thought, until they told me it died twenty years ago.

"What does it sound like?" asked an old lady cocking an ear in my direction.

"Like a dog singing," I replied matter of factly.

I'm not that stupid. Within minutes the word would have been out that I had been howling in the post office.

I thought my little investigation had done the trick because the Hound of the Basketcases had a couple of nights off, but then it was back on Tuesday around midnight.

I could hear it doing its worst right outside the front door, so I switched on the external lights and grabbed an umbrella just for good measure. The blast of icy wind knocked me sideways, I stood my ground but the dog had bolted.

The second I closed the door it was back, howling and running up and down the scales like a pooch possessed.

"It's the wolf at the door!" declared my wife from behind me.

Or at least it was the wind howling through the doorframe and doing an impression of a wolf.

Six feet of spongy draught excluder round the inside of the door and the singing dog was gone. Shame really, the singing door had less impact at the post office, apparently everybody had one.

One lady even had singing windows, "some nights its like the cats' chorus!" she said.

I'll stick with the door.

The Gloves

There are obviously certain words that men can't hear. 'Can you pick that up' I imagine are the five most popular. Generally speaking anything to do with womanly pursuits comes high on the list.

So when my wife asked me to buy moisturising gloves from

the supermarket I just heard the word, gloves. Apparently she had also said they were white cotton gloves but that probably just confused me so that vital piece of information was also filtered out and duly deleted long before it got anywhere near my brain.

I have a certain amount of history shopping in supermarkets for my wife. Normally I'll get a detailed list of items with either illustrations of the products or the actual packaging. Sometimes I'll even get a map of the store marking the exact location of the items. I've seen other blokes walking around dazed with similar directions and occasionally we'll meet up and swap hints and tips.

Just to keep us on our toes the supermarket will shuffle things around at night so even the day staff don't know where things are. "That's funny," they'll say, "they were here yesterday" then they go off and you never see them again. My theory is they go and ask a manager for assistance and then they have to sign the official secrets act.

Apparently stuff gets moved around so we'll pass things we never saw before and instantly buy them. In fact this is normally how I find really handy stuff I've never heard of that I didn't realise I needed.

My wife didn't bother with a shopping list this time, she said she didn't need anything then as I left she shouted about half a dozen things down the hallway and one of them was gloves. She then thought better of it and quickly retracted all the items apart from the mysterious gloves.

That was how they ended up, a pair of mysterious gloves.

I had my own manly shopping list, not actually written down, that would be far too sensible and organised, which is why I always forget half the things I need. At some point although probably not in the long run I think this saves me money so if I go home without sellotape for the third time in a row, who cares? I'm a fiver up and that's the main thing.

Once I'd bought all my stuff I started wandering around repeating the words 'mysterious gloves' to myself like a mantra, probably in the hope that if I said it enough times they would eventually present themselves to me as if by magic.

The previous week I'd had a problem with the word 'fad' on one of my wife's shopping lists. Up until then it had been a particularly good outing to the supermarket, I'd found absolutely everything right down to the last detail, but this 'fad' thing was really annoying me.

Again I kept saying it over and over hoping it would suddenly make sense but in the end I gave up and showed it to an assistant.

She was sporting the sort of microphone that you see popstars wearing when they're in concert so there was a chance we were going to have a bit of a sing song or even more promisingly she was in touch with a higher power that monitored daft blokes like me who were having a spot of shopping bother.

She looked at the list for a moment and then laughed to herself.

"Are you on a health kick?" she asked, raising her eyebrows at the amount of salads and fruit in the trolley.

"We've got rabbits," I replied flatly.

"We've got one," she replied, "well the kids have."

"Great, so what do you think of the word 'fad' any idea what that might be?" I asked.

"Fad," she said, "like a food fad maybe?"

Another assistant passed so she was shown the message list for a second opinion.

"Healthy eating day is it?" she asked pointing at my trolley.

"They keep rabbits," said the assistant with the microphone.

The other assistant gave a semi-interested nod and looked at the shopping list again.

"Maybe it's an acronym?" I suggested and made the assistant wince.

"My old man had one of them, dead painful it was," she said.

Another assistant arrived and she was now shown the list.

"Farthest Away Date," she announced and walked on.

A light suddenly switched on in my head, albeit a very faint one, more like an energy saving light really because I could vaguely remember my wife chanting 'farthest away date' at me on several occasions. But to be honest it was another three words that I couldn't hear properly.

"I'll have to go and change most of this stuff," I said to the assistants, 'the rabbits are very fussy."

Compared to dealing with enigmatic acronyms I reckoned

buying mysterious gloves would be a doddle but the gardening section proved a waste of time so I tried the women's clothing department and asked an assistant but she was baffled.

"They're white and I think they're made of cotton," I said, "my wife wears them when she does her Michael Jackson impression."

The assistant laughed and said they were moisturising gloves and that I would find them downstairs beside the moisturisers.

Quite how the two words - moisturising and gloves, had any business being together was beyond me. It was also beyond me finding them so yet again I had to ask an assistant for help.

She was speaking to a group of teenage boys when I interrupted and tried to ask her quietly where I could find them.

"Sorry?" she asked, so I mumbled again.

"Oh moisturising gloves!" she shouted, "this way Sir!"

The teenage boys giggled and sneered en masse as we passed .

In the next aisle the assistant pointed to the gloves so I thanked her and took a pair. Then she sidled up to me.

"Are they for you Sir?" she whispered suddenly, "because they're not very big."

"We've got rabbits," I said.

"Lovely," she replied and sped off.

Computery

When you come home and you're met by someone wearing a grave expression telling you that something terrible has happened I think you're entitled to think the worst.

I'd bustled into the house humming away to myself. I'd been at a theatre reviewing one of those jolly pop musicals about American High School teenagers who have an astonishing facility for singing and grinning in perfect harmony.

My wife on the other hand was the picture of discord. There were a few tense moments of expectant silence before she broke the vaguest of bad news.

Caught on the hop I was thrown into full terror mode and started running through my stock repertoire of disaster scenarios starring the usual cast of my wife and sons in the lead roles and the rest of our family and friends in supporting character parts. This can take many forms, from horrible accidents to natural disasters, but there's never a happy ending.

Once that's out of the way then the house gets it, the roof or the floor caves in, the boiler blows up and the garden disappears down an old mine shaft. This spreads out in a domino effect to encompass the village, the town, the world and eventually, before its too late my wife will tell me what's actually happened and I'll say, 'is that all!'

As a rule always think the worst and it will probably never happen, or as Brecht said, 'the man who laughs has not yet heard the terrible news'.

But there was something about the look on my wife's face that told me I might be wasting my time in the dread and doom department. Behind the look of complete dismay there was a glimmer of guilt and I was just about to ask what she'd done when she blurted it out.

"It's the computer!" she snarled, by which she meant her new pink Netbook. A mini-laptop that is so cute it could have 'My First Computer' written all over it.

It had been bought after a certain amount of discussion – actually about 10 years worth, in an attempt to disengage my wife ever so slightly from the 17th century. I knew it was going to be tricky because they didn't have computers in the 17th century but the main thing was the Netbook was small and a delicious colour, which meant my wife couldn't resist touching it maybe even opening it.

Or as I suspected dropping it. But to be honest I couldn't have cared less, no one had died and the house seemed to be intact.

"So have you broken it?" I asked casually, taking my jacket off. My wife looked perplexed, apparently the computer was fine and I was being cheeky for assuming such a thing. The problem it seemed was the story she had been working on for the following day's writers' workshop.

"It was almost finished," she said darkly, "and now it's gone."

She sat down on the stair and looked like a cartoon of sheer fedupness, so much so that I expected her to jump up and shout, 'and then I found it again and its finished, just a joke!'

But she didn't, instead the dismay was on the brink of turning into tears.

"How can it be gone?" I asked, "computers don't just delete stuff, not unless you've got a virus of course."

My wife shook her head and declared with all honesty that she was perfectly fine, although she had a slight sniffle earlier in the evening.

"Let's have a look," I said opening up the Netbook and peering at an apparently empty screen, "well it's short and straight to the point I'll give you that," I added.

A sort of low painful wailing started so I tried to assure my wife her story would not be lost. It was a personal piece and there had been a lot of deep digging to unearth it. Looking at the blank document I had a horrible feeling there would be a lot more deep digging to resurrect it.

"Maybe I should just stick to pen and paper," said my wife biting her nails.

I wasn't sure the planet could handle it. Every time she started a new piece for the workshop I could hear rain forests starting to tumble. Not because my wife wrote a lot but because her writing was huge, about a paragraph every A4 page so some of her stories looked like a series of signs or directions that would be viewed from a speeding vehicle.

When she typed her first piece on the Netbook she looked at it suspiciously and decided it was too short, even though it was over 1000 words.

"Doesn't look like much," she said frowning at the text.

The other problem was the screen, which was the wrong way round, "why is it not upright like a real page?" she asked and then, "what do you mean scroll, like a scroll of paper?"

Everything apparently is so much easier in the 17ᵗʰ century.

After an hour of staring into the Netbook I was ready to agree. I also had to admit I was baffled. I had found my wife's story, in fact I'd found several versions of it but they were all blank.

"You see that would never happen with paper," observed my wife, "the paper just wouldn't go blank!"

Somewhere on the computer lurked the original version of my wife's piece with all its wonderful text, but I wasn't the man to find it. My wife now looked resigned to the fact that all her hard work had gone forever.

"The police would find it of course," I said jokingly, "they can find anything on a computer."

"Really?" asked my wife perking up "you mean, if I took the computer to the police station they would find the missing story for me?"

"Absolutely," I said, "just take it to Lost and Found."

Threatening to hit your husband with a computer won't bring back missing files and telling your wife she's not a computery type of person will only make matters worse. Far worse. No matter what century she lives in.

The Turkey Trot

Ever since we started swimming again my wife's been fascinated by my legs. She's seen them before, in fact on a daily basis. But it's almost as if I've grown a new pair.

Maybe it was the light filtering down through the pool roof but apparently I had to show them off more.

"Bit nippy for the kilt," I said, "although I'd make an exception for Hogmanay."

My wife was busy studying my legs in our hallway as we were leaving to go out on a shopping trip. She had already told me that a lot of men have better legs than women and that I should be proud of mine.

"You don't want to hide your light behind a bushel," she added.

"Well you know what they say," I began, "a leg in the hand is worth two in the bushel."

My wife decided to ignore this.

"Lift up your coat," she commanded.

"Is this going to get kinky?" I asked hopefully as my wife bent down and began flattening my jeans against my legs.

"That's much better!" she announced, "you'll have to give up the old farmer thing with the jeans, baggy is out, skinny is in."

I liked the sound of skinny, although the old farmer thing rankled a bit.

"When's the last time you were at a farm roup bidding on agricultural equipment?" asked my wife.

She had me there, although I hadn't really pictured myself as a retired farmer up until then and now I was worried.

"You should have said something earlier." I moaned.

"It's never too late to be fashionable." Replied my wife.

An hour or so later she had me corralled in the gents' department of a large store, in fact it was the trendy gents' department, I could tell because it was staffed by young men that were so thin they couldn't be seen side on.

My wife had been discussing my bagginess with one of them and he was taking it worryingly seriously. He was wearing green trousers that were so tight he could have starred in The Nutcracker.

'That can't be good for you' I thought, 'keeping everything vacuum packed like that'.

"Sorry did you say something?" asked my wife, "the young man here thinks he's got just the thing for you," she added.

"Nothing too skinny," smiled the assistant, reading my mind.

While he was away I was told to be more enthusiastic. I was moving into a new era of contemporary male fashion. The old retired farmer would be put out to graze and a new aesthetically improved, younger me would stride forth with comfort and style. I was dubious about the comfort.

"Just like Dr Who!" said my wife, "you'll be regenerated into Peter Capaldi."

"He's older than me!" I lied.

The assistant was back with what looked like a pair of salmon pink surgical tights.

"Perfect!" said my wife, "you'll suit these, they'll take years off you."

I held them up to my legs. As long Johns they would have been ideal.

"Where's the rest of them?" I asked and was told to try them on.

In the changing room I couldn't get them passed my feet but my wife and the assistant didn't think this was a problem. Apparently it was just they were made and they would give.

"Give what?" I asked, "compensation after I've been strangled from the ankles up?"

More to the point they were pink and I reckoned I'd look like a turkey.

"Yes but at least you'll be a fashionable turkey," said my wife, making the assistant nod enthusiastically.

I had a feeling I was being trussed up for Christmas but my wife assured me there was a bright side.

"If you fly anywhere at least you won't have to worry about DVT," she said and again the assistant nodded wildly.

Back home the trousers refused to budge past my knees, but apparently it was a start and I had to persevere because it would be worth it in the end when I lost all feeling in my legs.

The following day I arrived home and almost collapsed when I saw two disembodied stuffed pink legs sitting on a chair in the bedroom. It turned out this was my wife's cunning plan to stretch the trousers. For added effect she'd stuck a pair of my shoes on the ends.

"Just give them a week," she enthused, "and you'll be skipping around in them to your heart's content."

'Turkey trot more like' I thought.

We lived with the stuffed turkey legs until I started hunting for socks and was told they had been used to pad out the trousers and that they were out of bounds.

"And some pants and an old T-shirt and a couple of jumpers," said my wife, "and your gloves, and maybe the odd scarf."

"Good!" I said, sticking the receipt in one of the pockets, "then they can trot back to the shop for a refund!"

The following day they were transformed into skinny draught excluders. There's a Christmas roup coming up. I can't wait.

Spray That Again

You don't get much colour choice with spray paint, which suited me fine. My wife only took half an hour to decide between the white, brilliant white and cream. If there had been the usual vast range of strangely muted colours to choose from like Vicar's Vest and Elephant's Breath we'd probably still be in the DIY store.

"Is this it?" asked my wife frowning at the meagre display of spray paint cans.

I had been tasked with painting a vintage Lloyd Loom chair and apparently you can't paint such things with a brush.

"But won't the paint just fly straight through the holes?" I had asked when my wife suggested using spray paint.

"Well, of course it will," she had replied, "so you'll have to be very, very careful. I don't want the garden or the house sprayed with paint!"

It actually sounded like fun at the time, but now, looking at the spray paint cans I was growing apprehensive.

I spent the time waiting for my wife to decide on the colour by staring mindlessly at an extensive range of fascinating adhesives. I had no idea there were so many ways to stick stuff together.

"It looks like that's the lot, amazing eh, how do graffiti artists manage?" she declared "so it's a toss up between the white, brilliant white and the cream, what do you think?"

I didn't think so it was the cream. But then there was a debate about how many cans we would need. Obviously there would be a certain amount of wastage, unless of course we had two chairs to paint and then I could put one behind the other and let it catch the stray paint.

"That's a great idea!" said my wife, "I know just the thing," and in a split second I had doubled my workload.

There was only one checkout open so we joined the long queue. The checkout was manned by an old chap who seemed to be taking his job very seriously. He counted people's change individually into their hands with great aplomb and concentration. Items were checked against receipts and bagged with impressive care.

He was just getting the hang of the system he told one woman who seemed to know him.

"Sometimes, the card machine is slower than me and that's saying something!" he said and they laughed.

"He never said a truer word," I muttered and was promptly elbowed in the ribs.

I stopped a passing assistant and asked about the possibility of another checkout being opened and he said we would look into it, but it didn't happen and the queue behind us grew longer and nastier.

"Does spray paint go off?" I asked my wife.

"I think he's sweet," she replied, "he's lovely with the customers. It's actually quite refreshing."

Eventually we presented our six cans of cream spray paint before him and waited as he polished his specs.

"Are we having a nice day?" he asked and we both nodded. It was like visiting Santa.

"Oh, someone's going to be busy painting," he continued, "spray that again, eh?"

We all laughed. Or at least I pretended to laugh.

"Do you have any identification?" asked the old chap suddenly, peering at us over his specs, his demeanour darkening.

"Sorry, can you spray that again?" I replied, but he just raised his eyebrows.

"It was funny the first time," muttered my wife, "did you say identification?"

"Yes madam, I need some identification." Replied the old chap.

I felt the weight of a collective sigh behind me slowly hit the floor. People shifted into a more comfortable position, laid heavy purchases down. A baby started crying. None of which boded well.

"Why do you need to know who we are?" asked my wife.

"It's the law I'm afraid," said the old chap, "it says here on the screen that I can't sell you the paint unless you provide satisfactory identification."

There was a strange, tense silence broken by a voice from the back of the queue, "it's an age restricted product!"

"Thank you Sir," replied the old bloke.

"So how old do we have to be to buy it?" I asked.

The old bloke peered at his screen for a moment.

"Two hundred and ten," he said, "sorry twenty one."

"Well there's quite a difference there," I replied, "which one is it?"

"Twenty flipping one!" shouted the voice from the queue.

"So how old do you think we are?" asked my wife, a smile beginning to bloom on her face.

"Well I think that's obvious otherwise I wouldn't be asking for identification," replied the old chap winking and making my wife go all coy.

For a moment I thought, 'is he so old that he thinks we might actually be younger than twenty one?' but I resisted saying it. Instead I produced my driving licence.

"Thank you very much Sir," said the old chap, "you may now spray away to your heart's content."

"I wonder if he thought we were both under twenty-one, or just me?" said my wife as we left the store.

By Royal Appointment

There was a time when the phone rang and you would have absolutely no way of knowing who was calling. This added a certain excitement to the event and an element of surprise. Sometimes of course it was an unpleasant surprise and you had to pretend you were someone else or that you had your coat on and you were just going out and unfortunately you couldn't take the phone with you. What a lovely thought.

Not that you would need to of course because the nice GPO had thoughtfully planted phones around the country and housed them in red boxes that smelled of stale cigarette smoke and urine.

Now you can decide who you want to speak to before you answer the phone. I must have lost my sense of adventure because if someone's name doesn't come up on my phone after it makes that stupid, strangely weary bloopity-bloop noise I tend not to take the call. If the number is blocked I make a point of not answering it out of principal.

There was however, something familiar about the number that called on Saturday morning so I answered it even though I was engaged in several disconnected activities, namely trying to catch up on my emails while cutting a plaster to fit the weird shape my left big toe seems to have assumed.

It was a beautiful day so I was sitting outside. I was also distracted by the arrival of the largest wasp I've ever seen which was trying to form a meaningful relationship with my exposed toe. This wasp was so big it couldn't fly properly, most of its energy seemed to go into making a noise like a buzz saw.

So when the phone bloopity-blooped I glanced at the number quickly and thought, 'who's that again?' and pressed the green button without waiting for an answer.

"Hi it's Jo," said a posh female voice, "Jo from the weary players."

At least that's what it sounded like to me as I was caught in mid plaster snip, while dodging a giant wasp and surveying the rash of incoming emails.

"The weary players?" I asked.

"I beg your pardon?" said the caller so I just moved on and asked how I could help.

Apparently I knew this lady and to back it up she rattled off the names of some local people in various arts and theatre groups I was acquainted with on one level or another. We had met she said several times at a local National Trust venue when I had been reviewing the choral society.

I still couldn't place her but then she played her trump card and said she'd recently bought a copy of my latest book.

"I've been tucked up in bed with you every night for the past few weeks," she said wistfully.

This always works. Now the sticking plaster and the emails were pushed to one side, although I maintained a keen vigil on the wasp, which had apparently fallen in love with a spare Band Aid.

"It's about the Royal wedding," declared Jo as if it was something blocking her drive.

I remained silent, trying to work out which Royal wedding she might be referring to.

"As you know it's fast approaching and..." she continued. Now I remembered.

"Am I invited?" I interrupted, but Jo barely missed a beat, "I doubt it very much," she said smartly then went on to explain how she was heading up the local Royal wedding gift committee and my name had come up at the last meeting. She stressed the word 'committee' as if meant something else, something much more meaningful and this worried me.

"The thing is, we wondered if you would care to make a special personal donation, either financially to the gift fund, in which case you and your family would be named on the reverse of one of the mats..."

"Mats?" I said standing up and moving away sharply from the wasp, "what, like beer mats?"

Jo laughed coldly. The mats she was referring to were of course handcrafted, highly decorative gilt-edged place mats depicting celebrated local scenes, painted in watercolour by Jo's husband Ron.

There was also an accompanying set of 'dinky' coasters, again gilt-edged. All of which had been specially produced for the forthcoming Royal occasion. I could peruse the designs at my leisure on the notice board at the community hall. Funny how I had missed that.

For a donation of £100 I could have my name added to the reverse of one of the place mats and for another tenner one of the coasters. There was a family discount available for £200.

"Do you think they'll like gilt-edged place mats featuring a painting of our post office?" I asked, "they're a young couple, did you consider personalised iPads?"

Jo was silent, I think she sensed I wasn't completely buying in to her Royal gift masterplan. But she had another trump card up her sleeve.

"What about a signed and personally dedicated copy of one of your books?" she suggested enthusiastically, "I think that would go down a treat."

"Do you think?" I said.

"Oh absolutely, they could take it with them on their honeymoon and dip into it when there's a lull in proceedings, they would love it!"

For a moment I pictured this scenario and to my surprise it worked rather well.

"In fact, what about one each with a personal inscription, perhaps you could supply them in a special commemorative slipcase?" she added.

"A commemorative slip case?" I asked, "do you mean like a Folio Society edition?"

"Brilliant, you'd have to be sharp though as we're running out of time," she enthused.

For a moment I tried to visualise exactly what form these Royal wedding commemorative slipcases would take and failed. You couldn't buy such a thing, I'd have to make them.

Nevertheless I agreed and took her address and full name – "Mrs King," she announced grandly.

"Very appropriate," I said and we laughed.

"Mrs Jo King," she added flatly.

I was back with the sticking plaster before the Royal penny dropped. Apparently some of my wife's friends will do anything for a laugh.

Solo Show

On my way to a student production I reckoned I had about two minutes to spare before the curtain went up but luckily I found a crater to park the car in that didn't have double yellows anymore. This is one positive aspect of our bombed out city streets.

Trotting into the venue I could sense the potent atmosphere of an audience that was wound up and raring to go. Joining them was the only thing on my mind. There were three young people behind a desk, students I reckoned, two boys and a girl all taking their jobs as the front of house team very seriously.

One of their phones went off as I approached and the place was suddenly filled with the Harry Potter theme tune. Panic and confusion now riegned as they had to deal with two things at once. First they had to decide whose phone was casting a spell, then they had to scold the owner – one of the boys for having their mobile on in the first place. A tense but suppressed argument now erupted that involved some shoving and elbowing.

Meanwhile I could see through the open double doors a young man with a big beard and an old baggy jumper walking slowly across the stage. For a moment I thought the play had started but then the young man began reading hesitantly from a piece of paper.

I reckoned he was the director because it sounded like he was making an Oscar acceptance speech, which luckily for me could run for some time, but we were in council premises and there was also a uniformed door lady tapping her watch at me.

"Excuse me," I said to the trio, "I'm sorry to interrupt but have you got a ticket for Roddy Phillips from the P & J?"

All three of them froze in mid-bicker and stared at me, then the one with the phone started texting. There was a worryingly long silence.

"What do you think, is that possible?" I asked.

"Sorry?" replied the girl while her friend stared open mouthed at me.

"Do you have a ticket for Roddy Phillips from the P & J?" I repeated.

The girl and the boy now stared blankly at one another.

As far as I knew arrangements had been made for a ticket and a programme to be left for me at the front desk. I could see a small pile of tickets with little yellow post-it notes stuck to them. I reckoned one of them was my ticket.

"It's probably in that pile of tickets there," I said pointing.

The girl looked down at the tickets.

"I don't think so," she replied, "they're complimentary tickets for our show."

"That's right," I said, "and hopefully one of them will be a ticket for Roddy Phillips from the P&J."

The boy in the middle started to say something but decided against it, then for some reason they were staring blankly at me again and their pal had now turned his phone off and joined them. In fact they looked non-plussed. This was obviously the group default expression.

I mentioned the fact that the show was about to start so it would be really handy if I could get my ticket, but they just looked at one another.

"Honestly, if you could just check that pile in front of you, I think you'll find there's a ticket in there for Roddy Phillips from the P & J," I said, glancing at the door lady who was looking as baffled as the kids.

"This is a student show," announced the girl, "yes, its a student show," chimed one of the boys.

I struggled with this for a moment and then finally a great fog seemed to clear before me. For some weird reason they thought

I had come to collect a ticket for a show entitled 'Roddy Phillips from the P & J'. I didn't know whether to laugh or cry. They obviously had no idea who I was, or even why I was there and I began to wonder myself.

If I was a show would I give myself a rave review? The door lady was tapping at her watch again and calling for me.

"Roddy Phillips from the P&J isn't a show," I explained trying to keep my face straight, "if it was it would be a pretty dull solo show I can assure you. Look, I'm Roddy Phillips and I've come to review your production, I'm a theatre critic."

They stared at me with growing distrust and then consulted one another.

"I think he's, like, a critic," said the girl, the end of her sentence rising to a questionmark.

"Do we want someone to write about it?" asked the boy in the middle.

"Of course we do its publicity," said wonderboy on the end.

"So who pays for the ticket?" the girl whispered. The boy in the middle shrugged his shoulders.

"Do you get in, like, for nothing?" asked the girl turning back to me.

"Totally," I said, everywhere I go."

"No way," said one of the boys, "that's like, so cool."

"So cool," echoed the girl.

"Ten seconds!" shouted the woman on the door.

"Look, I'm like, supposed to be the treasurer," said wonderboy, "so I'll sort it out."

"Good for you," I said, "so what are you guys studying, I hope it's not theatre management?"

"Politics!" they chorused. Very appropriate I thought.

"Enjoy the show!" they said.

"What about a programme?" I asked.

"They're like, a pound," replied the wonderboy flatly.

"Is that like a Euro?" I asked.

"Please have one for free," declared the girl presenting me with a programme as if it was a spare Kidney.

The bearded boy with the long baggy jumper was still on stage stumbling through his award acceptance speech. The audience were already in a light trance because he wasn't the director, he was the show.

The Chinese say 'the man in the free theatre seat is the first to leave'. Unless of course he's a critic.

The Wolf in the Boot

Turning into a supermarket carpark last week I stopped so a bloke could cross the road. He waved his thanks and as he passed he stared at our car, in fact for a moment he studied it, weighed it and had a good think about it.

"Maybe he collects registration numbers," said my wife.

As we passed him he continued to stare at the wheels on the passenger side, narrowing his eyes and tilting his head to get a different, possibly more revealing view.

My first horrible thought was a flat tyre or a nasty big dent I wasn't aware of.

"I think he just fancies you're car," said my wife as we stopped. I could see the bloke still staring in our direction.

The car had been in for an MOT and we had just collected it from the garage fifteen minutes earlier. It had also been cleaned and polished so it was looking quite spruce. Actually I couldn't blame the bloke for fancying it.

A new tyre had been fitted, rear brake pads and something that sounded as if it came from a garden centre. A brand new faint, but interesting noise had also been installed that so far only I had noticed because my wife had been on the phone most of the journey.

If I hadn't known better I would have said the mechanic's dog had managed to get itself stuck in our boot. Every so often the dog would give a little muffled woof, wait a moment for a response and then when nothing came it would give a dark menacing growl.

Whenever I turned a corner it would start whimpering and moaning then it seemed to fall asleep because there was a light snoring noise, which may have been a tractor. There is always an intriguing range of noises to contend with in the country, not all of which are produced by animals or machinery.

"Is that a dog barking alongside the car?" my wife asked at one point during a lull in her phone call.

I just shrugged and looked suitably non-plussed. It wasn't the time to tell my wife I thought we had a four-legged stowaway, as much as she likes dogs, or at least the tiny ones you can keep in a handbag.

Since the noise was intermittent I pretended that it would just go away eventually, hopefully sooner rather than later. It was probably just one of the new parts that had been fitted bedding in. Either that or there really was a dog in the boot.

I was dropping my wife off at the supermarket and then going for petrol so I stopped at the collection point and she nipped out. Within seconds the nosy bloke was back looking at the car. I decided this was a good time to get out and check the boot and anything else that might be wrong with the car, wheels hanging off that kind of thing.

The moment I got out the bloke was over. He was a lot older than I'd first thought and looked as if he might know a thing or two about cars.

"Is it 3 litre?" he asked nodding at the car while looking very serious.

He was asking the wrong person but I winged it, "could be, not sure to be honest," I said.

"I'm thinking of buying one," he replied squinting inside.

"What a car?" I asked and he laughed quietly to himself.

"So what's it like?" he asked.

"Fantastic!" I replied without missing a beat, "best car I've ever had, in fact I wouldn't drive anything else. It's so smooth you could be sitting at home on your sofa watching TV. And quiet, sometimes when I'm sitting at the lights I think I've stalled."

"That's what I thought," he said nodding away and looking suitably impressed, "and a very nice interior."

I was about to invite a complete stranger to sit in my car with me and I actually opened my mouth but fortunately nothing came out. Instead I said I had to go and got back in the car giving him a thumbs up as I turned the ignition key.

I had to reverse back to get out of the collection space and that's when I woke up the big dog in the boot. Only now it had turned into a nasty howling wolf. As I stopped the car it let a loud growl topped off with a spine tingling howl straight from hell.

The bloke was at my window so I lowered it.

"Is that your dog howling?" he asked.

"I hope so," I said, "for a moment I thought it was the car." Then I drove off to the sound of a poodle barking.

It was like driving around in my own personal Crufts.

When I stopped at the petrol station some kids in a suped-up Corsa looked impressed and came over to ask where I'd got the howling wolf noise from. I gave them the name of the garage and one of them said he knew them.

"It's called a Big Wooly Woofter," I said, they're on special offer.

I phoned the garage while my wife was shopping and explained how I'd been given a bonus wolfy sound effect and that it might be an idea to remove it before the next full moon, otherwise I'd have to shoot my car with a Silver Bullet.

The garage receptionist told me not to worry because it was probably just something bedding in.

"What, like a litter of Beagles?" I said.

An hour later I was driving one of the mechanics around waiting for the noise to start but needless to say it had vanished and I think he thought I was barking mad.

"We don't even have a dog," I said as we stopped at a set of lights.

Right on cue as I took off it sounded as if we were being chased by a pack of ravening hounds.

"Blimey! declared the mechanic looking over his shoulder, "that is quite lifelike."

Always good to get a professional opinion I thought.

Nudey

Basically my feet have never got the hang of walking. If nothing else this gives me an excuse to stop and whine while I'm out walking with my wife. Another trick is the loose bootlace. I have a lot of them.

Despite this we've covered a lot of ground during our walks. Over the past 20 years I reckon we've walked about 20,000 miles, which is the return journey from London to Sydney. Hardly surprising we've run out of country and taken to pounding through the local villages and towns. The principal aim of this is to see human beings, which are scarce round our way, but so far they've still proved illusive.

We see them as we pass houses that have conveniently left their blinds open sprawled in front of gigantic television sets, some of which are so big they must have been assembled inside the house.

Out walking one evening last week I was entranced by a particularly nasty cluster of blisters on both big toes and paused at the bottom of a steep road that seemed to snake away above me sniggering into a cul-de-sac. It was a dead end and I was dead on my fiery feet.

My wife was about two thirds of the way up and beckoning me to get a move on as she jogged on the spot. Then something seemed to catch her attention and she stopped in mid trot. I could see her peering ahead of her, then she turned and looked back at me.

It was probably some daft programme on one of the giant TV screens, nothing worth working up another sweat for, so I walked slowly and steadily up the road to meet her.

Standing beside her I tried following her frowning gaze but couldn't see anything remotely exciting about the three houses in front of us. They were at the top of the cul-de-sac about 100 yards ahead of us staring directly back down the steep hill to the main road. Each house had high hedges separating the front gardens. It was like a row of look-out posts.

The blinds in the front room of the middle house were wide open and a big overhead light blazed down despite the fact it was still daylight. This gave the room the appearance of a giant glowing fish tank.

"Everything OK?" asked my wife.

I was about to ask her the same question when suddenly we were off again.

"You know, I could have sworn I saw a bloke with...no never mind," she added.

Now I was intrigued and felt suddenly very energised. Mystery I find is an all-purpose tonic.

"What did you think you'd seen?" I asked. My wife stopped, grabbed me by the arm, covered her mouth with one hand and pointed at the illuminated fish tank room with the other.

There was a bloke with his shirt off standing behind what I took to be an ironing board. Even from about fifty yards or so his gym-crafted torso was very impressive. The board was positioned I assumed so he could watch his TV or get a clear view down the hill. Either way he was directly facing us.

Now I saw why my wife had stopped dead in her tracks so I suggested turning back. I had been dragged up a steep hill with nippy feet to see a half naked bloke, I'd seen him, my work here was done.

"No wait!" shouted my wife, grabbing my arm again, "look, here he goes!"

The bloke was obviously ironing because he was now holding a shirt, probably to put it on I reckoned. But no, he walked out from behind the ironing board and put the shirt down. He was now facing us stark naked.

No problem I thought this will only lasts seconds, he'll spot us and dive for cover and we can resume our walk in a forward motion rather than walking suddenly backwards at speed.

But the naked bloke stood his ground, it was after all his house.

"Is that legal?" I asked my wife.

"If it's not, it should be!" she replied.

The bloke now looked as if he was playing a vigorous game of tennis with an invisible racquet. It took a moment before I realised that's exactly what he was doing, but with a Wii and said as much to my wife.

"Now that should be illegal!" she declared.

I remembered the ugly naked guy that was in early episodes of Friends who behaved in a similarly unleashed manner in the apartment opposite.

"That isn't him," said my wife, glancing back at the svelte naked bloke as he went through the motions of a fast and furious rally with his invisible opponent. Personally I thought it looked slightly dangerous. Most accidents happen in the home and I imagine if you're going to prance around playing tennis with your kit off indoors that's a whole new ball game.

"I wonder if he's in some kind of club?" mused my wife.

"What, like a naked tennis club?" I suggested, "they could call it 'Love All',"

"No, a home nudist club!" retorted my wife.

"Still, 'Love All'," I said.

Concerned we might be accused of snooping we turned and trotted swiftly back down the hill, resisting the temptation to glance backwards, or at least I did. So basically the only person we had seen all evening was stark naked. As my wife pointed out it was certainly value for money.

"Fairview Road," I said as we passed the sign at the bottom, "thought as much."

Seating Arrangements

After more than three decades spent sitting in theatres and concert halls contemplating my review you would think I would have developed a generous critic's spread around the rear end. In fact the opposite seems to be happening, my behind is actually becoming finely honed or worn down whichever way you care to look at it.

Quite often during a longer performance or particularly if I'm sitting on a pew I'll have to take emergency action and lift one cheek higher than the other to give it a rest before it gives up the ghost and falls into a coma. Normally in theatres I'll just adopt a sort of slightly twisted side-saddle approach.

For some reason this seems to alleviate the direct pressure points and helps immensely but the danger is it can make me look as if I'm playing hard to get with whatever theatre production or concert I'm reviewing.

It can also give the impression that I'm very interested in the person sitting across the aisle from me. I normally always request an aisle seat so I can sit like this and sometimes the perfectly innocent audience member on the other side will start shuffling around and shooting me wary glances.

On one occasion it happened to be Prince Charles. The aisle between us was very narrow and he obviously thought I was planning a hasty exit. I caught his eye and he leaned over and said, "give it another fifteen minutes, it gets worse."

Or at least I think that's what he said. Time has a tendency to rewrite history. Prince Edward was in the production I was reviewing.

A couple of weeks ago I had to confess to a lady who shot me a dark look as we rose at the interval that I was having trouble with my seating arrangements and she looked very sympathetic.

"Is it piles?" she asked in a loud voice. We had just been bombarded by a particularly raunchy rock musical so I assumed she was over-compensating, but she turned out just to have a very loud voice.

"You should bring your own inflatable cushion, they work a treat," she shouted helpfully and held hers up.

Her pal nodded along in agreement and then turned to the lady behind her and announced, "he's got piles, Angela's telling him to bring in his own cushion, like we do."

Then they were all waving their cushions at me and making that long-suffering face that comes with the recognition of a fellow pain sufferer.

"Have you tried that new spray?" asked lady number three.

"Does that work?" enquired Angela, looking hopeful.

"It worked for Bob," replied her friend, "and you know what a moan he is!"

Angela looked suitably impressed as we walked up the aisle.

"I don't think its piles," I said, keen to set the record straight before this went any further and ended up the talk of the Stalls bar, "I think I've just got a bony behind."

"Well that's nothing to moan about!" declared one of the ladies laughing, "I'll tell you what, you walk up the stairs ahead of us and we'll give you a second opinion," she added and then we all laughed and I ducked into the Gents and left them wondering where I'd gone.

The Gents soon filled up so I washed my hands very slowly for a few minutes to be on the safe side but when I opened the door my three new friends were standing just a few yards away near the stairs looking through the show merchandise. So I had to sneak out and go back to my side-saddle seat.

"Oh here he is!" they chorused when they returned, then Angela leaned in close enough for most of my row to hear her.

"We've been discussing your problem and we think what you need is probably some kind of big nappy!" she announced then went back to her seat while the young couple next to me became suddenly fascinated by their programmes.

I could have done with that big nappy last week while reviewing a production of Harold Pinter's play The Caretaker. There are only three men in this play. It's typical Pinter, the language is often oblique and barbed yet it can be very funny and strangely moving. It demands full-on attention. If your mind wanders for a few seconds you're lost and it will take you ages to get back on track.

There was an unusually big queue at the box office when I arrived. But then most of the crowd left after collecting tickets for other shows.

"Quiet tonight is it?" I asked the chap in the kiosk, thinking Pinter might not be a big box office hit.

"Sold out mate," he droned, studying his racing paper.

This was bad news for me since the play was about to start and I would have very little choice of seats. However, as luck would have it there was an empty aisle seat a couple of rows from the front.

I couldn't believe my luck when the elderly chap sitting next to it told me it was free. I dropped down onto it trying to conceal my look of smugness and kept on going down until my knees were higher than my stomach. I saw the old chap glance at me. I think he was wondering why I was suddenly so short.

The seat then gently started listing to Port until I was convinced I would end up rolling around in the aisle. As a safety measure I grabbed the arm of the elderly bloke's chair and along with it his jacket sleeve and as the lights went down I stealthily pulled myself up.

This wasn't a long-term plan so eventually I had to let go and just hope my thigh muscles would hold out. After ten minutes the pain was substantial and distracting enough for me to wear a permanent wince on my face until I realised I could turn and sit at a right angle to the show and watch it over my right shoulder.

Pinter I have to say has never looked so good. If I could have just stood while driving home it would have made all the difference.

Take Cover

I was expecting to see Chris behind the counter of his record shop Vinyl Frontier, instead there was a punky young girl. Punky probably isn't the right adjective but my youth culture lexicon is forty years out of date.

"I see the tablets are working Chris," I said.

My wife rolled her eyes but the girl just gazed at me with a Poker face.

"Chris is normally a bloke," I explained to my wife.

"Well he's not today," she muttered and went off to seek solace with Joan Baez.

I think I said punky, more because of the girl's attitude as opposed to her vivid blue mohican, heavy black eye-liner and multiple piercings. She didn't look as if she suffered vinyl fools lightly. Apparently Chris was out to lunch and had left Miss Congeniality manning the decks. There was a sulky Leonard Cohen song groaning in the background that matched her face.

"I've got this album," I said to punky girl, "music to slit your wrists by, isn't it?"

The girl may have shrugged it was hard to tell.

Undettered by her charm offensive I explained how I was on a marketing drive for my writers' workshop and asked if I could replace the poster in the window with a new one. The current one looked like it had jaundice. But the girl didn't have the authority to approve poster replacement.

"I can sell records," she said very slowly, "and...um...yeah, that's it really."

So far our campaign wasn't going well. Earlier in a nearby newsagent the grumpy elderly owner had refused a poster on the grounds that he hated books.

"And writers!" he added before plunging into a phlegm-splattering coughing fit.

I put the poster on the counter and assured punky girl there wouldn't be a problem, but her attention had wondered back to her computer screen.

"Do you have any ukelele records?" asked my wife from the depths of the heavy metal section.

The girl was about to reply, probably to say something like 'just what's there' which is the stock answer to most questions asked in a record shop, when a woman bustled in with her young son. She seemed quite excited and was obviously on a mission.

"I really can't believe it," she began breathlessly, "this must be fate."

Punky girl and I looked at her with casual indifference.

"I wonder if you can help. My son wants to cover his bedroom walls with record covers and we were just discussing it when we suddenly found ourselves outside your record shop, it is a record shop isn't it? Anyway Toby's got this vision, haven't you Tobes?"

Sensing impending embarrassment Tobes had already dislocated himself from his mother and was trying to blend into the Jazz-Rock section.

"He wants a different decade on each wall," continued the woman, "I think it's going to be fantastic, we need, I reckon around 200 covers. Depends if we do the window wall. What do you think Tobes maybe we should leave that one? Anyway we'd like to buy some record covers please and lots of them."

Chris once told me that a bloke came into his shop with a machete and asked if he could sharpen it for him. It's this kind of thing that has always put me off working in collectable retail.

The punky girl said nothing for a moment. My wife and I meanwhile pretended to rifle enthusiastically through the 70's Prog Rock section.

Glancing at the girl I could see she was still sizing the woman up. Tobes had now thrown his lot in with us and was up to his nose in Tubular Bells. He looked about 10 or 11 years old when he came in, quite young to start a record cover wall. But on closer inspection I think he was about 13.

"The thing is," began the girl languidly, "this is a record shop and I'm only authorised to sell," she paused for a moment, "records."

"No problem then, because we don't want the records, just the covers, don't you keep a supply of spare covers?" replied the woman.

"The weird thing is right, for some reason people who buy

records also want the covers," said the girl very slowly as if she were explaining some complex abstract maths problem.

The woman looked genuinely surprised.

"Really, don't most people just leave their records lying around on the floor and forget about the covers?" she said, laughing to herself as if she was overstating the obvious, "you know, like you do with hardback books. I always lose the dust jacket, it's so unnecessary anyway don't you think?"

Again the girl sucked all this in and chewed on it. It was at this point that I began to appreciate how cool she was and not in an unflustered sense.

"There are boxes of cheap records underneath the racks," she said, pointing at one box in particular.

The woman lit up and started rummaging in the box, but the first record she pulled out was a Gary Glitter album entitled 'Touch Me'. Wincing, she turned sharply away from it as if it was painful to look at, then holding it at arm's length she pushed it quickly back into the box.

"Come on Tobes," she muttered, "we have to go."

Punky girl was smiling to herself as they left, but I wasn't. Outside I could see the woman peering at my faded poster and typing my number into her mobile. Time to take cover.

Sneezy

Normally you wouldn't be able to recall the exact moment a cold presented itself. By its very nature a cold drags you down by stealth, so there is rarely an element of surprise. The common cold has been designed in this way to give you time to waste money on pointless remedies while inadvertently passing the cold on to every one you encounter.

This period of uncertainty also allows you to enjoy the benefits of the phantom cold, or the hangover. How I fondly remember one of our sons reporting to his brother one New Year's Day morning, 'dad's got a cold...and a hangover."

I have to admit I had an inkling about my cold but as usual I decided to ignore it. I find this often works and as remedies go is absolutely free. Typically I go about my business with as much vigour as I can muster until that tickly throat, the runny nose, the aches and pains become figments of my imagination.

So when I started to feel less than my usual eighty odd percent – a hundred I find is now too much to expect on a daily basis, I couldn't think of a better place to go than one of the most popular orchestral concerts of the year, one that would be packed with people, but more importantly one that was being recorded.

As a critic you have to be an irritation free zone at the best of times, no coughing, spluttering, programme shuffling, no noisy sweetie wrappers, toe tapping nonsense of any kind. The concert hall would be hot and airless and probably alive with viruses of all shapes, but best of all I would have to be on extra special best behaviour because of those highly sensitive microphones.

The concert was sold out and of course the shops were open late so we had to park about a mile away from the Hall. This gave me a chance to test out my incoming cold theory as we struggled through an icy gale force wind to the venue.

In fact when we arrived I felt thoroughly revived and raring to go on Santa's musical sleigh ride. We were sitting in the front stalls so when the carol singing started I planned on being in fine voice and I probably would have been for about the first fifteen minutes of the concert.

It's not often you can say the arrival of a full-blown cold has been recorded for posterity or that it was shared by thousands people. If you happened to be listening to the BBC Scottish Symphony Orchestra's Radio Scotland concert at 3pm on Christmas Day you may have detected a strange noise during Jamie MacDougall's fine rendition of The Little Drummer Boy.

At the beginning of the second verse it probably sounded as if someone had decided to squeeze some air out of a balloon behind Mr. MacDougall. A reasonably festive, if slightly over zealous event you may have thought and in a way it probably was. Certainly as stifled sneezes go it was an astonishing work of art and a triumph of the will over nature.

It first appeared with a smarting in my right eye and quickly laid siege to my entire head flooding it with an explosive fizz until there was nowhere for it go but out towards the stage, the orchestra and the crooning MacDougall.

Two days later having thwarted the best attempts by the recording engineer to erase it, the blast would have fired out through your radio.

We were sitting about eight rows from the stage so at least it wouldn't have had far to go. However, perhaps driven by a sense of duty and possibly an element of panic I managed to turn the sneeze outside in and blast it back where it came from.

In order to achieve this I had to stand up for a moment then sit down again on a knife-edge as my lungs inflated and my face scrunched up in a knot. I was convinced my lungs were about to explode, but they coped manfully.

The resulting impact however, rocked me in my seat and I dropped my programme, which was only a few sheet of BBC paper, but it landed on its edge and sounded like distant ice cracking.

You may have heard that as well and just thought it was one of the little drummer boy's percussive stabs. Ever the professional Jamie MacDougall didn't miss a beat. My eyes now began streaming and since I didn't have a hankie I had to let them run.

An elderly lady sitting across the aisle from me shot me a smiling sympathetic look. She too had a tear in her eye induced by the moving tale of the little boy and his rum pum pum drum.

I felt another sneeze welling up and wondered where I could put this one. The bloke in front of me was wearing a top with a hood that was hanging down his back, if I leaned forward slightly I could probably use it to cushion the worst of the blast.

Attempting to get a proper grip of the sneeze it suddenly gave me the slip and escaped as a little whimper. The old lady across the aisle was gazing at me again and for a moment I thought she was going to nip over and give me a hug.

From nowhere my wife produced some tissues so I could dry my eyes. She then patted me on the knee and gave me the same look as the old lady. The sort of look that says, 'there, there son, you cry if you want to, let it all out, you're among friends'.
So I did.

"I think I'll have to sit at the back somewhere," I said at the interval, my eyes welling up again.

"It's that time of year," comforted my wife.

The strange thing is, when the cold was removed from the front line of the microphones it subsided. As cold remedies go it's probably not the sort of thing the BBC would encourage.

Speak to the Hand

I hadn't noticed the puppet. Although I suppose when you approach a shop counter and you see an assistant working behind it looking reasonably sane, if not downright efficient the last thing you expect to encounter is a hand puppet.

In any case I've become immune to the onslaught of strange stuff we encounter in antique shops and vintage markets. My 'guffometer' as I call it, is now set comfortably high.

It went way past the 'got it, sold it twice already' setting and was firmly stuck on 'full bloke' which is actually a couple of notches higher than 'absolute guff'.

This makes me screw my face up at anything my wife points at with excitement, particularly weird looking furniture that looks as if its been made during a therapy session. Anything she declares 'georgous!' is bound to provoke a derisory laugh.

I find this saves a lot of money, time and energy. In the past we would have bought the Victorian child's wheelbarrow that had been decoupaged with postcards of 1950'2 New York and after heaving it in and out of the car and into the house and then cleaning it for an hour, we would have wondered what kind of spell had been cast over us in the shop.

Shopping with the 'guffometer' full on may save money but it can be boring, so I've been breaking myself back in gently. Consequently I'd allowed myself to be seduced by a 1970's bookcase with blue and green sliding glass panels that even my wife had laughed at.

But even with the 'guffometer' at a relatively high setting the bookcase had decided it was coming home with me. First there was some bargaining to do with my wife.

"Well if you're having that, I'm having this!" she announced holding a standard lamp I think my Grannie once owned. It had however, been suitably upscaled - basically painted off white, thrown down several flights of stairs and then left to winter in someone's backyard.

"You're kidding?" I replied, leaning on my 1970's funky bookcase.

"Fair enough," said my wife, "I'll have this as well" she added producing a large hideous hat from behind her back.

"You wouldn't really wear that?" I asked.

My wife looked at it and then frowned at me.

It was a lampshade but it looked like a hat to me. I went off in search of the shop counter. This was easier said than done. The huge shop was really a series of small stands and displays with no link or sense of direction, typical of the sort of place you find in the Brighton lanes.

Eventually I found an island counter where a short woman with bubbly brown hair and red specs was writing in a big ledger book with a feather quill pen. All very Old Curiosity Shop.

I told her I was interested in the bookcase but she continued writing head down. I was about to try again when a white glove puppet appeared from under the counter. I hadn't cottoned on yet so I mentioned the bookcase again to the assistant and she nodded smartly in the direction of the puppet.

I think I'm secretly partial to a bit of wimsy. I wouldn't have expected this but as my wife often points out I have a soft spot for twaddle and I imagine the two are probably connected.

So I engaged with the puppet and it spoke back to me in a charming high-pitched voice with a vaguely American accent. Her name was Marcie and she was delighted to meet me. She also apologised for the rudeness of the assistant – 'you just can't get the staff!' she announced in her southern drawl. It was like being in the Muppets.

You could see how this sort of thing might not work quite so well if you were buying a bookcase in a department store, but in an antiques centre in Brighton I almost didn't question it. Even as we walked between the cluttered stalls and displays on our way to the bookcase threading our way between people and chatting as we went, no one batted an eyelid.

Once at the bookcase Marcie and I struck a great deal that included delivery. The assistant meanwhile looked otherwise engaged, dusting objects or greeting customers she knew. She wasn't American.

Back at the counter I felt strangely empowered. Dealing with Marcie had been fun but when my wife turned up with her standard lamp and a chair and asked if they could also be delivered we saw a different side of her.

"Now your taking the piss!" snapped Marcie while the assistant appeared to be on the phone.

Stunned, my wife looked at the assistant and then back at Marcie, who thanks to the counter now seemed unconnected.

"We have to speak to the hand," I explained, nodding at Marcie.

"What!" exclaimed my wife, then added "sorry I don't have time for this!"

Shaking her head she put the lamp and chair down. For a moment I thought she'd changed her mind.

"I'd like ten percent off at least and I'd like them delivered," she said and vanished.

"Some hope!" squeeked Marcie.

On the way out a bloke told us the puppet lady could re-assemble an AK47 in under a minute, blindfold.

"Is that with our without the puppet?" I asked.

Steely Dan

My wife was distraught. Apparently she'd done something terrible in the kitchen. I was confused, normally that's my job. Although I have to say my wife has form in the kitchen calamity department.

For instance some years ago while trying to alter the colour of a new laminate floor we had laid in the kitchen she inadvertently stripped the top layer off half of it. She quickly covered it with a rug and then hid in the back garden.

When I returned home and asked one of our sons who was about 10 years old at the time where mum was, he told me she was hiding in the back garden.

"Who's she hiding from?" I asked.

Our son shrugged, "possibly herself?" he replied questioningly.

We were so impressed with that response that the kitchen floor disaster paled into insignificance – for about two hours.

Last week's kitchen catastrophe was a little harder to spot, or at least it was for me.

"So what's happened?" I asked glancing nervously round the kitchen.

My wife was sitting at the table with her head in her hands muttering about how she had ruined it, absolutely ruined it and how stupid she was.

I couldn't see anything that looked remotely ruined to me and wanting to rescue the situation, said as much.

"But look at the cooker hood!" she wailed, "I've ruined it!"

I think it would be fair to say I hadn't paid much attention to our new cooker hood. I had a vague idea it was near the cooker, and sure enough there it was hanging above it. In fact I thought it looked rather nice. More to the point it appeared to be intact and said as much.

My wife shook her head slowly and threw her eyes heavenward, possibly hoping for divine intervention.

"Of course you'd think it looked nice," she said, "you're a man, in fact you probably think it looks fantastic."

There was no arguing with that. Walking over to the cooker hood I saw my blurred reflection gazing back at me.

"It just needs a polish," I announced, "so what does it do, is it broken?"

"No, its not broken, as you say it just needs a polish," said my wife calmly as she handed me a cloth. Arms folded she waited for me to start polishing, which I did, but nothing happened. So I polished harder.

I've had some experience polishing brass instruments over the years. They can be tricky because they're so bendy, but the cooker hood looked pretty straightforward to me.

"How's it going?" asked my wife flatly as I polished frantically.

I was breaking into a sweat but the more I polished the more the surface of the cooker hood seemed to blur. Somehow I was making it worse.

"Happy now?" asked my wife, "it's ruined!"

I was baffled. This was really my first close-up experience of the cooker hood and it wasn't what I was expecting. We had been waiting for a couple of weeks for the dust to settle after the decorators left and the big clean up was in full swing.

My wife felt confident enough to clean the new hood and the cooker and had set to work on both with strange results.

Baffled I turned to Google and typed in, 'my cooker hood won't shine'.

To my amazement hundreds of pages popped up with responses to the same question. All of the replies made the same point, namely that the cooker hood should never be cleaned against the grain. Even stranger, one of the most popular remedies for reviving the hood was Baby Oil.

"Did you know stainless steel had a grain?" I asked my wife who peered at me as if I had just grown an extra head.

"What do you mean a grain?" she asked, "it's not made of wood!"

I had to clean the cooker hood with warm water and dig out the magnifying glass, but there it was and if you clean against it you'll end up with a big smeary mess. I'm sure this isn't big news to a lot of people but it was a round earth moment for us.

We didn't have any baby oil but olive oil had also been recommended so I rubbed some on and then rubbed it off again and the hood came back to its soft mirror finish – for about half an hour.

So I ran out and bought special stainless steel cleaner and cleaned and cleaned until the only thing in my life was that cooker hood. I hadn't even thought about the cooker.

Meanwhile my wife got on with her life. Every now and then she would pop her head round the door and enthuse at my handiwork, which encouraged me to go deeper with my shine.

Once I had the hood back to its original gleam, I moved onto the fridge and then the microwave. Eventually all I did was shine stuff made of stainless steel.

Now I'm looking for more stainless steel things to buy. I'd like to say it's a hobby but its probably more like therapy.

"Exactly!" said my wife, "welcome to my world." Then added, "you missed a bit."

Aye there's the rub.

Podge

I've got to the stage in life where I've met so many people they're beginning to fuse together. Sometimes I fail to recognise people completely or I hail total strangers as close friends, possibly because they remind me of someone I've just seen in a film.

My wife seems to be afflicted by the same condition. For instance when Pauline joined my writer's workshop recently my wife decided she was a famous actress, possibly originally from Liverpool who in her latter years had decided to write her colourful theatrical memoirs.

This case of mistaken identity was exacerbated by Pauline's decision to remain anonymous – even though I knew her name. Pauline was being mischievous and in fact it unsettled the group slightly, particularly my wife who was now convinced that we had a celebrity actress among us.

"Actually," she began trying to conceal a smug smirk, "I think I know who you are?"

The group froze and stared at Pauline.

"Oh?" replied Pauline with some surprise, "have we met?"

My wife laughed, "have we met?" she said, "that's a good one."

My wife winked at Pauline and I changed the subject thinking it was better bottled than spilled so the group was now intrigued as to Pauline's identity. Similarly Pauline was intrigued about her potentially fictitious celebrity status.

Curiously I also thought I knew Pauline or at least I vaguely recognised her. But it could have been because she reminded me of several other people I've met. I suppose this is just a visual version of not remembering people's names, an area in which strangely I seem to be improving.

So basically I might not know exactly who you are, but I'll know your name, which is at least a start.

Pauline seems to have the same problem. Last week on the way to the writers' workshop I stopped at a junction about two hundred yards from the venue and saw Pauline approaching the kerb on the other side of the road.

I pointed at her and she looked round as if I was looking at someone behind her. Perhaps it was the distance or the fact that I was in a car but for some reason Pauline didn't recognise me. So I waved and gave her a big smile and slightly hesitantly she waved back, then she quickly looked round again to make sure I wasn't waving at someone behind her.

A few minutes later she came into the workshop and pointed her stick at me.

"That was you waving at me!" she declared, "I really thought my luck was in!"

There was only one other member in the workshop at that point, Chantal who is Swiss and speaks English with a charmingly inflected accent.

Chantal stared at Pauline who was still pointing her stick at me.

"This bloke pulled up in a big car, quite handsome actually..." continued Pauline.

I was already liking this, but it wouldn't last long.

"Looks a bit like the Dad in Downton Abbey and he starts waving and smiling at me. Well, I thought this is all right eh, then he drives off." Added Pauline.

"So was it the Dad from Downton Abbey?" Asked Chantal.

"No, it was him!" shouted Pauline stabbing the air with her stick.

Meanwhile I was trying to picture the actor who plays the father in Downton Abbey and remember his name. As usual I got his name but I couldn't remember what he looked like.

"Hugh Bonneville," I said, "he plays the Dad in Downton Abbey."

"That's him," said Pauline taking her seat at the table.

"What does he look like again?" asked Chantal.

"Like him!" shouted Pauline, "you know the actor, he's quite good looking but he's got a podgy face..."

"Podgy?" asked Chantal, "what is podgy?"

Pauline was about to explain when I interrupted.

"Hold on, hold on, what do you mean podgy?" I demanded.

But Pauline continued, "you know a bit soft and spongy, like a cushion, not really what you would call fat, just..." Pauline searched for the word, "podgy."

"Podgy," repeated Chantal, trying the word out with the benefit of its new found meaning while aiming it at me.

I laughed weakly and tried to change the subject by recounting the story of my Yorkshire doppleganger.

About 25 years ago on a trip to Harrogate I stopped at a petrol station and filled up my new Renault Laguna. Much to my surprise the bloke behind the counter commented on my car.

"You kept that quiet," he said smiling, "very nice," he added.

"Cheers," I said, "I'm really pleased with it."

The bloke stared at me and a woman joined him and asked if I was going to the barbecue on Sunday.

"I don't think I've been invited." I said and the woman jumped slightly, frowned at the bloke and then stared back at me.

Obviously it was a case of mistaken identity, the only problem was they were expecting a Yorkshire accent.

There was a moment of silence as the story was considered.

"Maybe they thought you were Hugh Bonneville," suggested Chantal.

"With the podgy face," added Pauline.

Fancy Dress

I think our sons may have some confusing memory images of their mother. Last week one of them asked if she had ever worked in a saloon. We were watching a western on TV at the time and I saw him glance nervously at his mother.

"It wasn't a saloon as such," I said, "it was more of a brothel."

Our son nodded sagely.

"Oh that's OK then," he said, "at least it wasn't just some dubious drinking den."

"So was that before or after you were a pirate?" he added.

We had to think about it for a few minutes but we decided it was in fact before.

The brothel in question was actually in a show – The Best Little Whorehouse in Texas, which as a curious twist of fate I ended up reviewing. Not only did I have to watch my wife along with 2000 strangers cavort around onstage in a state of undress with a lanky, bald cowboy I had to think about it and then write it up as a review.

In the end I didn't mention her, I took the view that she didn't need the publicity. As far as I could see she was doing a pretty good job all by herself.

At that time she was also working as a Lollipop lady and on some days when she was rehearsing she sported her harlot costume under the big white Lollipop lady coat. A few months later she was in a panto and there was a pirate's outfit under the big coat. It was winter so the layers also kept her warm.

For some reason she had a habit of playing pirates onstage, so much so that when a teacher asked our youngest son to draw his Mum he produced a picture of a pirate. It was brought up at parent's evening, along with a drawing of me lying prone on a couch. Apparently I had died.

To this day when anyone mentions pirates our sons automatically think of their mother. In hindsight we're lucky it was the pirates that stuck.

Which is why I was so surprised when she announced she would be going to Saturday night's Halloween party as a nun.

I had this theory that people default to their natural personality when they're in fancy dress, which is why I was slightly unnerved by my wife's decision to go as a nun.

"Does this nun, play a guitar, teach children songs and lead them to safety across mountains?" I asked.

"That's a great idea!" she replied, "I'll bring a guitar."

At the fancy dress shop the singing nun fell at the first hurdle. My wife emerged from the fitting room looking as if a huge black tent had collapsed around her.

"Does it come with poles?" she asked the assistant.

The assistant didn't think it came with poles. Then I remembered the conversation we'd had with our son and suggested my wife went as a pirate. But she wasn't convinced.

"I spent years as a pirate," she said, "But I've turned over a new leaf." She added looking at the assistant who smiled nervously.

"Looks like you've turned over a new tent!" I said.

The pirate outfit looked great, but my wife wanted a bigger hat and a more convincing hook, then comedy teeth.

"How much comedy do you want from the teeth?" asked the assistant earnestly as he led us to a display stand dedicated to horrible teeth. There were about two dozen sets to choose from, every one of them a stark reminder of the miracle that is modern dentistry.

Inspired by the comedy teeth and probably with Dick Emery in mind I decided I was going as a vicar, bearing out my theory about people reverting to type in fancy dress.

Curiously, at the party I was slightly dismayed at the amount of vampires, witches and zombies who after a certain amount of alcohol just assumed I was a real vicar.

"I don't suppose you're allowed to come in fancy dress.?" commented a young lady dressed as Catwoman, "are you allowed to drink?" she added swaying a bottle of wine in front of me.

"Only the communion variety," I replied and blessed her.

Personally I always find it tricky trying to a hold a conversation with a bloke who seems oblivious to the fact he has an axe buried in his head. However, I was on a mission to save as several partygoers looked like lost souls to me.

"What have you come as?" I asked one woman in black with bright blue hair standing on end.

"I haven't the faintest," she said, then added hicupping, "your eminence."

I could get used to this I thought.

But then I spotted my wife swashing her boisterous buckle with a group of ghastly ghouls, heartily skewering canapes with her hook, her eye patch folded up on her forehead like a third black eye. It looked more fun than being a nun, or for that matter a vicar. Sipping my sherry I made a mental note to stop reverting to type.

Steamed

My wife was standing in the doorway looking very pleased with herself. She had her bargain face on. This is the look she wears for about half an hour after she's wrung some extraordinary discount from some unwitting trader.

"Have you heard the one about the woman who went out to buy a mop and came home with a cleaner?" she asked.

"What do you mean a cleaner?" I asked, half expecting my wife to present me with a cleaning lady.

"Hold on a minute," she said and disappeared.

This didn't sound good. Then she was back.

"Actually I might need a hand," she said.

So it wasn't a cleaner, not unless they had to be carried around everywhere.

There was a large box in the hallway, bulging at the seams. Judging by the picture on the side I reckoned it was some kind of vacuum cleaner.

"Close," said my wife, looking especially pleased with herself, "in fact it's just what you always wanted!" she continued, opening the box with a flourish.

I stared at the contents and thought 'I bet its not a giant Scalextric set' so I just shrugged while trying to retain some enthusiasm. My birthday's looming and although I no longer acknowledge such meaningless non-events when someone presents you with a box and tells you it contains something you've always wanted you can't help raise a modicum of interest.

"So what is it? I asked.

My wife laughed and shook her head.

"It's a steam cleaner!" she said as if it was patently obvious to everyone except me.

"What a relief," I said, "for a moment I thought it was a Scalextric set."

"Now you know very well you can't steam clean laminate floors and windows and a multitude of domestic surfaces with a Scalextric set," replied my wife pulling at the box until a tangle of hoses and fitments broke loose and snaked around on the floor.

Strangely it looked sort of interesting.

"So how does it work?" I asked.

My wife shrugged her shoulders, "with steam," she said handing me the instruction manual which was incredibly thick for such an 'easy and fun to use' simple domestic appliance.

"Where does the fun part come into it?" I asked, pointing at the statement on the side of the box.

"No idea," my wife replied, "but I'm sure you'll find out."

The steam cleaner had been a display model, the last one in the shop so it was partly assembled. It was also a bargain that would transform the house, if not our lives.

For two days it did very little. Hunkered down in its bulging box, its jumble of attachments as mysterious as ancient artefacts, it moved apparently under its own steam ever closer to my study.

Eventually curiosity got the better of me. One afternoon last week while my wife was out I pulled the big instruction manual from the box. Most of it appeared to be in Sanskrit and the English section read like a PHD on artificial intelligence.

On the back of the box however, there was a simple set of diagrams for the non-mensa members. This was more like it.

The fact that I ended up building a scale model of an alien craft as imagined by HG Wells was I reckoned a bonus. If it had been fifty yards across I had no doubt it could have successfully invaded earth.

It certainly made the version on the front of the instruction book look positively boring.

Proceeding purely on instinct I cavalierly filled the body of the cleaner with water and pressed what looked like the appropriate buttons. A red light came on which might have been a standby light. Just in case it wasn't I pressed another few buttons.

The one thing that stood out in my mind from the instructions was a casual line about an initial dribble of water, but nothing serious. The main idea was to ignore the dribble and let the steam do its magic.

As I got to work on the kitchen floor I pictured my wife arriving home and finding me with my feet up reading the paper while every surface of the house gleamed around me.

Within seconds the new laminate floor in the kitchen was gleaming all right, it was gleaming under water. Trying not to panic I convinced myself it would quickly evaporate into steam and leave the floor totally dust free. But within seconds the entire kitchen was swimming and the water was slinking out to the hallway.

Switching off the steamer I ran for towels and began frantically drying up the floor. I think I used every towel in the house and every kitchen paper roll. By the time my wife returned I had dried and polished the floor and in fact it looked great.

"That looks fantastic!" she said, then added, "what happened to the box?"

I'd forgotten about the box. It had fallen victim to the mini-flood. When my wife picked it up it folded into a sloppy heap along with the instruction manual.

"Hurricane Sandy?" I suggested.

Life on the Edge

I'm no adrenalin junkie, but sometimes you have to live life on the edge, caution has to be liberally thrown to the wind, danger has to be laughed at and ice cubes slipped down the vest of fear etc.

For some reason, last Friday night's impromptu shopping trip seemed like as good a time as any for shuffling off the humdrum and quoting Blackadder.

"Lets go crazy!" I announced, "lets scan and shop!"

My wife stopped me in mid-flow.

At 10.45pm the supermarket was practically empty. There were two checkout operators in their pyjamas chatting at the end of a long row of vacant checkouts, while all around us shelves were being stacked by assistants shivering in their pyjamas.

"Doesn't this supermarket have a no pyjamas policy?" she asked.

"I don't think that applies to staff," I said.

The girl at the Scan and Shop section was wearing pink spotty pyjamas and oversized matching fluffy slippers.

"Aren't you cold?" asked my wife looking concerned.

"Freezing," Muttered the girl, then added with a big welcoming smile, "are you ready to scan and shop?"

"We sure are!" I enthused, "we're feeling pretty crazy tonight aren't we dear?"

My wife raised an eyebrow and asked the girl why all the staff were wearing pyjamas.

"Children in Need I think," shrugged the girl.

"Great!" I said, "so how does the scanner work?" I asked.

I'd seen people using the handsets and felt I was being left out. The handsets looked cool and high-tech in a Star Trek sort of way, which is about as high tech as I like it.

There were some introductory formalities, which I dealt with, meanwhile my wife lost interest and went off in search of the three items we had come in for.

The trolley had a special holder for the scanner handset, which I was particularly pleased with. It was like resting a raygun in its holster. I was practicing whipping the scanner out when my wife held up our first item.

"As long we don't get cheated," she remarked as I scanned the jar of decaffeinated coffee.

Then she changed her mind and I had to unscan the jar. This was quite tricky but eventually I found the delete button. At the end of the aisle my wife changed her mind again so I had to go back and get the jar of coffee and scan it again.

Just as I'd done it she paused for a moment but it was a false alarm and we were on the move again.

"Let's wait until you're absolutely certain we're going to buy something before I scan it." I suggested, but this was met with a look of distrust.

"I might change my mind after ten minutes, or I might just find something cheaper or better," she replied, "so I'm afraid you'll have to be flexible."

'Flexible' I thought, the dreaded 'F' word. I began to sense that living life on the edge was going to be a lot edgier than I had anticipated.

The three items we had originally come in for had now ballooned to at least a dozen. But I was enjoying myself. The scanner was unpredictable and required a certain dexterity in its deployment. You couldn't just point it at a barcode, its slim red laser bar had to be coerced into just the right position and then the button firmly pressed. There was no room for creativity or sloppy scanning.

The main thing was we wouldn't have to wait at the checkout when we'd finished our shopping, we also wouldn't have to suffer the indignities of the self-service checkout. There would be no unknown items in our bagging area. Everything would be pre-scanned and all we would have to do is bag it and pay for it.

Ten minutes later at the Scan and Shop section there was a six foot white rabbit waiting for us called Bruce.

"Hi can I help?" he drawled.

"I'll bet you're lovely and cosy in that outfit," replied my wife as I placed the scanner in the checkout slot.

Bruce removed it and asked if we knew about the spontaneous checks that were carried out. We didn't.

"So basically the supermarket doesn't trust us?" I asked, "that's not very nice, not what you might call 'adding value to your business'. But Bruce was focussed on the task at hand and carried on re-scanning our items.

"This is outrageous. I don't think we'll do this again." I continued, "what a complete waste of time, do you want to carry out a full body search, maybe have a rifle through my wife's handbag?"

"Essentially we've done your job for you," I added "and now you're doing it again."

Bruce remained silent as he finished re-scanning everything. Meanwhile my wife had lost interest and let out a huge sigh.

"Sorry Sir, but you had 14 items and your total was two thousand, three hundred and forty seven pounds and seventy two pence." Said Bruce, flicking a stray whisker to one side.

My wife sighed again.

"Did that include VAT?" I asked.

Fobbed Off

Ever since I accidentally delivered a bag of our best sheets and pillowcases to Dr Barnardos rather than the dry cleaners my wife has personally supervised our charity shop donations.

Probably just as well. The older I get the less attachment I feel towards stuff that I find at the back of the shed or in the loft, particularly if it doesn't belong to me.

The three black refuse bags we dropped off at a charity shop last Saturday afternoon however had my wife's full approval. One of them contained a large amount of my old ties, every one of which had several stories to tell.

"There's a book in here somewhere," I said wistfully as we filled the bag up.

"Let's keep all the books separate in a box," replied my wife smartly.

As I tied a knot in the black bag I waved a fond farewell to my Paisley pattern past. Little did I think we would meet again so soon.

Outside the charity shop I was delighted to find the 'loading only' parking space was free. But as I lifted the bag out of the car boot it must have caught on something sharp and ripped open all the way up. The ties sprang out in every direction like exotic snakes followed by a collection of flailing empty shirts.

As I tried to collect everything my wife appeared from the charity shop and accused me of secretly stashing stuff back into the car.

"Is that one of your shirts?" she asked pointing at the road as a van ran over a pink stripy number.

It's a pity I locked the car because we were only in the shop for a couple of minutes. Just long enough for the staff to giggle at some of my shirts.

"These are almost back in fashion!" chirped one of the charity shop ladies as she held up a dark purple shirt with a white collar.

That was when I spotted the traffic warden. He was crossing the road just as I turned round and glanced out of the window. Not a coincidence I thought. I find my traffic warden radar is becoming ever more refined these days.

I bolted out and explained how we were just dropping stuff off at the charity shop. The warden smiled and tapped his watch.

This was his way of tacitly reminding me that I was on the clock.

I nipped back into the charity shop in search of my wife but she was nowhere to be seen.

"Changing room dear," said one of the assistants. I went over to the changing room and knocked on the door.

"Get a move on, we'll have to make a run for it," I said.

"Ok let's go," said my wife suddenly from behind me.

"I beg your pardon!" said a brusque voice from the changing room.

There was no time for explanations. Outside the traffic warden was back chatting to a bloke on the other side of the street but I reckoned he had one eye on my car.

Pressing the key fob in my pocket to unlock the car, I was stopped in my tracks because nothing happened. Instead of the car springing into life and jumping to attention it sat in a dull sulk.

My wife told me to stop messing about but no matter which way I pressed the keyfob the car refused to respond.

"I think it wants a ticket," said my wife, "good luck with that." Then she was off shopping.

The warden arrived and gave me one of the looks as if to say your time's up mate, move it or else.

I shrugged and explained how my car had gone on strike. He almost seemed disappointed when I demonstrated. I couldn't even call for assistance because my phone was locked inside the car, along with my wallet.

"Its probably just the battery in the keyfob," said the warden, "just open the door manually," he added.

"Manually?" I replied.

"You know, stick the key in the door and turn it, just like in the old days," replied the warden miming the action.

I was baffled, I didn't think my car could be opened that way, certainly in the five years I've had it I've never unlocked it manually. Staring at the driver's door handle I couldn't even see where a key might go.

The warden peered at the door for a moment and then lifted a small flap.

"I would try the keyhole," he said.

So I pushed the key in, turned it and the door unlocked. It was like going back in time. The traffic warden smiled and walked off.

"Technology has brainwashed you," said my wife when I told her how I'd forgotten about using the car key manually.

The fact that the car alarm goes off every time I open the door is extremely annoying for all concerned, but it is very apt. In fact it may be a wake up call.

"It is indeed," agreed my wife, "and its telling you to wise up and buy a new battery for the keyfob."

The Accidental Burglar

I don't think I could live in a garden or basement flat, the lack of direct light and the constant threat of flooding would drive me up the wall, probably to the flat on the next floor

But for some reason I'm drawn to them. We were strolling past a row of basement flats during the interval of a concert on Saturday evening. Most of them had quaint, well-maintained steps down to their front doors, some lined with potted plants or ornaments.

Several also had their blinds or curtains open and their lights on, which we thought was very considerate of the owners. One had a splendid kitchen with the table laid for dinner and from our vantage point we could actually see what was cooking. We were discussing the menu when my wife, who was further up the road motioned for us to join her.

"If you had a garden flat of your own – not that you would because of the lack of light and the flooding thing, but if you did, I think that's probably what it would look like," she said, pointing downward.

The rest of our party beat me to it and started laughing, ruining any notion I had of a glamorous basement pad.

The window was brightly lit affording a perfect view of absolute and total, complete mayhem. Clothes, bedclothes, books and furniture fought together in a huge wild stew of stuff topped off by half an upside down bike.

"Excuse me!" I retorted, "I don't think I'd keep my bike in my bedroom!"

"How do you know it's a bedroom?" asked my wife.

There was a TV flickering somewhere deeper in the mess but I had spotted what looked like a pair of crumpled pyjamas and decided it was a bedroom, but I suppose it could have been any messy room in an equally messy flat.

I was about to make another quip about the mess looking like an art installation when my wife suddenly told everyone to be quiet and pointed downward again. We all peered over the railing but couldn't see anything remotely interesting.

"What are we meant to be looking at?" demanded one of our friends.

"Quiet!" whispered my wife, "there's someone down there."

Slowly a dark figure revealed itself hunched over the bottom of the windowsill. We all stepped back as a group, apart from my wife who was now transfixed.

I couldn't understand why I hadn't noticed the creepy looking figure earlier. Obviously I had been focussing on the monumental mess inside the flat. Apart from that, you just assume there won't be anyone hanging around outside a basement flat in the dark on a cold night.

I was now also gripped by the figure, who we assumed was a young man. He was dressed in a dark hoodie and jeans and was hard at work chiselling at the sash window. There was a determined, manner about him, so much so that he had failed to register us.

"He certainly looks as if he knows what he's doing," whispered one of our party.

"Yes, an expert I would say," agreed another as we looked on.

"Oh my God, it's a burglar," exclaimed my wife quietly, "he's trying to break in!"

"No way!" exclaimed one of our friends again very quietly.

"He can't be," I whispered, "the place looks like its already been burgled."

"Maybe he's a burglar with OCD and he's breaking in to tidy it up?" suggested our son Adam.

We all looked at Adam and he shrugged.

Meanwhile our potential burglar busied himself at the window, chiselling away up the right hand side of the frame.

"I wonder why he can't hear us?" I asked.

"Maybe he's listening to an ipod, probably something like the music to Mission Impossible," said my wife.

"That's not very professional is it?" I said, "a burglar listening to an ipod?"

"It can't be a burglar, can it?" whispered Adam.

Another couple I recognised from the concert joined us and wondered what we were staring at.

"It's a burglar," announced Adam and pointed at our hooded chiseller.

The woman's eyes widened and she covered her mouth as she stared down into the basement, meanwhile her partner removed his glasses and gave them a furious clean.

"Have you phoned the police?" he asked.

Probably because we were still savouring the Sherlock Holmes atmosphere we had completely forgotten to phone Inspector Lestrade.

"Do you think we should?" asked my wife and the couple nodded.

"Why don't you video him on your phone?" suggested the bloke. So I did.

"Isn't this some kind of invasion of privacy?" said one of our friends, "I'm sure the last thing he wants is to end up on YouTube."

At this point a girl appeared at the window and tried to open it. We all stepped back. Eventually the window flew upward and our young would-be burglar threw back his hoodie letting a mane of dark hair tumble out. Both girls cheered and clapped.

"Fresh air at last!" one of them exclaimed.

"The concert!" I shouted.

The Hogmanay Helicopter

Since our sons grew up and got sensible I've had no one to play with during the festive period. They try their best but I can see that their heart's not in it. Which is strange because I thought it was a family thing.

When I was seven I crept into the living room just after midnight on Christmas eve hoping to catch a glimpse of Santa making his long awaited delivery. Instead I discovered my father and my brother-in-law Eddie sitting on the floor encircled by the most amazing train set I had ever seen.

My father had the controls and was sporting a small stationmaster's hat while Eddie blew on a whistle. I just assumed that Eddie had opened his present early – my father was getting Old Spice aftershave and a lemon polo neck.

Suddenly my father looked up and saw me. He glanced at Eddie and for a long moment an uneasy silence linked us all. Until my father rallied.

"You're having a dream," he said in a very slow voice, "go back to sleep."

So I did.

"And in the morning your train set was back in its box and wrapped up as if nothing had happened." Chorused my family wearily last week.

This is one of the few times of the year I can reveal my gift age – probably about 8 years old, without shame or impunity. I've also reached that real age when I'm allowed to ask for a remote controlled helicopter for Christmas without being taken too seriously.

I had promised there would be no indoor stunt flying with the helicopter. Our newly redecorated house is not be messed with.

Judging by the large I was presented with on Christmas morning my wife had fulfilled her helicopter mission with a vengeance.

"I think that's the one you asked for," she said as I carefully peeled back the wrapping paper.

But as I dived into the box, removing layer after layer of polystyrene I could sense the helicopter shrinking. In fact the remote control turned out to be bigger than the helicopter, it also required two hands to operate it and according to the substantial instruction manual at least two brains.

"Not to be flown outside," I read out loud, "for indoor use only."

My wife leaned over so I could show her the instructions.

"Well you can play with it in your room," she said "and keep the door shut."

For ten minutes I sat at my desk and squinted at diagrams and instructions while throwing despising glances at the miniature 'indoor only' helicopter.

Eventually I couldn't resist it any longer. Grabbing the remote control I pushed the power lever forward, the helicopter lit up and the rotor blade started spinning until without warning it shot straight upward and clung to the ceiling.

Panicking I shifted the other lever and the helicopter swooped down narrowly missed my face and smashed into my desk, then it bounced up twisting with its blades still spinning and threw itself against the window with a resounding crash. Incredibly because of its ingenious structure the helicopter remained intact.

My wife came in just as I sat down again at my desk.

"Amazing sound effects eh?" I said as she glanced suspiciously round the room.

Obviously I had more studying to do before my next flight.

Unfortunately no amount of preparation could help me fly that helicopter. It took off and tossed around like a thing possessed before smashing into something even more fragile. I should have just asked for aftershave and a lemon polo neck.

I thought one of our sons would show me the ropes when they turned up on Hogmanay, but both of them produced the same potentially disastrous results.

We decided it was the size of the room.

While my wife was otherwise engaged we sneaked into the kitchen and set the helicopter down on the dining table. The prefect launch pad we thought for novice flying. In fact it was the perfect launch pad for wrecking the kitchen and almost blinding me.

When the helicopter buzzed up into my face the last thing I remember seeing was our youngest son Adam struggling with the controls as if he was fighting off a wild animal.

There was no serious harm done, or at least not to my face, but we'll have to replace a lampshade and I doubt if the Swiss Cheese plant will ever be the same again after its impromptu trimming.

When my wife appeared we started blaming one another, but she wasn't interested in excuses. Quietly surveying the damage she picked up the controls and was about to push the power lever.

"Oh I really wouldn't do that!" I warned, but it was too late, the helicopter sprang to vigorous life from between my legs and flew elegantly up across the room. After completing four mesmerising laps of honour round my head it paused in mid-air, then it banked, swooped off out of the kitchen and down the hallway back to base.

"Happy new year!" said my wife pushing the controls back into my sweaty hands.

It's going on Ebay tomorrow.

The Wardrobe

Generally speaking the mother of invention in our house is just sheer laziness, or as I prefer to call it – making life easy for yourself. With the house in a state of mild chaos after re-decorating I've been going for the easy life option with increasing speed, particularly with the festive season looming.

My wife on the other hand has gone into re-evaluation mode. Suddenly a radiator in the hall was supplementary to requirements and was promptly removed leaving large holes like eye sockets all over the beautifully re-decorated wall.

"Alternatively, we could have just turned the radiator off," I said surveying the Swiss cheese effect, while completely missing the point.

Apparently the hallway was now a more relaxed and happy space. Personally I had never found it tense or in any way anxious. It was certainly a lot breezier now it had relaxed, the holes bringing a refreshing icy draught down from the loft.

"We could do with a radiator in that spot," I said as the temperature in the hallway plummeted.

Paul the painter would fix it though and apparently he would be re-painting the big wardrobe in our bedroom, which was now the wrong colour.

Needless to say I couldn't see anything wrong with the colour, but then in my wife's world I'm classified as colour blind so I couldn't actually say for definite what the colour was.

A dull, pale greyish green is probably the closest I could get. One of those subtle, indistinct harmless colours expensive paint companies would call something like 'Twilight Blanket' or 'Priest's Beard'.

It had been painted that colour when we bought it and we liked it, but now it was oppressive and dominating the room. 'Tintagel Light' was the answer apparently, presumably freshly mixed by Merlin in his Cornish cave.

After that it was a domino effect of 'Paul could do this and Paul could touch up that' until we had stacked even more furniture and taken down the few pictures we had put back up.

Every room in the house including the bathroom now looked as if it had been burgled, but we consoled ourselves with the thought that it would only be for a couple of days at the most.

The funny thing about chaos is that you get used to it. Suddenly the constraints of normal every day life are broken and a sort of false liberty sets in. Particularly in the tidying up department.

So over that weekend prior to Paul's arrival on the Monday morning we relaxed our usual vigilant standards until it came to emptying the big wardrobe.

We stared at the contents, which included most of our clothes and shoes.

"So where do you think we should put everything?" asked my wife.

I had no idea, instead I came up with an 'easy life' plan involving leaving the contents of the wardrobe in place and simply covering everything with a large sheet of heavy polythene and then boarding and taping it all up with thick cardboard. It only took a few minutes but all of our clothes were now sealed up safe and sound.

We had taken a few items out, just enough to last us a couple of days.
Paul was impressed.

"Looks...impregnable," he said as we stood there beaming smugly.

Twenty minutes later I heard a distant screeching noise, which I took to be a car outside, then I heard it again so I looked out of the window but there was nothing to be seen. 'Maybe it was the wind howling through the holes in the hallway' I thought.

The third moan came from the kitchen so I thought I'd better investigate.

My wife was standing at the work surface while Paul was sitting on a chair with his feet up on cushions drinking a cup of tea.

'Bit early for a tea break' I thought.

"Poor Paul's put his back out!" declared my wife digging out the painkillers, "he's in agony."

Paul showed me the face of a martyred saint.

"It's an old problem," continued my wife, "he'll have to call the doctor and go home and lie down."

"Sorry about this," winced Paul, "I'll be back tomorrow."

"Poor Paul," I said surveying the chaos.

"Yes poor Paul," agreed my wife gazing at the half undercoated wardrobe.

"Never mind he'll be back tomorrow," I said.

"Oh, I'm not bothered about my clothes," replied my wife, "I'm just concerned about Paul."

"Absolutely." I said.

The following day Paul's entire left side was paralysed in a massive muscle spasm, he was on Diazapam and something else he couldn't remember the name of. He would be immobilised for at least a week.

"Poor Paul," I said surveying the unchanging chaos.

"Do you think we should get someone else?" said my wife.

As the days passed we crawled around this moral maze in the same two outfits until eventually my wife decided it was easier to replace her clothes than it was to replace Paul.

"After all, it is the season of goodwill," she said on her way to the shops.

The Magic Roundabout

I remember feeling slightly short-changed when I discovered there were only four children in the Famous Five. Who would have thought a small dog called Timmy would qualify as a full-fledged famous gang member?

I've never been that interested in dogs. I certainly don't share the level of fascination my wife seems to harbour for them, which borders on a sort of simmering mania. Only my wife could have spotted a tiny dog at dusk gambolling about in the middle of a huge landscaped roundabout.

"Did you see that cute little dog?" she shouted, making Joyce and Margot, our two drowsy friends in the back seat pop up and swivel round like five year olds. It's curious the dramatic effect the words 'cute little dog' can have.

"Go round again!" my wife shouted, "that lovely little dog looked like it was on its own, I hope it hasn't escaped from its owner."

"That's terrible!" chorused our friends.

Luckily the road was deserted so I wheeled round again and slowed down.

"There it is!" shouted my wife.

"Where?" chorused our friends.

"There, jumping around," replied my wife pointing at nothing in particular, "Oh my God, there's a whole cute family of them, go round again!"

Up until this point our festive holiday period had been delightfully low key on the fun scale of things, but now it seemed we had moved up several gears to full blown fever pitch.

"I'll bet they're puppies someone's got for Christmas and they've just abandoned them," said Joyce darkly from the back seat.

"A whole batch of puppies on a roundabout?" said Margot flatly, as usual keeping a cool head on the proceedings, "must be a magic roundabout."

"Well we're keeping at least one of them that's for sure!" said my wife, "go round again!"

"And I'm keeping another!" declared Joyce.

After the fourth time circumnavigating the roundabout I had forgotten why I was driving in circles. I was also starting to feel rather queasy so I pulled into a nearby carpark.

"It's definitely puppies!" declared my wife as we stopped.

I had to remind everyone that I was medically exempt from puppy rescuing due to my tennis elbow.

"I'll provide back-up," I muttered as they leapt from the car.

"If they are stray puppies I think I should get first choice, since I spotted them first!" shouted my wife as they headed off towards the roundabout.

I recommended caution since there was no visible pavement and technically a big roundabout is hostile territory to a pedestrian. It's certainly not the sort of place you might linger of a twilit winter afternoon. Just as well the roads were relatively quiet.

"Good luck!" I shouted, "text me if you need anything."

I watched as the three musketeers made their way valiantly across the road, forcing a white van to swerve and sound its horn. Clenched fists were duly exchanged.

Standing on the edge of the roundabout glancing around and scratching their heads the three amigos suddenly looked quite lost. I was toying with the notion of phoning an emergency escaped puppy hotline, if I could find such a thing online, when a police car appeared and slowed down.

You don't normally see three well-dressed women stranded on a roundabout and I thought the police showed admirable concern. A cursory glance and the police were off as the gallant puppy-hunters disappeared into the dense undergrowth.

Now I felt a pang of jealousy, then a slight sadness because I wasn't on The Island of Adventure and I began to wish I had gone with them. But there was the tennis elbow to consider and of course the car would have been recklessly abandoned in an unwholesome carpark.

It was also getting dark and cold. Against the dusky clear sky the roundabout made a vaguely sinister silhouette, almost like a volcano. In fact it looked more like King Kong's island. Five minutes later I was getting very nervous. The roundabout was big, but not big enough to warrant a base camp.

I called my wife but her phone was off so I tried Margot and she answered as if she was on the bridge of a Destroyer.

"Nothing to report as yet!" she shouted and hung up.

I've seen films like this where people vanish without trace, lured onto a roundabout by a band of evil prancing puppies only to end up in some secret underground lair. I tried Margot again.

"We've found some white rocks...what you might call a rockery I suppose," she said breathlessly, "can you see us?"

I couldn't so I turned the torch on in my phone and began flashing it at head height. It's quite powerful and Margot has spectacular eyesight for her age.

"Gotcha!" she announced and hung up.

The exact nature of the errant playful puppy was vehemently debated as we drove home. It was either a strange shy cat, a white plastic bag blown in the breeze or a ghost. The batch of cute puppies turned out to be some white stones.

"We could have been the famous five," lamented my wife.

"Woof!" I barked obligingly.

The Thingummyjig

Yesterday morning I found a mysterious clear plastic tube about ten inches long lying on my computer keyboard. A post-it note attached read, 'I think you'll like this'. I was delighted. Here was a ready-made excuse not to work, or at least not to finish painting the lovely Victorian washstand table my wife had decided should be bright red.

The tube appeared to contain a scrunched up egg whisk. Just what I always wanted. Still there was some kind of assumption that I would enjoy it, although my wife had written the note so that might not be the case. Without even removing it I could see how it could quite easily be employed as an instrument of torture.

With that in mind I held it at arm's length as I eased it free from its tube. When it sprang forth and splayed out like a giant wiry spider I was so impressed I stuffed it back in again and immediately had another go. My wife had been right.

I think the novelty began to wear off round about the fifth or sixth time. After that there didn't seem to be much to it. There was that nice wooden handle, six long curved silver legs and six shorter ones, every one of which had a tiny black plastic ball at the end. It made a really good springy noise on my desk though.

I was obviously meant to do something with it apart from bounce it up and down and stare dumbly at it. Google didn't yield much, but then I couldn't quite nail the description. 'Some kind of spidery wiry thing with a wooden handle' didn't really do it justice but I did learn a lot of fascinating stuff about Camel crickets.

Apparently there's an Australian species that eats one of its own legs when its really hungry. I was obviously barking up the wrong Gum tree.

I probably should have left it there but the thing had a mysterious otherworldly quality about it. Like Philippe Starck's classic lemon juicer it had the look of an HG Wells Martian about it. On the other hand it could have been a comb for grooming our pet porcupine, if we had one, or a personal mobile phone mast.

I decided to skype a friend and ask his opinion.

"Is it something you've broken?" asked Dave as I dangled the thing in front of my screen.

Actually it looks like a device for communicating with your home planet," he continued, "you can phone home now and ask them to come and get you. Does it make a noise?"

I made it scramble across my desk and Dave flew back from his screen wincing.

"Blimey, that's horrible!" he shouted and he was gone.

Looking at the strange marks it made on my desk it all became clear. My wife had left it deliberately because it was a tool for distressing painted furniture.

The washstand was sulking out in the vestibule waiting for its topcoat so I gave it a tickle with my spidery implement. The results were subtle to say the least and I think the experiment had more of an effect on the tool than the table. It now had little specks of red paint stuck to it so I cleaned it with white spirit.

While I was in the loo wiping it dry it occurred to me that it might be a new type of toilet brush so I gave it a swirl in the toilet bowl, which worked out well because it got rid of the last specks of paint that were sticking to it. But it didn't have much of an effect on the toilet bowl so I tried it down the kitchen sink plughole.

There's been a curious smell emanating from that plughole for the past week so I gave a it a rinse with some bleach and a thorough plunging with the thingummyjig.

I wasn't sure how much good it did but I certainly felt a lot better about the plughole and the strange smell had gone, replaced by the pungent odour of bleach of course.

An hour later my wife was standing behind me while I typed away on my laptop.

"So what did you think of this then?" she asked, dangling the weird toilet cleaning, paint distressing plughole plunger in front of me.

Before I could answer I felt an extraordinary tingling in my scalp. It was as if my head was being massaged by hundreds of tiny insects.

"You wonder who comes up with things like this?" continued my wife as I floated off to my home planet, "is that bleach I can smell?"

The Hot Rod

Our friend Derek was in the hot seat and enjoying every minute, "I love cars with heated seats," he sighed.

"So do I," muttered my wife from the back seat. My wife's not used to sitting in the back of the car and had already mentioned several times how thin my hair was getting around my crown.

But Derek needed that heated front seat more than my wife. Apparently his cigarette lighter had done something nasty to his back.

"How did your cigarette lighter hurt your back Derek?" asked my wife.

"Well, it was on the floor you see," replied Derek. There was a loaded silence, which neither of us could fill so Derek obliged, "I had to bend down and pick it up."

"Blimey, it's a miracle you didn't have a heart attack," I said.

"Ha, flippin ha," coughed Derek as he opened the ashtray, which I had forgotten was full of loose change. Derek shoved the coins aside spilling them into the footwell and pulled the lighter from its socket.

"Does this thing work?" he asked holding it up for inspection. All this talk about lighters had reminded Derek that he hadn't smoked a cigarette for at least 20 minutes.

"It's actually illegal to smoke in cars now Derek," said my wife, "fifty quid fine or life imprisonment."

Derek pushed the lighter back into its socket.

"You're too old to smoke anyway," I added as I pulled into a parking space at the beach front. But Derek was already rubbing his hands at the thought of lighting up.

As it turned out we should have known better. It was sunny but the wind was Shackleton force, even the seagulls were struggling to keep afloat. Derek produced a cigarette and lit it with great flourish but it was immediately ripped from his fingers in mid-drag.

For a couple of futile seconds he fumbled to catch it but it was gone, flying across the roof of our car and tumbling down the front windscreen straight into an air vent.

"What the heck Derek!" I shouted, "it's gone into the engine!"

"I know!" he shouted back, "it was the last one I had!"

"Is that serious?" Asked my wife.

"At eleven quid a packet it's catastrophic!" moaned Derek grasping at his back and wincing while simultaneously coughing.

"Actually I meant your fag flying into the car engine," snapped my wife as she joined me for a long hard stare down into the mysterious air vent.

"Where does that lead," she asked. I had no idea so I just said it was complicated.

"That doesn't sound good," added my wife, her voice rising an octave.

I had to admit it wasn't ideal.

"What's that smell?" asked my wife suddenly, "is that something burning?"

"I'm getting a bus," announced Derek, "I'm not getting in a car that might catch fire, not with my back!"

"Good idea, there's a bus every two days," I said popping open the car bonnet for a closer look. Meanwhile my wife was planning what to say when she phoned the fire brigade.

"Maybe we shouldn't mention Derek if it does catch fire," she said, "in case he gets arrested."

"Good idea," agreed Derek climbing into the back of the car.

"That's the petrol tank you're sitting on," I shouted making him jump straight out again, despite his bad back.

"Doesn't the petrol shoot forward when you press the accelerator?" asked my wife.

I had to think about that one for a moment and to be honest I'm still not sure.

"Maybe you should drive it somewhere secluded and see what happens, just to be on the safe side," continued my wife, "and we'll wait here, what do you think?"

"Ok...that might work," I replied as I tried to visualize myself driving a blazing car into the sea. It had a certain Viking appeal to it I had to admit.

"It's a shame I can't drive anymore," said Derek, "in the seventies things like this happened all the time."

In the end I drove the car the length of the beach front three times, taking a long slow detour round a large carpark with the air conditioning on full blast just for good measure. I wouldn't go so far as to say I was feeling heroic, but I felt as if I'd done the right thing.

When I got back Derek was smoking his cigarette. Apparently he'd spotted it on the ground as I drove off.

"We did shout after you," said my wife as she dived into the back of the car.

"There's no smoke without a fag," said Derek taking a lusty drag and then coughing with delight, "hot seat I think Jeeves!"

Hande Hoch

Normally I switch off whatever rubbish I'm watching on TV the moment my wife appears. Then we watch real rubbish. But the other night I thought I'd let my newly purchased DVD of Die Hard roll for a few minutes.

I'd only just started watching it but I'd already fast-forwarded it to that classic scene where Bruce Willis' grubby vested cop encounters Alan Rickman's suave German terrorist. At first it looks like Rickman's been rumbled but then he sneakily pretends to be one of the American hostages and Willis appears to be taken in by him.

"This is a really great scene," I said to my wife as she sat down. She was already glowering at the TV.

"Oh dear, is this Die Hard, that's such a lad's film," she said letting out a deep sigh, "we're not really watching this are we?"

"Hold on," I said, "this is a very tense bit."

Suddenly Rickman turned on Bruce and all hell broke loose, in German.

After a couple of minutes my wife finally cracked, "is it all in German?" she demanded.

"It's a special art house edition," I nodded enthusiastically, "isn't it great? They've re-released all of Bruce Willis' films like this, some of them are in Black and White, Die Hard Five's in French."

"They're going to do the same with all the Bond films," I added, "actually some of them are going to be silent."

My wife was now peering in disbelief at the screen, "did Bruce what's his name just ask Alan Rickman for some cake?" she asked, making herself comfortable.

My wife's language skills are obviously better than mine.

"It's actually quite good in German," she added.

She had a point. Alan Rickman and his band of crooked terrorists are in fact meant to be German so it worked out quite well for them. On the other hand there is something very peculiar about Bruce Willis speaking German with that cheesy half smirk at full blast.

I'd bought the DVD in a charity shop. There were two copies on the shelf, which I took to be some kind of omen, one of them was obviously intended for me. Unfortunately I'd picked up the version that wasn't because it was badly dubbed in German with no language alternatives. Just my luck, or as Bruce what's his name put it, "typisch fur mich!"

I wouldn't normally take something back to a charity shop but the thought of that other English version of Die Hard waiting for me on the shelf was irresistible. Much to my relief it was still there the following day.

The nervous young man behind the counter looked glumly at the DVD and shrugged.

"We don't exchange DVDs," he said dryly, "people watch them and then take them back."

"But it's in German," I said.

"Doesn't say that," he said flipping the DVD over. Obviously nothing was getting past him.

"Exactly, but take my word for it, the whole film's in German," I said.

He shrugged again and handed me back the DVD.

"You might be German for all I know," he said flatly and then started to serve the elderly bloke standing next to me.

I was trying to work out how German I looked when a tall formidable woman appeared behind the counter bustling with intent. I took her to be the manager so I gave her my story. She also closely examined the DVD, then handed it back to me.

"The problem is," she began disinterestedly, "you might speak fluent German for all I know."

"I wish I did, then I wouldn't be trying to exchange this DVD," I laughed trying to be charming, "ask me something in German, go on."

"Hande Hoch!" shouted the old bloke next to me.

Needless to say I started to put my hands up but then thought better of it.

"Look," I began, "I'm not German and I don't speak fluent German, admittedly I've seen this film at least half a dozen times, but I'd like to watch it again in English because that's how I like to watch films, its strange I know but that's just me. Unless of course it's an actual foreign film and then English subtitles are fine."

"Hande Hoch!" shouted the old bloke again.

"That's not helping," I said.

The old bloke shuffled off muttering something derogatory about the great German nation.

"Beethoven was German!" I shouted after him, "but not Bruce Willis," I added smiling broadly at the Manager.

I made a donation when she handed me the replacement DVD, which I don't regret even though Bruce is now badly dubbed in Spanish, "Solo mi Suerte!" he smirks. Exactly.

The Beastie Head

Normally if I see someone scratching their head I automatically start scratching mine. But when the sales assistant appeared from the back of the posh accessories shop furiously clawing at her head I was more fascinated than itchy.

The woman had burst through the door backwards with both hands buried in her thick dark hair. For a moment she stood before us shaking as if she was being electrocuted.

A younger assistant was about to serve my wife but she was also now scratching her head.

"You've got me at it now Sandra!" she shouted and we laughed nervously.

"I think its some kind of primal bonding instinct, like communal yawning," I said making my wife stifle a surprise yawn.

"This is the trouble with having long thick hair!" said the older assistant still grappling with her head and shaking it over the counter, "you get all kinds of flipping stuff in it."

"Stuff?" I asked, noticing that my wife had taken a few steps back from the counter.

"Yeah, I get beasties in it and they drive me absolutely nuts!" said the assistant digging her fingers further into her hair. We took another two steps back.

"Beasties?" asked my wife frowning, "I suppose it is quite thick, in fact I was just thinking how luscious it was."

"Thank you," said the woman smiling, "it is luscious, although I say so myself, but last week I had a cockroach in it and I didn't realise it. I went home and while I was unpacking my shopping I felt something wriggling and twitching on my head and then this horrible thing jumped out of my hair straight onto the pan loaf I'd just bought and I nearly died," she continued, shaking her head furiously, "I'm not letting that happen again I can tell you, this one's staying here."

The younger assistant tried to laugh and patted her colleague on the arm.

"The reptile shop next door shares our basement and Sandra reckons some of the bugs are on the loose," she explained, then made a weird madwoman face.

I had been wondering why the shop was empty.

"How did you know it was a cockroach?" asked my wife with a visible shudder, "it's quite a big insect isn't it, wouldn't you notice it?"

"Maybe it was asleep," I said and in an instant had an image of a cockroach on my phone, "did it look like that?" I asked holding it up for inspection.

Both assistants peered at the screen and grimaced, in fact I thought the younger one was going to be sick.

"I once carried a ladybird in the lid of a sugar free sweetie box on a train all the way to Edinburgh," said my wife making both assistants stare at her in silence.

"I was so scared it would get stuck on the train and wouldn't have anything to eat," added my wife, "eventually I let it go in Princes Street Gardens. I'd like to think it settled in quite quickly. Do you remember that?"

I nodded as I looked up grasshoppers.

"Yes, maybe you should go to a park and give your head a good shake," I suggested then showed the assistants the grasshopper on my phone.

"Does that look familiar?" I asked.

Everyone huddled up to the phone and the beastie head lady pondered over the image, scratching her chin with one hand and her head with the other.

"Could have been that," she said, "it was hard to tell, I ran out of the house so fast."

"So it might still be in your kitchen?" asked my wife.

Two other customers had now joined us at the counter.

"This lady had a cockroach hiding in her hair and she took it home and it escaped in her kitchen," my wife told them, "she never caught it so it could still be there. She's got another one now in her hair, but we think it might be a grasshopper."

The two women looked very concerned.

"That happened to me once coming home from Spain," replied one of them, "this huge horrible insect dropped onto my magazine as if from nowhere, but apparently it came out of my hair. They didn't catch it, I thought it was a cockroach but someone said it looked more like a cricket."

There was a round of general groaning.

"Why don't you go into the reptile shop next door and give it back?" I said, "it might be a lizard's lunch."

The scratching assistant paused for a moment.

"Why didn't I think of that!" she announced then marched off past us.

"Maybe there's a reward for it," said my wife scratching her head.

Car Bores

When I phoned roadside assistance a nice man with a cosy Yorkshire accent said there would be a technician along in half an hour.

"They're sending a technician," I told my wife.

"A technician," she repeated, "I don't think its that serious is it, why don't I try and start it? I don't think it likes you."

She had a point. Over the past ten years I've smashed, dented, scraped and scuffed my car to within an inch of my life.

I had to catch the nearby post office before it closed so I left my wife sitting in the driving seat frowning at the steering wheel.

Fifteen minutes later I was about to be served in the post office when she phoned to say the technician had turned up early.

"Did you tell him the car wouldn't start?" I asked.

"Hold on," she said, "did I tell you the car wouldn't start?" I heard laughter and some muttering, "sorry, Steve's been showing me photos of his really cute dog," she added.

"Great, that was nice of Steve, hopefully it's just the battery, could you mention that to him?" I interrupted.

Apparently it wasn't the battery. "It's much more boring than the battery," said my wife ominously.

She was standing at the car with Steve the technician when I got back. Steve was unexpectedly handsome and engrossed in a rather complicated form on his clipboard. Not very digital I thought for an automobile technician.

"So is it fixed?" I asked smiling broadly, hoping that might help.

"I'm afraid it's bad news," began my wife, "it looks like you've flooded your bores."

"What bores?" I asked, frowning and shooting bewildered looks between unexpectedly handsome Steve and my wife, "do you mean bores in the car?"

"Never mind that," said my wife holding up what I assumed was Steve's phone, "look at Steve's wonderful little dog, isn't she a sweetie, her name's Posie."

Steve glanced at his phone and showed us a perfect Hollywood smile.

"Posie," repeated my wife holding up the phone and kissing it. She offered it to me but I took a step back. Posie looked quite cute but she wasn't worth kissing a stranger's phone for and this wasn't the place or the time to get drawn into the ongoing 'should we, shouldn't we get a dog' debate.

"I don't want to be a pest but can you get my car going?" I asked Steve, "I mean your dog's lovely and everything but we really need to go somewhere, quickly."

"Like I said," began my wife, "you washed the bores out. It's a common enough error, so I wouldn't blame yourself completely. It's also a piston thing but luckily Steve here will show you how to avoid it in the future."

Steve flashed those sparkling pearlies again.

"So does the car start?" I asked.

"Absolutely," replied my wife, "it would have started in the first place, if you'd turned it on."

"So I just thought I'd started the car but for some reason I didn't?" I said, "why would I do that?"

"Only you know the answer to that," said my wife handing Steve his phone back and making him laugh.

"You do know my wife's not a mechanic, or any kind of technician?" I said, but Steve was already buried back in his phone.

"Maybe you were distracted and thinking about that scarf you couldn't find, you know the one you were actually wearing," said my wife.

I was getting worried. Earlier that morning I had spent half an hour looking for a scarf I had tied around my neck. Now apparently I'd called out an emergency technician because I'd forgotten to start my car.

"Look its quite simple," said Steve, suddenly springing to life and making my wife nod annoyingly in agreement, "you started the car but possibly accidentally, who knows, you turned the key back and the engine cut out before it had time to set itself up properly, this caused..."

The rest of that sentence was a long strange blur, but I remember something about pistons and bores getting a wash. My wife then supervised as Steve showed me what to do if it happened again, basically I just had to turn the ignition key with the accelerator hard on the floor.

"So next time, just START the car," said my wife to Steve.

I signed Steve's form with a little drawing of a dog and he started packing up.

"Thanks for the tip," he said to my wife as he climbed into his van.

"Any time," replied my wife.

"Little problem with his crank shaft," she added as we waved him off.

Side Effects

I love it when I go to the doctor with one thing and come out with another. Relief mixed with fresh trepidation is such a stimulating combination.

"How did you get on?" asked my wife when I returned from our local surgery.

"I had to buy a new blood pressure monitor," I said holding up said item for inspection.

"For a sep bladder infection?" asked my wife.

"Apparently the sep bladder infection doesn't exist," I replied unpacking the new monitor.

"And the rusty water colour challenge possibly caused by the non-existent sep bladder infection?" continued my wife.

"A mere pigment of my imagination," I said as I began filling the monitor with batteries.

My wife nodded sagely, "that monitor looks real though and ominous," she said.

I withheld judgement until I took the first few readings, although I had a good idea what to expect. I could still hear the doc's slow intake of breath as he pondered over the unexpectedly high numbers.

"So the old monitor has been lying?" said my wife as she stared at the slightly hair-raising results.

"And lulling me into a false sense of security so I could have a stroke," I continued.

We contemplated that thought in silence for a moment.

"Well, look on the bright side," declared my wife suddenly, "at least you don't have a bladder infection anymore."

For a week I had fun with the new monitor taking regular readings three times a day. For some reason I kept thinking the numbers would go down, but no matter how much I tried to relax they remained stubbornly high, or rather highish as I kept telling myself.

"My blood pressure's really low," said my wife as she stared at the numbers for the fortieth time, "really low. Anyway they'll just increase the strength of your medication."

But after a phone call to the Doc with the numbers he took another long intake of breath and added a different pill to my collection.

"Just report back to me in a fortnight," he said breezily.

"Ask him about the side effects," said my wife anxiously, so I did, but he'd gone.

Less than an hour later we were sitting in the car outside the pharmacy gazing at the tiny, lozenge shaped white pills, so small you wondered if they were worth bothering about.

"Size isn't everything in pill world," said my wife, "if that was arsenic you'd be dead in five minutes."

For a moment I felt a sharp pain in my chest and I could have sworn my heart tripped a beat, but it could have been trapped wind.

"Let's have a look at the side effects," continued my wife taking the packet and pulling out the leaflet.

Being computer programmed I immediately googled the new pill on my phone and quickly found a web page packed with disturbing side effects. Scrolling down the list there seemed to be hundreds so I went back to the top and had a closer look.

Some of them I already had, which was a relief, like for instance in no particular order: heartburn, indigestion, wind, confusion in large busy shopping malls, dizziness when bending down and picking stuff up, waking in the night at regular intervals and walking into sharp things on the way to the loo, weird dreams, dry mouth, a persistent annoying cough, mysterious aches in my joints – I've had that one since the onset of puberty, a strange sharp pain in my neck when I have to peer past someone at the theatre, a dull ache in just one specific part of my head, itchy eyes, odd ringing sounds in my ears, sudden deafness and strange rashes.

"I think you've already got most of this stuff," said my wife as she peered at the leaflet, "selective deafness, general impatience, a pathological allergy to dusting and cleaning, an addiction to 70's TV comedies that weren't funny then and aren't funny now…"

"Hold on, this isn't good," I interrupted, "may cause breast enlargement in men, mood swings, general irritability, skin reddening and hot flushes!"

My wife grabbed the phone from me and started reading.

"What the what. Well, I'm not living with a man who has a bigger chest than me, or who's fed up and flushed all the time," she announced.

"Neither am I!" I declared, feeling my chest for any signs of spontaneous growth.

Suddenly I felt my heart miss another couple of beats.

"I'll just borrow one of your bras as a starter!" I said taking a pill from the packet and swallowing it.

"Most men turn into their mother," comforted my wife, "at least the shopping will be fun."

The Great Escape

As I squatted over the spiked gate weighing up the chances of surviving the eight-foot drop on the other side, I was distracted suddenly by the chilling sensation of a sharp iron finger exploring the inner sanctum of my tennis shorts.

The exploits of Vlad the Impaler came to mind, then I heard Clive Dunn in Dad's Army shouting, "they don't like it up em!" as he brandished his bayonet.

And that was it for me really. My spiky gate climbing days were obviously at an end. In future unless I'm being chased by a T-Rex I'm taking the senior citizen route home.

It was also growing dark and I wasn't completely sure what was waiting for me on the freedom side of that gate. It looked a bit bushy and thorny to me. Perhaps not life threatening, but was it worth an iron spike in the fundament? In fact is anything?

I decided retreat was the better part of valour. We could spend the night in the park as far as I was concerned no problem at all. There were plenty of bushes for cover.

An hour earlier when the disheveled old bloke with the little yappy dog shouted something garbled at us across the tennis court it never occurred to us that he was the park keeper in disguise. Although I did think it was strange when he gruffly shouted, "please yourself!" when we gave him a cheery wave.

Eventually it became too dark to play so we packed up and left the court not thinking for one second that we were locked in the park.

I had never actually noticed the park gates before and I completely missed the whole park within a park thing.

When we found the first locked gate we were more amazed than anything. But as we encountered another and another we by-passed the amused phase and went straight for indignant with mild panic.

The gates were also getting higher and spikier and all the time we could see the main grounds of the park with its big open gates sniggering at us in the distant twilight.

"Don't worry dad," said Adam, "we can easily climb this gate."

I wasn't so confident, the gate looked about ten feet high to me. Luckily we've been watching the old BBC TV series of Colditz and I've learned to understand the role of a good escape officer.

"So what's your plan once you get on top of that spiky ten foot high gate?" I asked.

Adam pondered for a moment gazing upwards, "shout for help?"

I tried to think who we knew with long ladders and the appropriate long ladder transport, but I wasn't sure if our window cleaner did night calls.

"What about digging a tunnel, or phoning the police?" suggested Adam, "or you could stick your head in the railings and I could phone the fire brigade?"

Instead I decided enough was enough and I climbed the next spiky gate. I got up on top of it surprisingly easily, in fact I was rather impressed.

"We should have just done this in the first place," I announced, "instead of trudging round the park for half an hour!

A few seconds later that spike found its way inside my tennis shorts and I had a sudden rush of clarity. Once Adam had helped me down I eyed those spikes with a new found respect.

It was time for logic to prevail. It was reasonable to assume we weren't the first people to find themselves locked in that section of the park, so how did the other prisoners escape?

Using our mobile phones as torches we followed the iron railings into the undergrowth until it met the back garden fence of a house. Here sure enough someone had pushed that fence back just enough for a small child to squeeze through.

Down on the ground I slithered into the gap twisting and turning. At one point about half way I got stuck, but after a massive inhalation I managed eventually to pull myself through.

Adam had an easier time of it with me dragging him free from the other side. It was quite a moment, in fact there is nothing quite like the triumphant taste of freedom.

We were within sight of the car when it occurred to me that neither of us had our tennis bag with our new rackets.

It was a long way back, but at least Adam could be confident that he had the full support of his escape officer.

The Bride of Frankenstein

I've never really got the whole vampire 'Twilight' thing. But after taking my wife for a walk a couple of weeks ago I can now appreciate the primal power of the undead. My wife had undergone four hours of intense surgery at Guy's Hospital in London, during which her overblown thyroid gland was duly removed from her neck. It weighed one and a half pounds.

"Result!" she declared when her surgeon broke the news, "I'm one and a half pounds lighter!"

Now three days later she was standing before me like a living doll. Although a doll that was perhaps undergoing some repair. She had her very own bottle of blood that was constantly being filled from a transparent tube sticking out of her neck. There was a tiny pump hard at it inside her throat chucking out all that surplus blood, but apart from that I thought my wife looked great.

"She looks really great," I whispered to a nurse, "is that normal?"

The nurse smiled, "just make sure she takes it easy," she said.

"You look great," I said to my wife as I took her arm.

"You bet!" she said, "this whole cut throat thing is a good look for me!"

I'd been trying not to look too hard at the cut throat thing. It seemed to run round her neck from ear to ear and had apparently been double stitched with metal clamps for the full Bride of Frankenstein effect. It really looked as if someone had tried to give her a head transplant, changed their mind and just stuck the old one back on.

"Right let's get cracking!" announced my wife suddenly, making me jump, "I need some action."

As we passed the nurses at reception they gave me that, 'you better bring her back in one piece mister' look and frankly I've never felt responsibility weigh so heavily on my shoulders. We were only going for a walk around the hospital corridors but suddenly I was Special Agent Phillips and everyone, even little old people in wheelchairs were a potential threat.

"Did you notice one of the nurses was called Ebola?" asked my wife, "imagine naming someone after a plague?" she continued, picking up the pace.

Actually the nurse's name was Ebella but I was more concerned with catching my wife. She was already beginning to disappear into a throng of staff and patients.

I've never taken my wife for a walk before, normally I'm trailing behind her and obviously nothing was going to change. Within minutes we were in the bustling ground floor reception and heading for the doors.

I had noticed she wasn't blinking on a regular basis and obviously there had been the anaesthetic, the morphine and a week of trash TV to contend with so its possible she wasn't quite herself.

"I really don't think you're allowed out," I said keeping an eye on the incoming flood of people.

"It's fine," laughed my wife wierdly, "I've been out shopping already." For some reason all I kept hearing was the word 'shopping'.

As she glided ghost-like across the road clutching her bottle of blood I tried to stop non-existent traffic until I realised it was a pedestrianised area. For a moment I considered running back inside and reporting my wife's escape, but she was moving too fast.

Suddenly we were in a beautiful busy cloister with gardens on either side. I'm not sure if it was the big Frankenstein throat scar, or the tubes and the bottle of blood but people seemed happy to get out of her way. Mostly with a look of dread etched on their faces. Some of the children who saw her may never be the same again.

Across the road in a trendy Veggie café she met with a similar reception. Asking if they had a toilet the girls behind the counter stared at her as if she was holding them at gunpoint.

"No toilets here I'm afraid," replied one of them nervously.

"What's that over there?" asked my wife, pointing to a door that said 'Toilets'.

The girls spoke but nothing seemed to come out.

"Never mind," continued my wife, "let's go up the Shard!"

"Yes the Shard has toilets," agreed one of the assistants, while the other one mutely apologised to me.

Instead we went into the Borough Market, which was so busy it was like being in a Guinness book of records attempt.

A group of Goths decided my wife was the coolest thing they had seen and photographed her as she posed with them. Then my wife sort of folded and that was that, fortunately.

Back in her bed, she peered at me for a moment "did you know I was cool?" she muttered.

"Right from the start," I replied, but she was already asleep, clutching her crimson bottle for comfort.

The Soapy Opera

Originally we joined our local gym to stay in shape and watch rubbish TV but now it's turned into something of a social event with friends and neighbours popping up on the next Cross Trainer like the cast of a fitness-based soap opera.

I spent a lovely hour last week chatting to Bob the manager of our local post office while cycling to nowhere and back. Earlier we had both rowed for twenty minutes to nowhere and back so we knew the route.

I'm not sure how old Bob is but he took the post office job several years ago when he retired from the army. Facially I'd say he was probably around seventy, but from the neck down he looks about forty-five. I wouldn't really have guessed that until he joined me in the communal shower.

I have nothing against communal showers, but I probably wouldn't put them at the top of my Santa list.

"Mind if I join you?" asked Bob smiling broadly.

I could hardly say no, the shower room was empty, it's about 15 metres by 10 metres and has 12 showerheads, one of which is permanently cold. Bob immediately went for that one and turned it on full blast while I tried to find anything more interesting to look at. He gave it about a minute and then walked over to the shower next to mine.

"So, do you come here often?" he asked smiling to himself again as he started soaping his chest.

'It could be worse' I thought, at least he's not soaping mine.

It's difficult to describe Bob's shower routine in much detail as I spent most of the time trying not to notice how young he looked from the neck down. For a start he had an impressively panelled chest and an amazing six pack, actually that's as far south as I got. The rest is just soap and bubbles.

We chatted for a few minutes until another naked bloke turned up. It was Steve, who happened to be Bob's solicitor. Steve had been out running and just popped in for a shower. His legal practice is just round the corner from our house. I'd passed the sign often enough and now I told him I could put a face and pretty much everything else to the name.

Steve asked to borrow Bob's body wash as his had just run out. I offered him mine and for a few moments they were both mulled over.

"I quite like something lemony," said Steve rubbing his chin.

"Hold on," I said, 'I'll see what I've got!"

We laughed and Steve plumped for Bob's.

According to my wife this sort of thing doesn't happen in the women's showers, some of them have partitions and there's none of the Roman Bath camaraderie I was now trying to resist.

Bob was now enthusing about his Spanish holiday and Steve had given us a recipe for a fantastic chilli sauce he swore by. I showed them my freshly scalded left hand and that led us onto recent injuries, then operations and of course scars. Bob has a nice long one on his right thigh. Old army wound he told us and laughed.

The next time Bob serves me in the post office fully clothed I thought, I'll remember that scar.

Two boisterous young lads turned up, one of whom was singing, 'do you think I'm sexy?' at the top of his voice. At least they had the decency to go to the opposite corner. Or maybe they thought we had a little party going on up our end.

A short, chubby bearded bloke appeared wearing a striped business shirt, boxer shorts and socks. If only I'd known there was a clothing option.

"Oh hello Colin," shouted Steve the Solicitor, "how's the separation going?"

Colin gave us a gloomy thumbs up, "fantastic!" he shouted as he began soaping his shirt with Vosene shampoo. There then followed brief introductions and soapy handshakes all round.

After washing the clothes he was standing in, Colin disrobed and had a very aggressive shower, scrubbing and poking and soaping like a maniac.

"Colin's in a tiny bedsit," gurgled Steve as he rinsed his hair, "newly separated from his wife."

Colin gave us a long-suffering look as he rang out his shirt. For a moment I was struck by the amount of body hair he was sporting. It was thick and remarkably curly, like Coir matting.

At that point I sort of came to my senses and started to escape but Bob and Steve followed me.

While we dried ourselves Bob showed us some of his lovely holiday photographs on his phone. That's the most photos of Marbella I've seen, naked.

The Mysterious Traveller

There used to be a rule about not using the toilet on a train when it was standing in the station, but apparently that's no longer the case.

"Why didn't you go before the train started?" asked my wife as I was thrown back into my seat. I told her about the rule and she shook her head. Our son Adam meanwhile looked amused.

"Was it something to do with the smoke from the train choking you?" he said.

"It's just poor toilet training," replied my wife.

Modern trains may have stepped up their game in the toilet department but they need to do more work on the shake, rattle and roll. When you see people in films on trains they don't get thrown around like rag dolls in a storm.

Searching for a toilet that was actually working I rocketed through one empty carriage after another like a human pinball, bouncing off the edge of one seat onto the next. Eventually I found a toilet but just as I was about to open the door I was yanked into a seat right next to an old lady.

"That's why I sit near the toilet," she announced smugly, "you meet all sorts."

"Good luck!" she added as I made it back to the toilet door. But just as I opened it, the train lurched and pulled me backwards like a lifeless puppet. I was still holding onto the door, but fortunately my hand wasn't completely crushed against the wall.

In hindsight I should have just run along the train roof and smashed my way in through the toilet window. Next time, I'm on a train, I thought, I'll bring a stunt double.

The old lady was asleep when I was eventually thrown back out of the toilet. For some reason it felt like a rather efficient process. The very life had literally been shaken out of me, I had been spat back out and now I was raring to go.

The journey back to my seat was reassuringly familiar and I managed to crumple my right side against a seat so now I had a matching set of bruises. When the train stopped at a little station I made a dash for it but got caught between carriages when it started up again, lurching back and forth.

By the time I got back I was needing the toilet again, but I didn't have the stamina for an another expedition. To my surprise there was a large, glamorous middle-aged woman sitting in my seat looking very pleased with herself. As far as I could see the carriage was empty, yet here she was smiling knowingly at me over her well-thumbed copy of Fifty Shades of Gray.

"How did you get on?" she asked, as I sat down opposite her, "did you manage OK?"

I smiled weakly at her, trying to work out if I knew her then I glanced at my wife and Adam for help.

"I was just telling this lady you had to go searching for a toilet," explained my wife, her eyes, telling me a different story, something like, 'this lady seems nice but she may be bonkers so just play along with her'. It's amazing what you can get from a single stare. I nodded and then asked my wife for hand sanitiser.

"Did you forget to wash your hands?" asked our new friend, lowering her book to reveal an unusual amount of cleavage, "naughty, naughty!"

"It's very warm in this carriage don't you think?" said my wife suddenly, giving me a loaded stare.

"The next carriage has air conditioning," I said, "shall we move?"

"What a great idea!" declared the woman suddenly, "lead on Macduff!"

We all stood up slowly, smiling at one another in silence, then slowly rattled and bumped our way into the next empty carriage.

"Here's the perfect seat!" announced the woman waving her book in the air.

"Excellent," replied my wife, "why don't you have those seats all to yourself and we'll sit here."

I piled in next to my wife and Adam but the woman followed and filled the fourth seat, mostly it seemed to me with cleavage.

"Oh I do love a smutty book don't you?" she said, getting herself comfortable with Mr Gray.

For ten minutes she giggled to herself and then just as I was beginning to wonder if we were being held hostage by some kind of passive-aggressive dominatrix, the train stopped and the woman got off without a word.

"Next time," said my wife, "just go to the loo before you get on the train."

Which reminded me.

The Four Checked Shirts

I had fallen into a cosy reverie, which I was actually enjoying, not quite a bonafide daze but I was working on it. Suddenly my wife grabbed my left knee and started shaking me back to reality.

"Oh my God!" she whispered intently into my ear, "you'll never believe this."

"Believe what?" I whispered, now on full alert. Obviously something absolutely staggering had just happened and typically I had missed it. I quickly glanced around but couldn't see much in the way of interest.

"This is amazing," continued my wife pulling our son Adam into her confidence. Adam I assumed had also been in his very own private zone, he certainly looked as if he had travelled a great distance when I caught his gaze.

"What's happened?" he whispered anxiously, "is everything OK, what's going on?"

My wife was looking very pleased with herself as she glanced at us both in turn, "You two need to pay more attention to what's happening around you," she said.

Adam and I shared baffled looks. The tension was now beginning to annoy me so I demanded to be put out of my misery.

"Well, don't get too excited," began my wife, trying her best to conceal the triumph in her voice, "but there are three men right in front of us, sitting very close together, all wearing the same short-sleeved checked shirt and all of them are bald."

Now normally that would hardly have been edge of seat news but believe me in the circumstances it was like winning the lottery. Adam I both immediately sat bolt upright and started scouring the theatre audience for the three bald, check shirt wearing men.

I found two, but Adam had them all and pointed me in the direction of the third man.

"Weird," I said and made the woman in front of me turn round with her best steely face.

"Amazing," added Adam making the woman's husband turn and give him a matching stare.

"Sorry," I whispered to the couple, "but there are three bald men wearing matching shirts more or less in front of you."

The couple started looking round for the three men. They seemed delighted once they had found them and then the bloke came back with the startling news that there was a fourth.

"There can't be!" said my wife, making almost the entire row turn round, including one of the check shirted bald men.

"I've got him!" announced Adam, "he's up there in balcony."

Sure enough there was our fourth bald man in that now very familiar short-sleeved checked shirt.

Meanwhile something was happening onstage involving someone's trousers and a garden hose that had gone missing.

"Twenty five quid I've paid to watch someone's trousers fall down while they were looking for a garden hose!" grumbled Adam during the interval.

"But there was that fascinating subplot about the neutered cat," I said.

"And the four men in the audience wearing the same shirt," added my wife, "don't forget them."

I had a feeling that Adam wouldn't be accompanying us to the theatre for at least the rest of his life. We discussed escaping but after examining the heavy rain outside and remembering that I was reviewing the play, we decided to stay for the second act and see how many more men we could find wearing matching shirts.

"I found them first," declared my wife as we related the story to a friend we met in the foyer.

Peggy said she would keep an eye out for them during the second half.

"I'll tell you what," she added, "we went to a London theatre last week and saw Lord of the Rings, it was much better than this, in fact it was absolutely amazing."

Somehow the stage version of Lord of Rings had obviously passed us by.

"The dancing was out of this world, their legs went like this," Peggy then made fast twisty movements with her fingers, "sometimes their feet were just a blur," she continued, "they have microphones in their shoes so you can hear them properly. What a great show, you must see it!"

"Lord of the Rings, the dance version?" said my wife.

Peggy nodded enthusiastically.

"Is it as good as the book or the film?" I asked.

"Never read or seen it," said Peggy, "but I'd go back and see that show again."

"And the dwarves and elfs were all dancing?" asked my wife.

"Everyone was dancing," said Peggy, "like this." She then started Irish Step dancing, arms rigid by her sides.

At least this gave us something to mull over as we returned to our seats.

"Why didn't we go and see that?" demanded Adam, "I love Irish Step Dancing and Hobbits."

Sweet Enough

My wife doesn't need a supermarket loyalty card, she already has one, hard wired into her brain. If she likes a product then she literally can't get it enough of it and if it happens to be an own brand, like a certain type of diet ginger beer then the supermarket has hit the loyalty jackpot.

"I had to buy 18 cans," she said last week, "it's really annoying, the shop keeps running out."

The supermarket keeps running out because my wife is bleeding them dry. There's probably a special area in the supermarket's warehouse with my wife's name on it. Just as well its only certain food products or soft drinks, or vital things like baby wipes and not designer shoes and handbags.

But carrying all those cans of ginger beer up 39 steps to our flat on an almost daily basis is taking its toll on my knees. So I couldn't believe my luck when my wife declared she was taking her latest batch back to the supermarket for a refund.

"Thank goodness for that," I said, "drinking ginger beer by the gallon can't be good for you."

"It's not the ginger beer, that's bothering me," said my wife, "it's the Aspartame, the side effects are terrible apparently."

"Does it cause obsessions with certain soft drinks and baby wipes?" I asked staring at the list of ingredients on the side of one of the cans and failing to find any mention of ginger or beer.

"It's really annoying," continued my wife, "they take the sugar out so we won't get fat and replace it with a sweetener that drives everyone nuts!"

"It's banned in a lot of countries," I said gravely, chipping in my tuppence-worth while looking up Aspartame on my phone, "oh dear, it says here that it causes…"

But the list was too long and my wife just nodded sagely, "I know and I've been drinking it by the gallon."

"Well maybe not quite the gallon," I said trying to play it down.

We agreed not to mention it to the supermarket management.

"It's not worth it," said my wife, "I'll stick to fizzy water from now on."

Music to my ears but the Aspartame thing was bothering me so the moment my wife put the cans down on the customer care counter and asked for a refund I was off.

"It's your own brand and its got Aspartame in it, a chemical that's banned in half the countries in the world because it drives people nuts and causes panic attacks."

The assistant looked surprised.

"Sorry what's it called?" she asked.

"Honestly, it's fine," said my wife, "if I could just have a refund that would be great."

"Yes and we'll resist suing the supermarket," I added.

"Would you like me to get the manager?" asked the assistant.

"No thank you, that won't be necessary," said my wife kicking me in the shin.

"Are you ok Sir?" asked the assistant as I winced.

"It's the Aspartame kicking in," I groaned and then hobbled off.

Armed with my new artificial sweetener knowledge I thought it my duty to scrutinise the ingredients of every item we bought.

"It won't be in garlic bread," said my wife as I peered at the label on a baguette, "Or in semi-skimmed milk," she added taking the milk from my hand and placing in our trolley.

Meanwhile I was trying to work out how much money the supermarket was going to lose now my wife was off the diet ginger beer. Their share price might even be affected.

"You might want to check your favourite diet lemonade that you can't live without," said my wife and for a moment a nasty little icy wave of panic overtook me. This particular own brand of diet lemonade is a vital ingredient in the making of vodka martinis. So obviously a life essential.

I made straight for it in the next aisle, grabbed a bottle and ran down the ingredients.

There was the usual carbonated water, lemon juice from concentrate and then a pile of stuff that sounded like the ingredients for a home made car battery and finally Sucralose, but thankfully no Aspartame.

"Sucralose!" declared my wife, "that's worse!"

I quickly looked it up and it wasn't good. I particularly didn't like the part about Sucralose penetrating the blood barrier around your brain, allegedly.

"Fizzy water?" asked my wife holding up a bottle, "that will be ok in a vodka martini won't it?"

I considered it for a moment.

"I'm going to live dangerously thanks," I said, placing four bottles of diet lemonade in the trolley, "it's a dirty job but someone's got to do it."

Knees Up

I was going to get a T-shirt made saying, 'I hurt my knee playing tennis', but my wife didn't think I was going far enough.

"How about, I hurt my knee," she began thoughtfully, then paused as she plotted out the words on her imaginary T-shirt, "during a really dangerous mission to save the world, but I don't like to speak about it, or complain about it to anyone ever, because it's very top secret?"

"Bit long for a T-shirt," I said.

Anyway to keep the cost down I had to order a minimum of 36 T-shirts and when I thought about it I don't really wear a T-shirt that often. Except at the gym and that's one of the few places you get genuine respect for a sports related injury.

"Tennis," I said to one of the iron men at the gym when he pointed sympathetically at my trussed up, mummified right knee.

"Warming up is so important dude, particularly when you're that bit older," he replied slapping me on the back and making my ancient dusty bones rattle.

Actually it's just as important to make sure you place your specially made support insoles into your tennis shoes in the correct feet. Apparently this tiny error of judgement distorted my hip/knee/ankle alignment and increased my chances of injury. A lot of people have found this fascinating.

Just to add injury to injury I'd also put the insoles back in the wrong feet in my ordinary trainers and then walked around in them for two weeks, making my knee worse. When Phil my favourite Podiatrist inspected the insoles for wear and tear he held them up and frowned at them. I thought it was the odour but then he gave me that, 'you're a bit of a prat aren't you?' sympathetic smile.

"So it wasn't the tennis?" began my wife, "you tore a ligament in your knee because you can't tell the difference between right and left!"

True, but still not a great T-shirt slogan.

Technically I was actually playing tennis when that first fiery stab of knee pain stopped me in mid-forehand smash. I thought I'd been shot or struck by lightning, the sky was a touch on the broody side.

Three weeks later I'm still hobbling and wincing at almost every step. Getting in and out of the car is the worst. The twisting action brings tears to my eyes so I have to swivel my legs out like some fifties Debutante.

"That's a very demur look," said one of my friends as I slinked out of the car in front of him, "I think it suits you. Can you walk with a book on your head?"

I can't but I can tell you the number of knee replacements I've heard about it.

"My granddad had a knee replacement," said a woman in a queue in Marks and Spencer, "he had no end of trouble with it."

"Apparently it's a very painful and long recovery for older people," said another woman, giving me a long sympathetic look.

"Is it housemaid's knee?" asked the first woman making the check-out lady wince.

"Ooh I had that for years," she said through ill-fitting dentures, "that's why I stopped going to church."

The other evening at our local cinema I saw the manager watching me as I limped slowly towards the box office. Although we had set out together my wife had beaten me to it, bought her ticket, had a pre-emptive comfort break and was waiting for me in the foyer, she tapped her watch as I hobbled past.

The manager didn't mention the limp but he gave me a consoling discount of two quid. When I paid him the £5.50 I gave him a knowing wink.

We were there to see the film '45 Years' starring Charlotte Rampling and Tom Courtney and the little cinema was a snowstorm of white heads.

Just before the film started the assistant manager turned up to make his usual announcement about mobile phones.

"Right, listen up, I know it's probably past your bedtime," he began cheekily, then turning to me said, "but do your best to stay awake during this one. And anyone caught throwing a Werther's original will be carried out forthwith," again he looked directly at me. Everyone laughed.

"How much was your ticket?" I asked my wife.

"£7.50, how much was yours?" she replied, but the film was starting so I kept quiet and shoved a Werther's original in my mouth.

I thought the T-shirt might say something like, 'I'm not over 60 but I accept discount'. Although the limp and the constant pained wince seems to say it all.

Hard Times

About a quarter of a mile down our road I had one of those epiphanies, 'wait a minute!' I shouted, as I slammed on the brakes and leapt out of the car. My wife meanwhile barely batted an eyelid and continued rummaging in her bag for the mysterious stuff she rummages for.

To be fair she's used to these occasional sudden stops. Normally it's a strange sound or an odd smell coming from the back end of the car that I just have to investigate before we get too far up a country road without a mobile signal. There's never anything there of course, apart my imagination working overtime.

Two minutes earlier I'd put my briefcase in the boot and we'd set off from the house without a care in the world, but something was niggling at me. Something I just couldn't put my finger on until my wife asked if we were going to the gym that evening. Then for a moment I saw an empty space in the car boot, shaped like my gym bag.

I now stood scratching my chin over that space. My wife's gym bag was there but for some reason mine had vanished. Back in the car I pulled over and phoned the gym. While I waited for my call to be answered I told my wife about the bag shaped space.

"That's funny," she said, "I remember seeing it last night and wondering if you'd left a damp towel in it."

A girl answered the phone and I asked if a battered old black gym bag had been handed in, but it hadn't.

"Well if its been nicked you'd better keep an eye out for any thieves that might be availing themselves of your facilities," I laughed, "because my gym card was in it."

The girl was silent for a moment.

"We don't tend to get many burglars using the gym," she said.

My wife was now investigating the boot. Suddenly I heard a faint shriek.

"Sorry," I said to the girl, "I'll have to go, my wife's screaming."

"You never said the boot had been cleaned out," said my wife when I joined her.

Apart from my wife's gym bag, my genuine Russian fur hat and one old trainer, the boot was in fact empty and strangely tidy, almost as if it had been vacuumed.

"Where's my other trainer gone?" I said, picking up the remaining one and giving it a proprietorial sniff.

"Never mind your smelly old trainer!" shouted my wife, "where's everything else, where's the picnic stuff and the bag of clothes we were about to drop off at the Red Cross shop?"

"What about the workshop and art class posters!" I shouted.

It was a real cliffhanger of a moment but I quickly started to feel as if I'd fallen off the cliff.

"We've either been burgled," I announced, "or, this isn't our car."

"Good point, "said my wife, "even if it isn't our car, I assume you locked it last night?"

In fact I'd been having trouble with the remote locking system and couldn't be certain that it had been locked. It was however parked up our drive, with the boot facing the pavement. Which meant someone either knew the car was unlocked or they had gone up the whole street trying every car until they hit the jackpot with ours.

"What I don't understand is, why they didn't take your gym kit or my best Russian hat?" I said, pulling on the hat.

Judging by my wife's expression this wasn't a question worth answering. True my gym bag was decrepit and contained half used body wash, shampoo and deodorant, a pair of pound shop specs, a damp towel, smelly socks and an old T-shirt, but there was also my favourite fluorescent orange shorts and matching headphones.

Back in the car looking for an emergency packet of Rennies my wife opened the glove compartment and nothing fell out because it was empty. In fact the front of the car was completely devoid of anything, including around £10 in loose change, our sunglasses, a dozen classical CDs, a half eaten Snickers bar and a load of other boring but sometimes handy things you might need during a car journey.

"Hard times," muttered my wife, "unless of course you dumped your gym bag to get out of going to the gym and then cleaned out the rest of the car to make it look like a burglary."

"That would explain why your gym kit was left," I replied running my fingers around the empty door compartment and finding one mouldy licorice allsort.

"Case solved," said my wife, "drive on Watson."

Bagged

I had a street fight on Saturday afternoon. I say street fight because that was how it seemed to me, but in reality I suppose it probably looked more like a brief altercation. Certainly the passing community policeman just kept on passing by. He probably had it down as a mild disagreement, although for the few fleeting seconds when he slowed down he looked more concerned for my welfare than the old lady's.

She had just exited the shopping centre as I was approaching it for the second time. The first time I'd just reached the door when I remembered I'd forgotten to bring a carrier bag with me as usual, so I had to go back to the car and get one from the boot.

Normally I would just throw caution to the wind and either buy yet another bag that I could add to our expanding collection, or go carrier bag commando and walk back to the car balancing everything I had bought in a precarious pyramid. After a close call with a bag of clementines and a bottle of vodka I decided that I had to take my food shopping more seriously.

There was an impressive selection in the boot, about twenty or thirty flimsy 5p jobs of various colours and brands and enough bags for life to last at least a dozen lifetimes.

I'm not sure how the bag for life promise works if the shop you bought it from goes bust at some point in the distant future. Maybe there's some kind of special bag for life fulfillment insurance in place. It does make you think twice though about shelling out an extra five pence for a slightly thicker, slightly bigger bag with a nice design on it.

I was only nipping into Iceland so naturally I grabbed the nearest Marks and Spencer bag and shoved it in my jacket pocket.

Back at the shopping centre door my phone went as the old lady approached. I pulled it out and saw my M&S bag flying momentarily between us. Cool as you like without batting an eyelid the old lady snatched the bag and tucked into her shopping trolley bag.

"Excuse me," I said, "I think that was my bag."

The old lady stopped and frowned up at me. "You think that was your bag?" She asked, "you just think it was yours, so you're not completely sure?"

It was my wife on the phone so I told her I'd phone her back. She managed to squeeze in an order for six iceberg lettuces before I cut her off.

"Actually I'm fairly certainly it was my bag," I said, "so if you don't mind I'd like it back."

The old lady was still frowning at me although it may just have been her natural facial expression.

"Was it a Markies bag by any chance?" she asked.

"Absolutely," I said.

"Then it was mine!" she declared and started moving off.

The government says that the carrier bag mountain has now been greatly reduced but I can tell you it hasn't, its just been moved to our house. I suppose it is a cheap form of insulation but lately we've been thinking about having our collection professionally recycled.

We reckon we've got enough for a bench and probably a complete set of sturdy garden furniture, the sort you see in laybys for picnickers who enjoy the jeopardy of a family meal within a few feet of a speeding juggernaut.

So I thought to myself, I didn't build one of the largest carrier bag mountains in the West by letting some frail old lady run off with one of Markies' finest. I could see the bag sticking out of the trolley so I made a subtle grab for it but she was too quick for me and pulled it away.

"Look," I said, "I'm sorry to bother you but that's my carrier bag, I just went all the way back to the car for it, then it flew out of my pocket when I answered my phone and you very kindly picked it for me, but now I'd like it back."

"I've seen you somewhere before!" snarled the old lady as she pointed a shaky finger at my face.

That's when the community policeman passed by, glanced at us, probably thought, that nice man's trying to help that garrulous old lady with her shopping but she's having none of it and walked on.

Which is just as well because that's when it got heated. I got my bag back though. At the checkout I pulled two Markies' bags out of my pocket. Still, I'm five pence up.

One Day I'll Fly Away

Apparently as you grow older you lose the ability to hear high-pitched sounds. Unfortunately that doesn't seem to include the hair-raising squealing noise that's been keeping me awake at night.

You would think some night prowling sadist was at work on our bedroom window with a lump of polystyrene. We're 39 steps up in a top floor flat so they'd have to be pretty agile.

"It's only seagulls!" shouted my wife as she re-adjusted her earplugs.

Maybe it's just me but earplugs don't work. The average fledgling seagull has been genetically refined over the millennia so that its mother can hear it shrieking for grub on the other side of the earth. A couple of fiddly bits of foam aren't going to stand between a mother and her young.

"So no point in moving!" shouted my wife.

I've got some history with seagulls and most of it, in fact all of it, is bad. I've been attacked, harassed, entangled, dumped on and stolen from countless times over the years.

Last week at the seafront I engaged in a tug of war with a couple of seagulls the size of small dogs. The first giant gull appeared from nowhere and pinched a baguette sandwich I was about to eat. Fortunately the baguette was shrink wrapped and too heavy for the seagull to fly off with, so it called for a mate to give it a hand. I had to step in and pull it from the thieves' beaks, only they wouldn't let it go.

A bloke sitting nearby jumped up and for a moment I thought he was going to lend a hand but instead he started videoing the potentially hilarious scene on his phone.

"I'm only here for the week and so far this is the best fun I've had!" he shouted, "can you look a bit angrier?"

In the end I got the baguette back but the seagulls weren't happy. As they flew off I could see them marking my card.

Lying awake listening to that stream of skull cracking squeals it was obvious they had sent their kids to annoy me.

"I wonder where they are?" I said outloud to myself up at the window, peering into the feeble darkness. My wife was asleep by this time, she is a year older than me so its possible she's become more immune to those high pitched sounds.

Her eyesight must be better though, because the next morning she was pointing excitedly across the road at our neighbour Tom's house.

"I've found one of the culprits!" she shouted.

Joining her at the window all I could see was Tom manfully trimming his hedge. Tom is one of those busy octogenarians that make me feel lazy, but somehow I just couldn't see him up squealing in the middle of the night.

"Not Tom you twit," said my wife, "up on his roof!"

There is a small flat area on the top of Tom's roof and suddenly a ball of grey fluff appeared on the edge. It pushed out a pair of little wings, gave them a nervous flap then tumbled backwards out of sight.

"Oh its so cute!" said my wife, "it's trying to fly."

Again the baby gull appeared, flapped its little wings, and fell backwards. We were hooked. This must have been what it was like before television.

Over the next few days I warmed to Terence, don't ask, I suggested Steven (Seagal), George (Segal) but was shot down. Terence certainly had pluck and as he grew larger by the minute – weight, which seemed to play against his escape plan. His parents meanwhile kept an encouraging eye on him.

"Eventually he will join a nursery flock where he will play and learn vital skills for adulthood," read my wife from her iPad, "and he can drink both fresh and sea water."

Who would have known?

One morning there was tremendous excitement when Terence made it onto Tom's chimney top. I took a photograph but it just looks like the chimney's wearing a little grey hat.

But now I could put a name to the midnight squealer it didn't seem so bad.

Then Tom asked us if we had by some slim chance spotted something strange on his chimney. We were so excited to share Terence's antics we gave Tom a detailed account of the fledgling's movements over the last few days. I was about to show him the photos on my phone when I realised Tom was looking at us with faint alarm.

"We just happened to notice him, in passing," said my wife.

"Because of that high pitched squealing noise," I added.

"Squealing noise?" asked Tom.

Bin Here

We've bought the same two Sunday papers religiously for years but they've obviously outgrown us because ninety percent of them ends up in the recycling. We say the same thing every Sunday when we dump them in the bin, it's like a Mantra designed to soothe rather than motivate.

"You wonder who reads all this stuff?" I'll say.

"Hopefully someone at the recycling centre," my wife will reply.

We were late home last Sunday night and the bin was so full I had to press the papers down just to close the lid.

Half an hour later, my wife was looking for a magazine I had just accidentally thrown out. There was more recycling to go out, so I volunteered my services, plus I wanted my money's worth with that magazine.

"Technically speaking that magazine cost us around £1.50," I shouted to my wife from the landing, "and the bin gets emptied tomorrow morning."

Our bins sit in a neat little walled area off the path. You can still see them from the pavement but at least they're all neatly lined up, shoulder to shoulder, although the recycling bin being much larger has to stand on its own. I always think it looks slightly smug and probably looks down on the other common or garden waste bins. Or at least it did when I last saw it half an hour earlier.

Even though the bin wasn't there I still stood for a minute or so in front of the empty space holding my bits cardboard and my bag of plastic bottles. Open mouthed – because that's what you do under such extraordinary circumstances, I swiveled around in search of the errant bin.

'Maybe,' I thought, 'it had rolled off somewhere', which was impossible of course. But nevertheless I checked round the sides of the house with high hopes of finding it hiding from me. I even looked around the car, which was up the driveway. Then I expanded my search to the immediate pavement and the street, all the while still holding on to my little bundle of recycling.

When I got back the bin was still gone, I had no alternative but to go back upstairs with my recycling.

"Did you try calling for it?" asked my wife.

"Seriously," I said, "it's gone, along with that magazine."

My wife's face darkened as she went to the window, even though you can't quite see the bins from there.

"That's a pity, I was looking forward to reading that magazine, in fact it's the only part worth reading," she said.

I don't think my wife completely believed me, in fact I wasn't sure I believed myself, so much so that when we went downstairs to check I was surprised to find the bin hadn't returned.

"It can't just have disappeared," said my wife standing in front of the empty space repeating my open mouth look while swiveling around in case the bin had decided to go for a little trundle.

"But it was jam packed," she continued, "half an hour ago!"

Which was a good point. Not only had someone nicked our recycling bin they had nicked our recycling.

"This is the sort of thing the secret service do when they're investigating someone," added my wife darkly.

"Or just some builder who needed an extra wheelie bin," I said, "who else would be fit enough to lift the bin into a van?"

"If they had a van. Maybe one of the neighbours has pinched it because their bin's damaged or nicked," suggested my wife, "maybe we're part of some missing wheelie bin domino effect."

"Well it stops here!" I declared, "I'm not stealing someone else's bin just because ours was nicked."

"Good for you," replied my wife, "that's how wars start. Plus when you think about it the bin has fulfilled its destiny by being recycled."

I mentioned all this on the phone to the bloke from the council waste department. I also told him our car had been recently burgled. He was surprised to hear that and the bit about the secret service.

"And you're sure you haven't mislaid the bin?" he asked.

I tried to picture that for a moment and wondered if we had checked under the bed, or down the side of the sofa.

"Actually we were thinking of putting up missing posters," I said dryly, "you know, with a nice photo of the bin, maybe with a sad face painted on it."

"You could try that," began the bloke, "but if the posters blew away they would be considered litter and technically you would be held responsible."

Might bin that idea I thought.

Sticky

Sometimes the urge to fix things is overpowering, particularly if the amount of effort involved will be minimal. If the item in question belongs to my wife then even better because it usually guarantees a decent return for little investment.

Quite often I fix things by default because for instance the screwdriver I lost five years ago turns out to have been living at the back of my sock drawer, or as happened to me last week a tube of extra strong glue attached itself to my hand while I was rummaging around in a cupboard. It was like winning the lucky dip.

"Aha!" I said, smiling to myself, "now I can stick some things together."

Top of the list had to be one of my wife's trainers. I had a vague memory of her stubbing her toe and the front sole of this hand crafted designer trainer coming away and here I was with a tube of super powerful glue about my person. Actually it was attached to my person but it was still fate.

The excitement was almost too much as I hunted down this trainer. By the time I found it I had managed to detach myself from the tube of glue and had already begun planning my next sticky situation.

The main thing about using really strong glue is remembering to treat it with respect and a degree of focus that only comes from wearing one's specs, so on they went. A few carefully placed drops of glue under the end of the sole and the trainer was good as new. In fact you would never have known there had been anything wrong with it if it hadn't been for the bloke wriggling on the end of it.

I was holding the trainer in my left hand and pressing the sole together with my right while blowing on the glue in the rather optimistic belief that it would dry faster. Which it did, a lot faster in fact.

When the tube of glue stuck to my hand earlier it had been a playful, casual sort of attachment. It was nothing serious; both of us knew that from the start. It was fun while it lasted and when the time came for us to move on we did so knowing that it was the right thing to do.

The trainer on the other hand seemed to be interested in a long-term commitment. When I tried the surprise approach – tugging my fingers away, my pinkie broke free, but the other three fingers and my thumb decided they wanted to bond with the trainer and refused to budge without leaving their prints behind as evidence.

By this time I was laughing out loud, partly because I'd never seen anything so stupid but mainly through a growing sense of dread. You don't see many people gainfully employed with a ladies size 4 brown trainer dangling from the end of their right hand.

It makes all kinds of social activities tricky. Driving would be out of the question for instance and almost anything else I can think of.

At least I could answer my mobile. When it rang half of me thought 'hurrah' help is at hand, if you know what I mean, but the rest of me wanted to go into hiding.

As it turned out it was Bob from the local garage telling me my car was ready to collect.

I was on the brink of turning the conversation towards the subject of super glue antidotes when Bob asked if I could nip round for the car sooner rather than later because he was running out of space.

"I'll be right on it," I said with surprising authority, "I just have something to attend to first."

Remembering what Freud said about the shoe being the ultimate sexual fetish object I decided the trainer just had to go. A mild wave of panic cruised up the back of my neck as I saw before me an excruciating trip to A&E. It wasn't as if I could hide the thing.

There's just nowhere you can conceal a trainer about your person, not for any length of time. Even if it had been big enough for me to wear I would have had to lurch around like some knuckle scraper.

I had just reconciled myself to losing the skin off my fingertips when I was literally saved by the doorbell. It was my wife, she had forgotten her keys.

Glancing down at the trainer she snatched it from me and made off with it mumbling something about throwing the pair of old things in the bucket.

It's strange but at the time the only thing I felt was relief.

Sofa so Good

I asked my wife recently if she thought she had made indecision into an art form. She thought about it for a minute, during which I could see her struggling to come to any sort of firm conclusion and in the end she had to admit she wasn't sure.

"What else could it be apart from an art form?" she asked, looking puzzled.

It was never intended to be a multiple choice question so I told her to forget it and concentrate on the job at hand which involved deciding whether we should go for the three seater or the two seater sofa.

It was a tough decision to make. It had already taken a month to talk ourselves out of our first choice of colour, a strange but compelling pale green. Only it wasn't pale green because when you held the sample swatch up to various light sources it changed tone. Then there was the denim type blue. It was quickly cast aside in favour of the snappier, more provocative ambiguous green blue. But somehow the original blue made a comeback.

Just in case, the samples were tacked to the current sofa which is apparently well passed its smell by date and mulled over and for at least a week the whole thing was off.

"Who needs a brand new sofa in a dining kitchen anyway?" said my wife.

Thinking this was some kind of trick I agreed and shook my head at the same time just for good measure.

"Sorry, was that a yes or a no?" asked my wife.

I just made a vague wheezing noise. I'm too long in the tooth for absolutes when it comes to domestic purchases.

But now finally we had come to a decision, it was the two seater, no three seater, in green, sorry in blue, yes blue, possibly.

"Tell you what," said my wife, "let's measure everything again and get the samples out."

"Or," I said, pretending I wasn't losing the will to live, "lets phone the sofa company up and buy the blue three seater?"

My wife suddenly looked very nervous, "OK go for it, three seater in blue, no green, no blue."

Nick was very enthusiastic about our purchase. Although he did ask if it was a surprise for my wife or partner. Apparently not many men buy sofas over the phone.

"Its all good Nick," I said reassuringly, "my wife's standing by in case I cave under pressure."

Nick was from somewhere in the north of England and apparently we were about to buy his favourite sofa, he'd sold hundreds of them, not many over the phone, he had to admit so he recommended going into the shop's nearest branch and giving the sofa a test drive, so to speak before we committed ourselves.

As my wife left the room I told Nick in no uncertain terms that if I didn't buy this sofa in the next ten minutes I would be committed.

"What's he saying?" asked my wife as she came back into the room.

I just shook my head as I listened to Nick telling me how comfortable the sofa was, in fact probably the most comfortable sofa he ever sold. He would have one himself but he still lived with his parents, although they were thinking about buying one.

"Can I pay by card?" I interrupted, but there was no stopping Nick. Now he wanted to know where the sofa would be.

"Is it fussy?" I asked.

"I'm thinking of light," said Nick, "will there be direct sunlight?"

"That's a question I ask every day," I replied.

"The problem is fading," explained Nick, "and of course I have to warn you about sitting on the arms of the sofa, that might cause damage, also if you sit on it with damp jeans there will be a chance of dye transfer."

"We don't have jeans," I said, " and no one will sit on the sofa, never mind on the arms in damp denim!"

"But if that should occur you would be completely covered by our five year..."

Suddenly my wife was looking anxious.

"Why are you talking about damp jeans?" she asked.

"So anyway Nick, here's my long card number, are you ready?" I said.

"Sorry did you say the sofa would be in a dining kitchen?" asked Nick, "because there might be a chance of spillage or food stains, now I should tell you about our..."

I started reading the card number. To be honest I don't think I've bought anything with so much conviction.

"Wow, that was easy," said my wife smiling, "while you're in the mood, how about a new free standing fridge?"

The Bench

I was disappointed last week to see one of my favourite benches lying dismembered on the pavement like a bundle of firewood.

No doubt the relatives of the bench's dedicatee Miss Barbara Simpson 'loyal friend of this parish' would be even more distressed.

I say it's a favourite bench but I've never actually sat on it. I had however, earmarked it as a future possibility and here it was in wrack and ruin.

"Maybe it's self assembly," suggested my wife as we stared at the wreck, "probably only take you about a week."

"I'd like to reassemble whoever did it," I grumbled darkly.

It looked as if the bench had been torn from the pavement and then dropped from a great height. It's the kind of thing some monster might do in a film to get a super hero's attention.

"Let's hope no one was sitting on it at the time," said my wife as we glanced back at the sorry scene.

When it was intact the bench sat outside a rather grand house directly across the road from a private school so its demise I assumed would not go unnoticed. It did however go unreported.

Four days later it was still lying in a broken heap, gathering sodden leaves around its various parts for comfort.

"Maybe the bench police are busy at this time of the year," said my wife, but I was already on the phone to the council.

"Oh hello Mr Phillips," said the bloke at the other end, "it's Michael here, what have you got for us today?"

"Is that your pal?" asked my wife who had been listening in.

"He's not my pal," I replied smothering the phone into my coat, "sorry hello...Michael, I'd like to report a vandalised bench."

"Oh dear, just give me a minute Mr Phillips so I can get your official file up onscreen," replied Michael, "I don't think that's been reported. How did you get on with your seagull?

"What's he saying, can I help?" asked my wife.

"He wants to know about the seagull," I said, again smothering the phone. My wife thought for a moment.

A few weeks ago we encountered a seagull sitting at the entrance to a block of flats. It seemed to be uninjured and looked as it was having a think about something, probably where it's next meal was coming from. It looked up at us when we spoke to it but then quickly lost interest.

A bloke in a tracksuit appeared from the front door and stepped over the bird. Pausing for a moment he looked back at us.

"Is that your seagull?" he asked.

"We were hoping it was yours," replied my wife but the bloke just shrugged.

"They all look the same to me," he said and jogged off.

It was getting dark and we were concerned for the inert seagull's welfare so I phoned the council but Michael advised the RSPB. Apparently the council don't have an official position on seagull rescue.

"What about the paint spill in the middle of the road you reported Mr Phillips?" Michael was back, still trying to get my file onscreen, "you said it looked like a map of New Zealand."

"Still there," I replied, "I can't believe no one has reported this broken bench," I continued, "it's a very nice neighbourhood and there's a private school across the road."

"Well, not everyone is as civil minded as you Mr Phillips," said Michael.

"What's happening now?" asked my wife, hoping back and forth, "it's getting cold!"

"Maybe I should get a tight blue lycra suit and a red cape," I said to Michael slightly smugly laughing to myself.

I could hear computer keys being tapped.

"That's entirely up to you Mr Phillips, now if you can just confirm the location once more for me."

So I did, adding that it looked to me as if someone had been jumping up and down on the bench and it had given way. There was a strange silence during which I imagined Michael picturing me jumping up and down on the bench in a blue lycra suit and a red cape, possibly in an attempt to take flight.

I checked around but there were no cctv cameras in sight.

"Obviously I didn't jump and down on the bench and break it," I said making my wife frown and shake her head, "if I had done..." Suddenly my wife snatched the phone from me.

"Hello, Michael, it's Mrs Phillips here, I'd just thought you should know that all these things my husband reports are things he's done himself, basically just to get attention and he really shouldn't be out, we're so sorry to have wasted your time," she said as I tried to retrieve my phone, "Oh and the seagull flew off and lived happily ever after," she continued, "and there's a broken bench that requires urgent treatment. That's the end of today's report. Thank you very much."

My wife then handed me back my phone. There was no one there.

I had an official file and everything.

Busy Doing Nothing

I had been casually watching our neighbour Tom for about half an hour. I was working in my study, but Tom was obviously more interesting than the piece I was writing. I'm not sure how old Tom is but he's certainly old enough to be my father. He's also quite petite, not a word you would often use to describe a man, but it seems to fit Tom.

I paint this miniature pen portrait of Tom because he had been working on his ten-foot high beech hedge like a six-foot bodybuilder a quarter of his age and I couldn't help following his progress.

It had occurred to me to nip over and lend Tom a hand, the article I was writing wasn't going anywhere fast and I was looking for an excuse to escape from it. But Tom seemed to be coping very well on his own, in fact remarkably well. The hedge didn't stand much of a chance.

It was also rather cold and miserable but the weather doesn't seem to bother Tom. He's seen it all before, been there, done that and bought the thermal vest.

There was also the matter of my tennis elbow to consider. I've been nursing my right arm for several months now and it would have been a shame to spoil its progress for a five-minute fumble with a beech hedge.

Which reminded me, the strap, or brace I was wearing on my forearm required some adjustment. It was at least half an hour since I had fiddled with it so I slipped it off and without thinking took it apart. Considering it fulfils such a basic function – essentially it shortens the length of the extensor muscles, it's quite a complex piece of kit.

In fact just to remind myself how efficient it is I Googled it and found a fascinating article that drew a clever analogy between the physics behind the brace and playing the guitar, fingers shortening strings etc.

"That looks really boring," said my wife from behind me, making me jump, "I thought you were really busy, don't you have a deadline to meet?"

I explained how the arm brace had suddenly fallen apart and that I was in the midst of an emergency repair.

"Thrilling," replied my wife, "that'll get your piece written."

"I thought you were painting?" I said.

"Tom must be very strong," said my wife, peering out the window, "amazing when you think he must be old enough to be your father," she continued.

Apparently she had also been distracted by Tom's Herculean task.

"He must have a lot of stamina," she added, "and think of all that exercise and fresh air he's getting."

"Tennis elbow anyone?" I said holding up my right arm and wincing, "and anyway we don't have a hedge."

Suddenly there was great excitement. Another neighbour, Margaret, had stopped to speak to Tom. She had her two Collies with her and for some reason she pointed at our house. For a moment they both stared at us staring back at them. We ducked down and when we surfaced Margaret had gone and Tom was sweeping up.

"Better get on with our work," said my wife smartly.

I had a about an hour left to finish my article so I made another cup of Cinammon and Apple tea, read the back of the packet again, hovered over a box of Jaffa cakes and then went to the loo.

For some reason the toilet seat wouldn't stay up properly. This was disappointing as it's relatively new and I only fitted a couple of months ago. With great difficulty as I recalled. Curiously it now seemed to have slipped over to one side.

You would almost have thought someone had removed it and then put it back on squint. An investigation was called for.

My wife looked at it and shrugged.

"It was always squint," she said, "I just didn't like to say."

Baffled I had a closer look and discovered I had fitted it wrong. Obviously I couldn't leave it like that so I got some tools and dismantled it.

The structure of the seat was almost as interesting as my arm brace, it turned out there were several different ways it could be fitted. After going through them all I discovered that only one really suited the shape of our bowl, a subtle point I had failed to grasp on my previous encounter with the seat.

Once I was happy with its new position I invited the inspector through to give the seat the once over. My wife was impressed and asked if I could tighten the door snib so I did and then I hoovered the toilet, the hallway, the kitchen, the living room our bedroom and my study.

By the time I got back to my desk I only had twenty minutes left to finish my article. I was flushed with panic, but the article poured itself out. I used to think a tight deadline was the best thing for focusing the creative mind but procrastination is actually much more productive.

Cold Play

So far I haven't had a cold this week. I didn't have one last week either, or the week before, but apparently that didn't count. I now have to date all my future colds to last Saturday. That was the day I was introduced to the magical anti-cold spray my wife has been using in the privacy of her own nose.

I thought there was something sniffy going on. Every so often my wife seemed to have a blocked or runny nose but it was always waved away as something that would pass and it did.

I just thought she was constantly under attack from cold bugs and her immune system fought them off. I didn't realise she had a secret little helper until I walked in on her with it up her nose.

"Everything OK?" I asked, "what's that you're putting up your nose?"

"What this?" she sniffed, holding the little bottle as if it had just appeared, "its just some anti-cold spray I thought I'd try."

"How does it work?" I asked.

My wife just shrugged and said she wasn't exactly sure about the science behind it but so far it seemed to be working, she hadn't had a cold since she started using it. A few puffs up each nostril every day kept the common cold at bay.

"If it's that good," I laughed, "you'd think everyone would use it."

"Everyone does," replied my wife, "well everyone I know."

Suddenly I felt as if I hadn't been picked for the football team, which I never was so at least it was a familiar feeling.

I asked if I could try the spray but it was slipped quickly into my wife's handbag, which is the equivalent of seeking holy sanctuary.

"So what's in it? I asked.

"Just loads of different stuff," said my wife vaguely.

"I assume all this different stuff is legal?" I said.

My wife sniffed and then started coughing. Her eyes were bleary and she seemed slightly unsteady on her feet.

"Packs quite a punch," she said then sneezed so loudly I saw stars.

"Wow! that was a good one," she continued then blew her nose loudly

"So a couple of squirts of that stuff and you have an instant cold," I said once I'd got my hearing back.

"Pretty much," replied my wife through a coughing fit, "but it's a fake cold that only lasts a few minutes and then you've got this amazing shield against real colds."

Normally I would have run a mile in the opposite direction from anything that gave me a fake cold but I was keen to try the magic nasal spray that boasted dozens of active ingredients. However, my wife didn't think it was a good idea.

"Cross infection!" she declared, shaking her head and backing away.

So sharing wasn't an option but my wife said she would buy me my very own magical nasal spray that afternoon.

When I thought about it I wasn't sure I wanted to risk a fake cold, no matter how many minutes it lasted. I was feeling fine, in fact I had felt fine for at least two hours and if I could avoid the usual round of minor household accidents, there was a slim chance I could go a whole afternoon.

But my wife had bought me the spray and presented it to me with a certain gravity.

"Use it sparingly and wisely," she warned.

I couldn't help noticing that the bottle was different for hers. Mine looked like the junior version and on closer inspection it seemed to have only two ingredients, salt water solution and gel, neither of which sounded particularly active. When I asked why it was different my wife smiled sagely.

"You can't just jump straight into the strong stuff," she said laughing, "you have to acclimatise yourself and build up to it gradually, then go for the real thing."

For some reason I believed this so I squirted salt-water solution and gel up my nose 4 times a day for three days. Nothing happened, not even a fake sneeze.

I reckoned it needed something a little extra, something to give a nice little kick so I tried some Olbas oil in each nostril and then used the spray.

I think it would be safe to say it reached parts of my face I didn't realise existed. For about five long minutes I went on a Fantastic Voyage round the mysterious tunnels and caverns of my head. At one point my neck and even my hair started burning. Then it stopped and nothing. I was back to normal.

Online I compared the two magical nasal sprays and discovered that my wife's was five times more expensive.

"How many colds have you had this week?" she asked when I showed her my findings.

"None that I can remember," I replied.

"Exactly," she said, "and just as importantly, think of the money you've saved."

My wife's now on her second bottle, so at the moment I'm cold free and at least ten quid better off. What a week.

Antiques

There was a very smart elderly lady waiting for me at the door to the hall. She was in tweeds and was brandishing a clipboard as if she meant it. From the end of the path I thought she was wearing a crash helmet, but it turned to be her hair, which had been energetically whipped up into a frenzy and then completely immobilised. Close up it looked as if it had just come out of a freezer.

I wasn't surprised to see the clipboard. I assumed this was Miss Barron who had approached me to speak to her 'seniors' group and give them a little insight into my column. Miss Barron and I had exchanged a couple of very professional emails about the engagement, she had even sent me a gentle reminder that morning.

Apparently she was quite a fan of my writing and she was so looking forward to meeting me. It would be a treat, she had said, for her members and a memorable experience for all concerned. Which actually put me off slightly. I wasn't sure I could be memorable and the last time I told my wife she had a treat in store we ended up in Casualty.

But here I was outside a small church hall in a strong November drizzle trying memorably to shake Miss Barron's hand.

"It's so wonderful to meet you at last," she said smiling broadly, "I just love your food columns. I meant to ask, will you need access to the kitchen?"

"Thanks but I've actually had my lunch," I said and made Miss Barron laugh.

"Very funny," she said tapping me with her clipboard, "I meant for cooking or preparation."

I was baffled. "I don't have any food with me," I said, "should I have brought food?"

"Sorry silly old me!" said Miss Barron smartly with a slight whistle on the 's', "you're not the food chap, you must be antiques."

"That's no way to speak about your members," I said laughing but Miss Barron was frowning at me and then at her clipboard.

"Not antiques, right you are, how about gardening...curling...small animal vet?" she asked looking up after each category to check for a nod.

"Oh dear, I'm still on October's list," she continued shuffling some papers on her clipboard, "so sorry Philip, back on track now, let's go inside and I'll introduce you to everyone."

"This will be interesting' I thought. But in fact it wasn't because the moment we were in the hall Miss Barron vanished and left me staring at seventy-three senior strangers. I was given the exact number by another older lady whose name escapes me but at least she had a vague idea who I was meant to be.

"You must be Philip," she said offering me a cup of tea and a Bourbon, "you've got a full house, there's seventy three of us today, congratulations!"

Just the thought of it made me nervy so I slugged the tea and my toothache reared up again. It had been behaving itself for the past few days but the hot tea must have set it off and now it was pounding away.

"Two minutes Philip!" declared Miss Barron as she passed waving her clipboard.

It was time to nip to the toilet and apply some of the toothache gel I'd bought earlier. I'd never tried this stuff before so when it failed to have much of an effect I dolloped it on.

By the time I was sitting on the small stage the gel was starting to tingle. Miss Barron began introducing me as Philip but ending up calling me Mr Philip. Which I thought was close enough.

There was a vague ripple of applause after which I started to speak but my mouth was suddenly immobilised like Miss Barron's hairdo. I apologised and tried to explain how my mouth was frozen but it probably sounded like I was speaking with a sock in my throat.

"What did he say?" someone shouted.

"Has he had a stroke?" someone else asked.

"Who's had a stroke?" asked another frail voice from the back.

"Not me!" came the reply, "not yet anyway!"

Everyone laughed which I thought was promising but then the hilarity stopped dead.

I should have read one of my columns as an opener but to stall for time while my mouth came back to life I asked if there were any questions. After my third attempt the penny dropped and more than half the audience put their hand up. 'Could be here for a while' I thought.

I picked an elderly chap near the front. He tried to stand up but fell back into his chair. He had confused himself so his pal asked a question instead.

"Do you make it all up?" the bloke asked bluntly.

I often get asked this question so I gave my stock answer about how I only write about real events but allow myself the luxury of embellishment. The crowd looked uniformly underwhelmed.

"Is it too hard to make things up then?" continued the old bloke.

I just laughed and asked for the next question but there weren't any. There had been around fifty hands, but only one question.

"Maybe go with the antiques next time Philip," said Miss Barron at the door. It was still raining outside.

Spring Heeled Jack

At first I thought it was a black coat someone had dropped. In the darkness from the other side of the road it could have been anything, a bin liner or a giant vampire bat. But then it moved and took human form.

"Is that a man dressed in black lying on the pavement across the road?" I asked pointing at the dark shape.

My wife and our son Adam peered across the dimly lit road. I think my wife was about to say it was just a rubbish bag when she decided it wasn't and took off, shouting, "it's not a rubbish bag!"

Adam beat her to it and was bending down trying to get the bloke's attention when we arrived.

"I'll handle this," he said firmly, and advised us to stay back, his medical training coming to the fore. It was like being an extra in Casualty.

To my untrained eye the bloke looked as if he was taking a nap. It was late, just after 11pm on Halloween and it had been raining so the pavement was damp and not ideal for a good night's sleep. But for some reason the bloke looked very comfortable.

Adam tried to speak to him again, but there was no response.

"I think I'll phone an ambulance," I said and took out my mobile.

"I'm fine," muttered the bloke.

Startled, but relieved we bent closer and stared at him hard.

"I don't think he's fine," said my wife shaking her head, "he's very pale, he's got dark rings round his eyes and his lips are blue, is that blood?"

"I think that might be make-up," I said taking a closer look.

"I'm fine!" snapped the bloke making us all jump.

It was like having a conversation with a ratty ghoul.

Adam asked the bloke if he was diabetic and if he was in pain but the bloke insisted he was fine.

"I think he's fine," I said, "he's just taking a well earned nap from a busy night's haunting."

Just then a pair of inebriated young witches turned up, wobbling merrily. When they spotted the bloke one of them screamed making the other one scream back with fright.

"Do we know him?" one of the witches asked us.

"I don't know," replied Adam, "do we know you?"

"Shouldn't there be three of you?" I said.

The witches looked baffled and then started rummaging for their phones.

"Phone something," one of them blurted, "phone a thing, what do   you   call   it?"

"An ambulance," drawled her pointy-nosed pal.

We explained that the bloke seemed to be fine so maybe we should just phone the police.

"Yes!" shouted witch number one, "we don't know him and he's fine, so phone the police."

At this the bloke suddenly leapt straight up and without a word bolted across the deserted road. It happened so fast all of us gave a communal double and then a triple take.

"That was awesome!" croaked one of the witches.

Awesome wasn't the word I used. Just a few weeks ago while walking home at midnight we encountered a naked bloke on a bike. According to my wife, he was awesome.

At the end of the road we looked back and saw the witches still gazing around them wondering where the man in black had gone.

"Did we know him?" we heard one of them shout.

We were still discussing the strange supine somnambulist ten minutes later when we spotted another dark human shape lying on the pavement ahead of us.

"Do you think it's a different bloke?" asked my wife, "because I couldn't stand it if he jumped up again, I haven't recovered from the last time."

"Could be some kind of dangerous cult," suggested Adam and warned us again to stay back.

It was the same bloke. He was even lying in exactly the same position.

"I wonder if it's some kind of public art installation?" I said as we stared down at the dark figure, "he could be a famous performance artist for all we know. It's certainly different."

"It's not very entertaining though is it?" replied Adam as he knelt down for a closer examination.

"He seems to be OK, but maybe we should phone the police just to be on the safe side," he added, "what do you think, should we phone the police?"

"Yes let's phone the police!" I added loudly and we all stepped gingerly back.

Right on cue the bloke jumped up and sprinted off like a modern day Spring Heeled Jack.

"It's not much of a performance, is it?" said my wife, "I mean, if you've seen it once that's pretty much it."

A few minutes later a police car appeared out of nowhere and crawled past us, the officers inside peering out as if they were searching for someone or something.

"He went that way!" shouted my wife pointing in the opposite direction the bloke had run, "Well, he wasn't all bad," she added looking at us, "you can't blame him for being a bit jumpy, it is Halloween after all."

Spicy Cure

Despite a level of hygiene that would have been the envy of Howard Hughes my wife and I have been playing pass the parcel with a particularly nasty stomach bug.

We can't remember who had it first but I certainly had it last.

"We need to stop this now!" Declared my wife when I started complaining of stomach cramps for the third time in two months. She was frowning round the kitchen as if it was haunted by bacteria.

"Maybe we should move house," she continued.

"And burn this one down!" I interjected, "along with all our goods and chattels, in fact shouldn't we bury everything in a lime pit first and then set it alight?"

"Let's not get carried away," said my wife, "I'll buy more hand sanitiser first and see how we got on."

"Can you drink hand sanitiser?" I groaned, "Because that might do the trick."

While my wife was out at the hand sanitiser shop I consulted Doctor Google. One thing was for sure, whatever I had, it was a lot worse online. Within seconds I only had a few months to live, possibly even weeks. In fact according to some of the results I was probably already dead.

Unsurprisingly my stomach cramps immediately got a lot worse and I broke out in a clammy sweat. My abdomen now felt like an old red hot accordion playing the funeral march. I had to lie down on the couch because my head went off on a slow spin cycle.

Rousing myself for a second assault I typed in 'cure for stomach cramps' and up popped 'Cinnamon'.

'Really?' I thought, 'just cinnamon?' But then there were another few pages about the magical combination of apple and cinnamon. Now we were getting down to the nitty-gritty.

Actually cinnamon sounded like it knew what it was doing and with my intestines tying themselves up in another squelchy knot I was game for anything. After scouring the kitchen cupboards I phoned my wife and asked where the cinnamon was hiding.

'You're not baking are you?" she asked, "its not all Paul Hollywood you know."

I don't think my wife has ever seen me baking but last week she caught me watching the Great British Bake Off at the gym. Which is where it belongs.

"I've made a start to our Christmas cake and I can't find the cinammon," I said.

There was a static-filled tense silence while my wife tried to work out if this was actually feasible. Finally she admitted we had no cinammon. Frankly I was amazed but then I can't remember the last time I saw my wife baking either.

"So it's for stomach cramps," she said, "now that's fascinating."

I should have known by the tone of that 'fascinating' what was coming.

An hour later my wife was unpacking several large bags on the kitchen table, every one of which contained cinammon in one shape or form, in fact you wouldn't think cinammon could take so many shapes or forms.

"This is a lot of cinammon to have in one room, do you think its safe?" I said as I rummaged through the bottles of tablets, packets of powder, sticks, teas, biscuits and a rather tasty looking cake.

"Thirty eight quid!" I shouted after rapidly counting up the receipts.

My wife unfolded a leaflet and held up the finger of silence.

"Arthritis," she began grandly, making sure she had my full attention, " bladder infections, cholestorel problems, colds, heart disease, immune system problems, the flu, longevity, weight loss, indigestion, pimples and stomach cramps."

She then handed me the leaflet as if we were in some courtroom drama. Just as well because I'd lost the plot after the words, 'heart disease' set my stomach cramps to full blast.

"All from cinammon." I mumbled, "who would have thought?"

I unfolded one of the packets and dipped a tentative finger into the powder. Just a tiny speck blew a hole in my tongue about the size of a 5 pence piece. I may never taste savoury things again.

"I'll bet that took your mind off your stomach cramps!" said my wife.

As my eyes filled with water I opened one of the boxes of cinnamon and apple tea and had a sniff. It wasn't good news. My money was on the cake, but it was a no calorie no taste job, apart form the distinct rasp of cinnamon of course.

"I can't wait to try the tea," said my wife switching on the kettle, "let's have a cup each."

We stood facing one another for several minutes like duellists, the dangerous aroma of cinnamon hanging between us like a veil. I managed to hold my breath for the entire time.

"Didn't Hitler and Eva Braun do this in the bunker?" asked my wife as we raised our mugs.

In fact it wasn't all bad, just in parts, but I can report that it eased the cramps.

"Maybe we should wait for the arthritis before we try it again," said my wife quickly packing our cinnamon stash into a cupboard.

Fifty Shades

Sometimes in charity shops my wife inexplicably suffers a massive taste bypass. She'll start pointing excitedly at the weirdest things. Earlier this week it was a tray featuring three Chihuahuas sitting in teacups.

For a moment I thought I'd have to phone for an ambulance as she appeared to go into a state of shock. But then her head cleared and she decided the tray was silly, even though it was only four quid.

I saw her throwing sly glances at it as I grazed on the DVD section.

"Just buy it," I said, "and put yourself out of your misery."

"It's ok," she replied, "I've seen something much better."

"Really?" I asked, "better than a tray with Chihuahuas in teacups?"

"Sorry, where did you say that tray was?" asked a woman from behind me. My wife pointed at it reluctantly and then shrugged at me.

"Too late now," she said, "but look at this!"

She was holding up a pale blue jumper on the front of which had been knitted a portrait of the 1970's pop singer David Cassidy.

"Six quid!" announced my wife, kissing David on the lips before draping the jumper over my shoulder, "I'll see you both in twenty minutes."

"He's still alive you know," said the woman with the Chihuahua tea tray as she passed.

This was great news but I was more interested in a film I had just spotted. If my wife could buy a David Cassidy jumper I could buy a DVD of Beneath the Planet of the Apes. I was fairly confident this was a classic terrible film so I had to have it.

Then I went really wild and snatched up an LP of Pinky and Perky's Hit Parade. On the record cover the loveable falsetto piglets looked pretty much as I had left them fifty years ago.

However, I managed to hide this lot behind my back in one swift movement as an acquaintance loomed up. For some reason I always want to call this bloke Roger even though I'm fairly sure that's not his name.

Roger is the type of person who takes a script with him to the theatre so he can spot any mistakes the cast are making. I didn't think there would be much room on his cultural high ground for old Pinky and Perky.

"Oh hello there, find anything interesting?" he asked in a vaguely patronising manner, "I'm just here sheltering from the rain."

I think I smiled weakly; it didn't look like it was raining to me. Roger was holding a book but I couldn't be bothered asking him what it was. We were edging towards the counter so I ushered him forward.

"Oh no, after you I insist," he said showing me that peculiar smile that always makes me feel like a special case.

"Did you get to any of the Proms this year?" he continued over my shoulder, "or the Edinburgh festival. I think I overdid it. I'm suffering from opera overdose. Do you ever get like that?"

Discreetly I produced my trove and laid it on the counter, making sure the singing piglets and David were face down. A large elderly assistant in tweed appeared. She had the bearing of a Headmistress so I immediately straightened myself up. It was like prize giving day.

"Right now what have we here?" asked the Headmistress grandly and very loudly.

"Did I tell you I'm writing a play about the Higgs Boson?" continued Roger as the Headmistress picked up David Cassidy.

"Now here's a rather good looking although slightly effeminate young man knitted on the front of a lovely jumper!"

Just in case the whole shop were in any doubt she held the jumper up over her bulky chest and stared down at David.

"An absolute bargain at six pounds!" She continued whistling through her false teeth.

I glanced over my shoulder and caught Roger raising a pair of quizzical eyebrows.

"Beneath the Planet of the Apes!" announced the Headmistress peering at the DVD, "now that does sound fascinating I must say. Have you read The Naked Ape?"

"I actually met Desmond Morris," said Roger leaning in over my shoulder.

I was about to grab the LP but the Headmistress beat me to it.

"Pinky and Perky's Hit Parade!" she announced with relish, "what an exciting time you're going to have!"

You would have thought she was running an auction. I'm sure no one was interested apart from Roger but it felt like the whole shop had been brought to a standstill and the bus queue outside were showing an uncommon interest.

"They're presents actually," I muttered as I hastily paid for them.

"I'll keep you posted about my play!" said Roger as he squeezed out that strange pitying smile again.

I was at the door when the Headmistress picked up Roger's book.

"Fifty Shades of Grey!" she declared, "oh dear that doesn't sound very colourful."

Not half as colourful as Roger's face. I could only see his profile but he looked about fifty shades of red to me.

The Mobile Flasher

Either my eyesight is going or street lighting just isn't what it used to be. Walking home around midnight on Saturday you could see why the streets were deserted, or rather you could guess why they were deserted.

Long canyons of solid blackness were punctuated by cold spotlights that fervently lit the base of the lamposts and not much else. Three yards in any direction and you may as well have been blindfolded.

"I quite like it," announced my wife, "it's atmospheric."

"I know," agreed our son Adam as he walked into a bush, "it's like being in a film noir."

"It's like being in a bush you mean," I said, there was a chance Adam hadn't noticed because it was so dark.

He was however, first to spot the bloke on the bike.

"Is he topless?" asked Adam pointing down the road.

"Who's topless?" I replied peering into the gloom and struggling to see much of anything.

"Probably just a flesh coloured T-shirt," said my wife.

"Who's wearing a flesh coloured T-shirt?" I demanded, searching my pockets for my reading glasses, which weren't that helpful as it turned out.

"Actually I think he's naked," said Adam making me spin round and peer desperately in every direction.

"Don't look Mum, he could be some kind of pervert!" shouted Adam covering his mother's face with his hands. In the ensuing struggle and flurry of flapping hands I don't think either of them saw very much.

But I turned round just in time to see a naked bloke ride past on a bike. He looked very serene and as he cycled gracefully into the bright pool of a streetlamp I couldn't help noticing he had the gym-fit body of a thirty year old, but the face of a sixty year old.

"I didn't see his face," said my wife glaring at Adam, "in fact I didn't see anything!"

They were still squabbling so sensing the possibility of an

impending column I felt duty bound to catch the rear view.

"Nice bike," I said, "quite expensive, no lights on though."

"That's ridiculous!" declared Adam, "imagine riding around at night with no lights on!"

"I know, but at least he's not wearing anything black," I said watching the naked figure dissolve into the velvety blackness.

"He couldn't have been completely naked," said my wife.

"You've got to hand it to him if he was," I said, "I mean, it's tricky enough riding a bike at the gym with shorts on, never mind in the buff. That's quite a feat considering the obvious dangers and discomfort. Although he looked quite happy to me I have to say."

My wife winced and we all laughed.

At this point the pavement narrowed and Adam led the way. He was the first to stop at the next deserted junction.

"Personally I think he could have been a mobile flasher," he shouted as the naked cyclist re-appeared before him right on cue.

Adam leapt back and grimaced, but the cyclist didn't seemed to notice him. He was far too busy looking up at buildings and glancing behind him while consulting a piece of paper.

"That's strange, " I said, as we watched him ride off into the darkness, " I didn't see that piece of paper the first time, I wonder where he was keeping it?"

"He is quite fit isn't he?" said my wife.

"If he's looking for an address, do you think he's visiting somebody else who's naked?" asked Adam.

"Maybe he's a delivery man," I suggested, "and he works nightshift. Delivering very, very tiny parcels."

"Let's ask him," suggested Adam making me turn round just in time for another full frontal.

For a moment I thought the naked cyclist was going to stop and ask for directions. He hovered for a while before coming to a standstill about ten yards from us. He was still scanning the houses and consulting his piece of paper. Then a phone appeared in his hand from nowhere and lit up his face.

"He's not that old," whispered my wife, "he's probably only around forty. In fact he's actually quite handsome."

I was more concerned about where the phone had sprung from. I was also still wincing at the thought of riding a bike in the altogether when suddenly he started moving slowly towards us.

We rustled up our friendliest, 'we see naked blokes on bikes all the time and we're not bothered in the slightest' faces but you would have thought we were invisible. To be fair we weren't standing directly under a streetlamp so he probably thought he was alone. Although I don't think he was that bothered.

As we stood and tried not to watch him I felt like a Peeping Tom, my wife on the other hand was fascinated.

"I wonder if he has hot flushes," she pondered, "and has to strip off."

I started walking and the bloke past me within seconds still holding his piece of paper. The phone had gone.

"It's OK, don't panic, he's wearing a pink thong!" announced Adam loudly.

"There's always a catch,' replied my wife as the darkness swallowed us whole.

The Five Quid Watch

When the watch my wife has worn for the past 12 years finally disintegrated last week, I knew she wouldn't dash out and buy the latest Rolex. The word 'expensive' isn't part of my wife's vocabulary, which is one of the things I find so attractive about her.

She tried three charity shops and almost bought a Gent's diving watch, which was huge apparently. This suited my wife because she likes to tell the time at a glance without the use of a magnifying glass.

"Very fashionable," enthused the elderly assistant as she showed my wife the giant watch, "all the girls in pop videos wear big watches."

It was only £10 but when she tried it on my wife couldn't lift her arm, not on a regular basis.

"Such a pest," she told me looking disappointed, "it told you the time, the date and how much oxygen you had left all at a single glance from a distance of about ten feet, underwater. It would have been really handy."

I had just picked my wife up in town and we were sitting in the car.

"Don't worry," I said soothingly, "there'll be plenty of other cheap watches."

"I know," she said trying to suppress her excitement, "I bought one, for a fiver!"

"Brilliant!" I replied, "did you haggle for a discount?"

"I sure did!" she declared rummaging in her bag.

"Did you get it?" I asked.

"No, but I got a free pen, which I thought you'd like," she said holding up a surprisingly substantial silver pen.

"What a woman!" I said taking the pen and examining it, "a five quid watch and a free pen with the name of a famous discount store emblazoned on it. Perfect, it's like Christmas!"

The pen had writer's block, but apparently it had worked in the shop, so maybe it was just nervous. While I tried to cajole it back to life my wife produced a rather smart looking plastic box from her bag.

For a five quid plastic box it looked pretty good to me and there was even a watch inside it, a very impressive, stylish watch with a stainless steel casing and a strawberry red strap.

My wife held up the receipt and pointed grandly at the price. I leaned over for a closer look. Five pounds, it barely seemed possible.

"And...it's got a three year guarantee," she announced, unfolding a piece of paper, "although it says here that we have to enclose a cheque for £7.50 to cover the return postage for the replacement watch."

We thought about that for a moment.

"Well it is quite heavy I suppose," continued my wife.

"Try it on!" I said, "it looks great!"

My wife opened the box, which I already had my eye on. I could see it on my desk holding stuff I never use like giant purple paperclips and those noticeboard pins that snap and stab you the moment you put any pressure on them.

"I think its stuck!" said my wife as she struggled to free the watch. For a moment she turned the same colour as the strap.

"Let me have a go," I said, "there'll be a special technique for releasing it."

Unfortunately there wasn't. The watch was wrapped tight around another piece of clear plastic embedded in the box.

"This is why it was a fiver!" said my wife, "its glued into the box."

My face now also matched the red strap, but the watch just refused to budge. I was baffled. After five minutes I was on the brink of doing something I would later regret in court.

"Do you think you need to take it out of the box?" I asked shaking, "I mean, you can still tell the time."

My wife thought about this for a moment then snatched the box back, punched it several times and tried to strangle it before burying it in her bag.

It was after 6pm on Saturday and the shop my wife had bought the watch from was closed all day Sunday. We were busy on Monday so for two days my wife carried the watch around in its box. At one point she strapped the box to her wrist with masking tape for handiness. Eventually on Tuesday we took it back to the shop.

"Is this watch meant to stay in its box?" my wife asked the assistant.

The girl peered at it and then carefully opened the box. For a few minutes we smirked as she tried to cajole, tease and threaten the watch free but it wouldn't budge. Then she vanished, returning a few minutes later smiling with the watch, but no box.

"What happened to the box?" I asked.

"Box?" asked the assistant.

"The box the watch was stuck in about a minute ago," I said.

"He's got plans for it," chipped in my wife.

Suddenly the assistant remembered she had to break the box into hundreds of small pieces. All we got was a shrug.

"I wonder if the box was covered by the guarantee?" pondered my wife as we left.

The Lock-In

Holding a writers' workshop in a pub has interesting advantages. For a start it gives me an opportunity to hone my table waiting skills. I'm quite adept now at balancing a laden tray while climbing two sets of stairs. Three or four heavy trays is quite a nice little workout of a Friday afternoon.

Sometimes the collective shape of the tables just isn't right and rearranging the layout is a personal favourite, although it has to be properly timed. Normally I wait until everyone is settled for the afternoon, notepads and iPads at the ready before I make the disruptive move.

Then there's shopping to be done in Waitrose next door while the writers work on their timed exercise. I find 20 minutes is about right for a quick sweep round the aisles.

If the pub had a dartboard I could probably fit in a couple of games but it's not that type of establishment. It's ancient and stuffed full of atmosphere.

Last Friday I left 11 writers fired up and beavering away in the function room at the Lamb Inn while I headed off with my shopping list. However, on my way down the stairs to the bar there was a sudden change in the otherwise charming ancient atmosphere and the stairs grew darker.

It was 2.45pm and sunny outside, but the pub was gloomy, almost as if a fog had settled inside it.

I felt a low rumble around me or above me, it was hard to tell but it seemed to be coming from the walls so I hurried down the stairs remembering the poem Antigonish by Hughes Mearns:

"Yesterday, upon the stair, I met a man who wasn't there. He wasn't there again today, I wish, I wish he'd go away."

I reckoned I had found the exact stair that inspired that poem and I was about to leave it sharpish. Convinced some invisible force was following me I think I jumped the last four steps.

Meanwhile, overhead the sinister grumbling grew louder. The bar was empty so I was happy to see Natalie the manager.

"Oh hello," she said chirpily while staring at something over my right shoulder, "what's happening here?"

Nervously I glanced behind me but there was nothing there, no ghost, no stairs, nothing. Just a silver wall. Apparently I gave it a cartoon double take.

"What the what!" I shouted, "I thought there was something weird happening, where's the rest of the bar?"

"Oh it's still there," replied Natalie calmly, "it's just that we can't see it for that steel security shutter."

Suddenly I saw a headline that read; 'Writers Trapped in Pub Refuse Offers of Help'.

"Uh oh, the lights are out and the till's off, must be another power cut," said Natalie, "but don't worry it will come back on shortly, your writers probably won't notice any difference."

"Let's hope they don't!" I said remembering there was a well-stocked bar upstairs in the workshop room.

Suddenly I saw another headline; 'Writers Trapped in Pub Drain it Dry!'

Rather shaken I went off to Waitrose next door but it was also affected by the powercut so I couldn't buy anything. Customers floated around aimlessly with half empty trolleys as if they too had been disconnected. The staff had already gone into holiday mode and were huddled at the checkouts laughing nervously.

"Can't I buy anything?" I asked a managerial type.

He shook his head. "Unfortunately not sir, but you can still browse."

Meanwhile back in the pub the writers worked away completely oblivious of the fact that they were quite possibly locked up for the afternoon.

"Look on the bright side," said Natalie as she leaned against the steel shutter, "at least there are toilets upstairs and bedrooms if the worst comes to the worst and of course there's always the fire escape."

'The fire escape!' Of course, the fire exit door was just a few yards from where the writers were sitting. Hurrying outside and round the side of the building I bolted up the fire escape and knocked on the big heavy door. Then I knocked again and again. I didn't want to panic anyone but I thought I'd just run the idea of the fire escape past them.

Eventually I heard someone say rather disinterestedly, "Do you think we should get that?" So I knocked again.

"Can't be for us," someone said, "could be seagulls."

So I banged louder.

Suddenly the door flew open and my wife was staring at me.

"Oh it's you, what do you want, we're busy," she said.

"I just wanted to let you know that if you were ever trapped in here by some strange twist of fate, you could use this fire exit," I announced while the whole group stared at me as if I had two heads, "its quite safe and easy to climb down."

"Fascinating," replied my wife and closed the door.

"What did he say, is that part of the timed exercise?" I heard a muffled voice ask.

"I hope not," said another voice, "I'm half way through mine!"

Satisfied I had done my bit for health and safety I went for a rather pleasant walk, and savoured the surprisingly sweet taste of freedom.

Shoplifting

It's probably some primal instinct that kicks in when I'm grazing around food and small domestic appliances, but I'm just not that keen on being watched while I'm shopping.

It was just after 10pm but the supermarket was practically deserted. Maybe the rain was keeping the crowds away. My wife and I had gone our separate ways at the door agreeing to meet in about twenty minutes. In my wife's world that's about an hour.

I had blank CDs front of mind and one of those history magazines that explains everything with wonderful illustrations as if you were 10 years old.

I was engrossed in a fascinating illustrated article about trench warfare when it suddenly occurred to me that I was being watched, if not actually spied on. But after glancing up and down the empty aisle I decided it was just my overactive imagination.

A few minutes later I was all trenched out so I moved on to a magazine about Cats and as I opened it up something white caught the corner of eye. I stared up the empty aisle at a display of children's party masks and shuddered. With their soporific music and surreal lighting empty supermarkets can be quite spooky places. Certainly a great place for a haunting when you think about it.

I was only a few seconds into an article about Cats who act in films when the white flash again disturbed me. This time I was quick enough to catch a glimpse of a bloke in a white shirt, in fact he was a security guard.

Round the corner I found him leafing through birthday cards, he was at the Dad section and laughing at the verse in one of the cards. I stood nearby and had a look through the Congratulations Your Blood Test Was Negative section. When he'd gone I checked the card he was laughing at and it was blank.

I didn't think much of it until I was at the DVD section and he appeared behind me. I could see his reflection in a video screen that was showing a silent trailer for the film Frozen on a loop.

He appeared in a scene with Olaf the snowman and Princess Anna and stood between them like a ghost. Slowly he turned and looked at me watching him in the screen while ABBA sang Knowing me, Knowing you.

This is great stuff, I thought. John Le flipping Carre would have struggled to dream this up. I decided to start acting suspiciously just to test him, although quite what that would have entailed I really had no idea. So instead I thought I'd try the siege strategy and wait him out. He could only re-arrange PlayStation games for so long.

Eventually after about five minutes I threw in the towel. This bloke had been well trained. He had stealth, patience and silent shoes, everything you need to combat retail crime.

I moved round the end of the aisle but it was full of toasters so I quickly changed my mind, turned back and walked straight into him. For a brief moment we made bodily contact. He was wiry with ginger hair and not as tall as I thought. He'd recently eaten a mint. We made our muffled apologies and parted.

He then tailed me round the store while I looked for my wife. I found her sniffing pears in the fresh fruit section

"Don't look now but I think I'm being followed," I whispered.

My wife automatically glanced around as an old lady shuffled towards us with her trolley.

"I see what you mean," she whispered back, "she does look slightly shifty."

"Not her," I replied as the security guard appeared, "him!"

"Oh, he's probably just bored," said my wife and went back to her big pear debate.

"He was reading a blank birthday card and laughing to himself," I said.

"Why would he have a birthday card with him?" asked my wife.

I explained how the security guard had been using the greetings card display as a cover so he could scope me out.

"Scope you out?" repeated my wife slowly just as the security guard passed.

He was now carrying a PlayStation game but I wasn't fooled. I was sure I saw him smirking so while he was still in view I made a big show of placing my 'purchases' in our trolley.

"I'll just put this stuff in our trolley darling, so we can pay for it at the check out like normal people," I announced loudly, making my wife sigh heavily.

Down at the assorted nuts the security guard was back again in full hover and I was beginning to bristle so I decided to take the bull by the horns.

"Excuse me," I began, "can you tell when the store closes?"

Slightly startled he thought for a moment.

"Oh, at midnight," he said.

"Good!" I replied, "I've still got an hour and a half left to nick stuff."

The bloke looked surprised, then smiled broadly.

"Knock yourself out mate," he said, "I don't work here."

'Yeah right,' I thought.

Call the Midwife

We now have a large plastic box in the kitchen packed full of pills and potions and plasters and lots of other medicinal stuff that doesn't start with a P. We keep it all in the same big box so we know where to go in an emergency, apparently.

"We don't want blood dripping all round the house while you hunt for a plaster do we?" said my wife when she consolidated the various plasters and pills I had inadvertently distributed about the house, although she missed the stuff in the loft.

Personally I always thought this was a convenient arrangement. In my experience pain can strike when you least expect it in different parts of the house, not just in the kitchen. Quite often painful things happen to me in my study for instance, which is why I had such an eclectic mix of first aid supplies in my desk drawers and cupboards,

Now if I've maimed myself with a chunk of razor sharp plastic packaging I have to bleed all the way to the kitchen, work out which cupboard the big medicine box is in, drag it out and then wrestle with it until it decides to open. All the time of course I'm bleeding over everything, which wasn't really the plan.

This hasn't actually happened yet, but I conducted what you might call a dry run last week when I was gripped by something far more insidious and enigmatic. While working at my desk my stomach found something sharp to play with. I tried ignoring it but eventually I was forced to start rifling through my desk drawers for a quick fix. Then I remembered the big box.

"It's probably just trapped wind," I announced as I dragged the heavy box out of its cupboard with both hands.

"Sorry to hear that," replied my wife, 'but if you can untrap it elsewhere that would be much appreciated."

Ten minutes later I had completely emptied the plastic box over the kitchen worktop and was sorting through its contents like an archeologist on a dig.

"What's that for?" I asked holding up some pink stretchy fabric that smelled vaguely of TCP.

"Nothing to do with me, thank you very much," said my wife after a quick glance.

If I hadn't been in pain I would probably have enjoyed this. There were things I hadn't seen for years and new stuff that looked really exciting. There was an ear cleaning kit that looked particularly tempting.

"Rubber tubing?" I announced, holding up a length of brown snake-like rubber.

My wife just shrugged, "again, all yours dear," she said.

Quite frankly I was amazed at the amount of different plasters and bandages we had, there was enough supplies for a mini MASH unit. This was nothing compared to the number of stomach related products. At a rough count there appeared to be more than two dozen completely different packets and bottles. All in duplicate. Obviously someone had filled out the requisition form wrong.

Despite the fact that I was now struggling with the fencing match in my stomach I decided to take the time to divide the stomach pain remedies into two camps, stuff to make things happen and stuff to stop things happening.

"There's a number in there for hypochondriac's anonymous," remarked my wife as I worked.

After a few minutes of sorting and examining I had two big piles of medication in front of me. Maybe it was the increasing sharp pains but I couldn't quite work out what to take. Was it something that needed to be released immediately or gently talked down?

Suddenly the pain started rising towards my chest.

"I wonder if I'm having a heart attack?" I moaned clutching my now inflated stomach.

"In your stomach?" said my wife reviewing my bump, "looks like you need a midwife to me. Is there something you want to tell me?"

Since the pain was getting worse I decided to play safe and take at least one of everything.

Some big chalky tablets for indigestion were first down the hatch, another handful for wind, a couple from a strip without a packet which I think said something about IBS, two senokot tablets in case it was the egg sandwich I had for lunch that was bunging me up and a generous swig of some pink stuff that that turned out to be three years out of date.

"One way or another," I said "that should get a reaction."

A few minutes later I was lying on the couch about to expire with my wife dangling a bulging polythene bag over me.

"This lot's going in the bin. Hopefully you've counteracted everything you've taken," I think she said, although it was hard to tell over the garbled noise coming from my stomach, which had now assumed a thrilling life of its own.

"The midwife is running late," added my wife, "but she said, just start without her."

I got up groaning for another rummage through the big plastic box. I wondered if that ear cleaning kit would work at the other end?

Old Hotlips

I didn't notice the couple at first, I was probably too busy laughing at the trailers for forthcoming films featuring flying people blowing up giant flying robots. But after the fourth trailer full of exploding buildings and screaming people my eyes started wandering, searching for something more interesting, something that wasn't being blown up or firing a gun.

We were on the end of an aisle and the two seats in front of us were empty. There was an older couple in the next row. I'd seen them come in, a thin, bald bloke who liked he was on his last legs and a woman with orange hair and a walking stick.

They took a while to settle down and now seemed to be chatting because the woman was staring at the bloke. In fact she may have had her head on back to front because I could almost see her whole face, which was slightly creepy.

For a couple of minutes my attention bounced between the couple and another exploding trailer, during which the orange haired woman didn't move a muscle, apart from her eyes which seemed to be mapping the bloke's face as he stared at the mayhem on screen.

I thought they looked like an older couple from a French film, perhaps on a secret date, re-kindling an old affair after accidentally meeting one another in a characterful street café. They probably hadn't seen one another for forty years but when their eyes met across a croissant it was as if time had stood still.

You can tell how interesting the film trailers were.

As the woman stared at her old lover she was perhaps waiting for a response to a deep question about their relationship, the man meanwhile mulled over his reply. At one point he opened his mouth and I thought he was going to speak but instead he filled it with a hand full of popcorn. The woman just gazed longingly at him, almost as if she was amazed he was there.

After a few minutes of this slightly unnerving waxwork show I began to think there was something odd going on. I assumed the woman was breathing but it was hard to tell in the half dark. So I nudged my wife for a second opinion. She took one look at them and just shrugged.

"The film's starting," she said quietly.

The couple however, had started their own film and as I suspected it was very French. It's a long time since I've seen people snogging in a cinema so at first I thought they would stop after a few seconds. But that's not really the point of a cinema snog.

I reckoned they would have to break for air or some lip balm eventually but they were locked solid. Maybe the woman was giving the man the kiss of life, or maybe she was feeding him, like mother birds feed their young.

I nudged my wife again but the couple weren't really in her line of sight so she wasn't interested.

"Leave them alone," she whispered, "they're not doing any harm."

"But they're older than us," I replied, "much older than us."

"Don't get any ideas," warned my wife, "this film looks good."

I couldn't tell. I only had eyes for the vintage snoggers. Glancing round no one else seemed bothered so maybe it was just me. I wondered about speaking to a member of staff.

"Excuse me," I'd say, "there are old people snogging in front of me and I can't concentrate on the film."

"No problem Sir, leave it to me, I'll split them up," the staff member would reply.

Then something strange happened. Suddenly the woman had gone, vanished into this air. After about five minutes she bobbed back up again.

I pointed this out to my wife but she reckoned the woman had probably just dropped her sweets and was looking for them.

"For five minutes?" I whispered.

I decided to move seats.

The cinema was very busy but there was an empty seat standing on its own at the back. I think this is a disabled seat and I was ready to vacate it at any moment.

Unfortunately these seats always have lights right above them, possibly so you can read if you're bored. At least I could see my clementine when I peeled it.
This is the perfect cinema snack, silent, fragrant and refreshing.

After a few minutes I noticed a bloke in my old seat.

'What a cheek' I thought, 'probably some pervy voyeur who spotted Hotlips and her pal and wanted a close-up view.'

This meant there was an empty seat and in fact it wasn't far away so I quickly moved and sat down in it. I was quite pleased with myself until I realised the couple next to me had obviously starved themselves for at least a week. They were now busy working their way through every noisy snack imaginable, including a giant community size sack of crisps.

I decided I'd visit the loo before resuming my special, brightly lit Billy No Mates seat. I had no idea what was happening in the film, when I sat down again I didn't even recognise any of the characters. I could see the snoggers had gone back into 'staring at one another' mode so I hadn't missed much.

"What a lovely film," enthused my wife as we left, "very moving."

"Certainly moved me," I moaned.

The Rule of Thumb

I made some very interesting discoveries earlier this week, all purely by chance, which is so often the way. Scientifically speaking I should probably try and repeat my findings but I'm quite satisfied the results were conclusive.

In a nutshell I discovered that no amount of screaming will help you close your front door while your thumb is stuck in the jamb. What you might call a general rule of thumb.

I would imagine however, that the same would go for anything that was stuck in a doorjamb. So far I've resisted trying anything else.

At the time of 'thumbgate' as I like to call it, I was involved with several other matters, namely searching for my ringing phone while checking if I had everything with me before leaving the house, car keys, briefcase, brain etc. Obviously the brain part had been left on the kitchen table.

Which would explain why my thumb was loitering in the jamb and why it remained there for so long while I tried to force the door closed on it.

As I understand it, pain is a warning that something isn't quite right so it was interesting to discover that my nervous system seems to have a two or three second delay. About enough time for me to give the front door another hard tug.

"But why did you have your thumb in the doorjamb?" asked my wife as she pulled a bag of ice from the freezer.

"I have no idea," I winced, "it's never been there before."

"And you closed the door on it twice?" continued my wife, I just nodded and she shook her head adding, "amazing!"

"How could I be so stupid?" I said as my thumbnail starting turning purple.

There was a long painful throbbing silence so I repeated the question.

"Oh, sorry I didn't realize that was a genuine question," replied my wife then added, "maybe it was all just too much for you. Closing the front door at the same time as you were leaving the house must have been tricky."

In my defence I haven't done anything quite so stupid since I fell out of a tree after sawing through the branch I was standing on. It was a complex sort of tree.

The main thing was I could almost move my thumb so it probably wasn't broken, just severely stunned into submission. I had made myself late for an appointment so I got my phone out and tried to operate it with my left hand and promptly dropped it.

This was the second astonishing discovery. I'd always considered my left hand to be the equal partner in a very handy and versatile double act. It plays half a piano and half a guitar and even table tennis but here it was wandering around my phone like it was an alien planet. It was almost as if it belonged to someone else.

In the end my wife took over with the phone while I fought with a packet of painkillers. Again the screaming thumb wanted to come to the fore and push the tablets out of their foil wrapping. But it was useless. This time the left thumb stepped up and fumbled around until a paracetamol torpedo flew out and hit me in my left eye.

If I'd tried to do that deliberately if would have taken me a week.

"Oh dear, what have we done now Sooty?" asked my wife in her worst Matthew Corbett voice. But I was in no mood for glove puppets.

"That looks very nasty," my wife continued staring at my thumbnail, "it reminds me of someone, its got an unhappy face," she looked up at me for a moment then added, "that's going to get a lot worse and you might even lose the nail, the best thing we can do is get rid of all that blood right now, I'll heat up a needle."

If I ever need to wake up in a flash that's the line I'll play over in my dozy head. A part of me thought my wife was kidding, but another part of me that is very familiar with this woman's work knew that she wasn't.

"Remind me again why we need a hot needle?" I asked backing away nervously with my ice pack, "sounds like you're adding insult to injury if you ask me."

"Well I'll have to heat the needle to make it sterile," replied my wife raking through one of the kitchen drawers, "you don't want any dirty old needle piercing your thumbnail and infecting with you with goodness knows what. Anyway all that trapped blood will pour out in seconds and you'll be pain free. Works a treat, every time."

Which is another interesting discovery. Apparently all it takes for me to leave the house in under two seconds without slamming any stray body parts in the door is the sound of my wife rummaging in a drawer for a needle. I'm going to add that to my motivational self help book when I write it.

The Case of the Extra Case

The girl behind the airport check-in desk asked if I'd packed the suitcase myself and for some reason I had to think about it. You'd think I'd know better because diffidence and uncertainty never go down well in airports these days, it just makes you look suspicious.

It's an even bigger mistake if you look concerned or furtive when you go through the final gate and have your photograph taken, the last thing you want is your shifty mug stuck on some global database for future scrutiny by international security forces.

The suitcase packing thing always amuses me because I haven't packed a case for about 35 years. I get to lay stuff out near the case or suggest stuff I'd like to go in it, but actually packing it is another matter.

The same embargo applies to bags at supermarket check-outs. I used to be allowed to pack our shopping, but at some point I must have lost the knack or maybe packing standards went up. Either way I'm not to be trusted.

"Sorry Sir, did you pack this suitcase yourself?" repeated the girl.

"Oh, absolutely, the whole thing, right to the top!" I replied. I was about to add, 'no drugs, bombs, guns, machetes, exotic endangered animals, illegal immigrants' but thought better of it.

Sarcasm is another thing you can't check in at an airport. I think it's probably a bona fide offence.

"Just the one suitcase you're checking in today sir?" asked the girl.

"Yes that's right," I said and then remembered our son Adam also had a suitcase, a great big thing inside which I imagined were the entire contents of his flat and quite possibly some of his mates.

All the way to the airport I kept thinking I was driving in too high a gear and when Adam heaved his case from the boot of our car, the vehicle lifted visibly and gave out a gasp of relief.

"What on earth have you got in there?" my wife and I asked in unison.

"Just the bare essentials," replied Adam, turning puce under the strain of lifting the case.

The girl at the check-in desk didn't like the look of it either.

"You've only got one suitcase booked so I'm afraid this one will be extra," she said.

We looked at one another like Dumb, Dumber and Dumbest so the girl explained how we had only allocated ourselves one suitcase when we booked our tickets online.

"Yes, one each," I said.

The girl shook her head, "just one in total I'm afraid, so if you want this case to go it will be extra."

Again we shot one another that look Oliver Hardy used to give Stan Laurel when he accidentally covered him in paint or landed him in jail.

"You're not bothered about your case going on the plane are you Adam?" I said.

"Well let me see, it's a tough one, but do you know what, I think I'll have to take the case with me," he replied.

By this time the check-in girl had both cases tagged up so it was going whether he wanted it or not.

"Right," said the girl, "that's £360."

I started to speak and words may have left my mouth but they didn't add up to much, certainly nowhere near £360.

"Thirty-six pounds?" asked Adam.

"No, three hundred and sixty pounds," replied the girl.

"Really?" stammered my wife, "that can't be right?"

Then we were all laughing. Hysteria tends to have that effect.

The girl explained how there was a £30 charge for the extra case and then £10 per kilo on top of that. Adam's case weighed in at 33 kilos.

We asked the girl to check with her manager but after a brief phone call we were still £360 out of pocket. Company policy apparently. Unfortunately it was our company policy not to pay it. On the other hand the flight was closing in five minutes so we launched into something resembling a scene from the Generation Game.

The object of the game was to lighten Adam's load as quickly and as publicly as possible. Amazingly we had 4 kilos to play with so we started stuffing Adam's perfectly packed clothes and accessories into our case and hand luggage. Everyone in the queue behind us seemed to enjoy this part of the proceedings. Up until then we had just been three prats holding them up, now we were actually supplying some laughs.

"How many pairs of jeans have you brought?" and "fourteen pairs of pants!" were just two of the memorable lines. After Adam donated his set of free weights to the airport we got the cost down to £220, which I tried to pay until my card was rejected. Curiously it would work two hours later.

Growing more frazzled by the second I reached into my now bulging briefcase for my specs and pulled out a single leg.

"Should have kept them in their case," advised Adam. He paid the £220.

Struggling with overgrown hand luggage and loose items of clothing – my wife was carrying a pair of Adam's boots, we made our way to the security gate.

"No need to take your boots off Madam," declared one of the security men, too late as it turned out because a couple behind my wife were already holding their shoes.

"Laptop Sir?" asked the security bloke.

Opening my briefcase I could only find 14 pairs of Adam's pants, which I then removed unceremoniously.

"No need to take your pants off sir!" quipped the security man.

I dumped my laptop in one tray and Adam's pants in another. If they had photographed me then I'd probably be on the FBI's most wanted list.

I had to be stopped, scanned and lovingly patted at length first. Something had set the bleeper off. It turned out to be the buckle on one of Adam's belts that I'd stuffed into my back pocket.

I think we made it onto the flight by the skin of our teeth. Brucie would have been proud. Scores on the doors - £220 short of a family nervous breakdown.

Sleeps like a Bat

Strange things happen at night while I'm asleep. Sometimes I wake up and all the furniture seems to have been moved around or replaced with slightly different, creepy versions. The wardrobe is the worst culprit. It's big and white and has the ability to transform into a foreboding, dimly lit corridor.

In my half waking dream state I'll gaze at it in puzzlement wondering why I had never noticed there was a corridor in the middle of our bedroom wall. Should I get up and wander down it and see where it leads?

So far I've managed to resist further investigation by falling back to sleep or waking up and staggering to the loo down the real hallway.

It's not all scary stuff though. Occasionally the bedroom just looks like it's been redecorated. This wouldn't surprise me because my wife is quite handy with a roller and she does have a habit of staying up later than me.

When I mentioned all this to her last week she was concerned enough to look it up online.

"Here we go," she began as she peered at the computer screen, "nocturnal hallucinations, blah, blah, blah, oh dear."

Suddenly I was interested and tried to squeeze myself in front of the screen.

"It's nothing," interrupted my wife, "basically you're Hypnopompous, but then I could have told you that."

Essentially my imagination goes into hyperdrive as I wake up but it doesn't bother telling my brain. The effect only lasts a couple of seconds so maybe it's not worth bothering the old grey matter with dubious information.

Having said that, I was very impressed a few nights ago by the persistence of one of my nocturnal delusions.

I had been dreaming about a giant rabbit or some kind of animal with big ears although they could have been horns.

Responding to the usual bladder alarm call I managed to drag myself partially awake and in the dawn light saw a pair of giant rabbit ears just inches from me. Which in some strange dreamlike way made sense. I was fascinated but assured myself they weren't real and fell asleep again for probably just a few minutes.

Nature's ardent call however, soon had me awake again and staring at those giant rabbit ears. I lay for a moment and waited for them to evaporate, but they didn't.

'My wife will never believe this,' I thought to myself and then wondered where she had gone. Suddenly the rabbit ears moved and rubbed themselves together and I realised they were my wife's feet.

Apparently I had turned 180 degrees in my sleep so now I was lying with my head at the foot of the bed. This was clever stuff because not only had I taken my pillows with me I'd also had the foresight to move my bedside cabinet with its light and pile of books. I had been busy.

Not content with hallucinating about rearranging the bedroom furniture I had actually done it. Better still it had been effortless because I had done it in my sleep.

I had obviously moved everything else, including the window and the door but at the time I didn't think of that. I had more important things to do like rushing to the toilet before I sustained permanent damage.

I was a lot more awake when I returned to the bedroom but I still thought I was seeing things. My wife it seemed had decided to move her pillows to the foot of the bed and sleep upside down.

I stared at her for a few moments just to make sure I wasn't being Hypnopompous again and she mumbled something.

Baffled but relieved the giant rabbit ears had turned out to be just my wife's feet I rolled back into bed. For a moment I toyed with the idea of also sleeping upside down just to straighten things out but I couldn't be bothered. I also resisted tickling my wife's feet and instead fell asleep.

In the morning we seemed to wake almost simultaneously which was interesting.

"I had a strange hallucination last night," I yawned at my wife's feet, "I thought you were sleeping upside down."

My wife's head appeared at the foot of the bed, weirdly disembodied. With half shut eyes she peered at me and smiled weakly.

"If you were a native American Indian you'd be called 'Sleeps like a Bat," I said.

My wife yawned and smoothed her hair.

"If you were a native American Indian you'd be called 'Snores so incredibly flipping loud his Wife has to sleep upside down like a Bat," she replied sleepily, then drummed on my head with her feet.

Apparently this top to toe arrangement is the shape of nocturnal things to come. Armed with her bespoke earplugs my wife says the couple of metres she has now put between us in bed makes all the difference, acoustically speaking.

"If you could hear yourself snoring," she said, "you'd do the same, believe me."

I'm going to stick with being Hypnopompous. Too much excitement at night tends to keep me awake.

Dumbfounded

I have a great system for storing our important personal and household paperwork. Everything is carefully filed in separate A4 wallets and then catalogued in chunky box files.

It's very sensible and ordered. It's just a shame I can never find them. I know they're somewhere safe because that's where I put them. Unfortunately my idea of somewhere safe must change, possibly on a monthly basis.

My wife meanwhile keeps different important stuff like appliance guarantees and instructions in her own safe place, which of course never changes.

So the idea of keeping everything together seemed like a good one, needless to say it wasn't mine. I think the word my wife used was consolidate. I was impressed but I had misgivings.

"Isn't that a bit like keeping all your eggs in the same basket?" I suggested looking for loopholes so I could avoid spending a couple of hours rooting around in cupboards or up in the parallel universe we call the loft.

"Who said anything about eggs?" asked my wife.

I started in the loft. In my defence stuff does tend to get rumbled around when you've moved house as many times as we have.

To the uninitiated our loft probably looks like vaguely organised mayhem. But I can show you the part that's frozen around the late seventies and there's another part that is very much in the early nineties. Maybe I should sort through everything and lay it out properly in decades.

It was while wading through the early nineties that I unearthed what I naively thought were the box files I was looking for. They were a lot more bashed than I remembered and the first one had a £34 electricity bill from February 1991 but I was still excited. I was 23 years out but at least I was on the right track.

In another box file stuck to a TV licence for 1992 I found the remains of an IQ test.

Around that time I had written an article about Mensa and I'd sat some IQ tests. The results were very interesting, basically I was so stupid I really shouldn't have been out on my own.

One question in particular had held me, my family and my friends in a mind numbing strangle hold for days, possibly weeks.

Today of course you would type it into Google and get the answer in seconds. I resisted that and instead decided to test my wife's memory.

"Did you find the box files?" she asked when I turned up in her studio doorway.

"A man, looking at a painting," I began solemnly, "says to himself: brothers and sons I have none, but that person's father is my father's son." Who was the person in the picture?"

My wife stared at me wide-eyed and started to mock cry.

"Oh my God, not that again!" she screamed as she slumped in front of her painting.

It was as if time had stood still for twenty odd years.

"Wait a minute, did you say 'Person'?" said my wife rousing suddenly.

I read the question out loud again.

"Last time you said, 'that man's father is my FATHER'S son', now it's a PERSON, that's a completely different question!" shouted my wife as she grabbed the test paper from me.

"And your final answer was, HIMSELF," added my wife, "ha ha, all that flipping anguish and arguing and you had the question wrong in the first place!"

"I think you're splitting hairs to be honest," I said snatching back the test paper as my wife started hitting me with it.

"Incidentally, it's his daughter," she added smartly as she returned to her easel.

I thought about it for a minute but my head started to hurt.

"OK, how about this one, is it legal for a man in Russia to marry his widow's sister?" I asked.

"No, he's dead you twit!" shouted back my wife.

I picked up a pen and wrote that on the paper over my original 'YES' answer.

"Your mother's brother's only brother-in-law is asleep on your couch. Who is asleep on your couch?" I shouted excitedly.

There was a long silence and for a moment I thought our chances of a Mensa family membership were slipping away.

"Your father!" shouted my wife.

I'd written, 'your mother's brother's only brother-in-law'.

"Right, try this one," I said, "a man builds a house with four sides, each side faces south. A big bear comes along. What colour is the bear?"

Again there was silence so I repeated the question.

"Well he must have built the house on the North pole don't you think?" said my wife making me nod blankly, "although I can't think why, but anyway the bear must be a Polar bear, so it's white."

I took her word for it. I'd left that one blank.

"Last question," I began dramatically, "a man fills two large box files with important paperwork and loses them, why did his wife allow him to do that?"

Like I said twenty years ago, a high IQ isn't all it's cracked up to be.

There is no Show

It must have been the excitement that sent our collective bladders into overdrive. Suddenly at the Manse gate all seven of us were desperate for what my wife calls, 'comic relief' and there were dark mutterings about the minister's Rhododendrons.

"Just hold tight," I advised as I rang the Manse doorbell, "there's bound to be a toilet."

"Hopefully two," added my wife, nodding at the huddle of scrunched up faces.

We'd been told by our friend Judith, who was performing in a promenade play about the Suffragettes, that the Director would be on the door and that she probably wouldn't let us in if we were early, under any circumstances.

Performed across two floors of the Manse the period play would plunge the small, select audience right into the middle of the action so there would be no nipping off to the loo during a quiet moment. Not unless you wanted to end up as an extra.

I rang the doorbell again and heard it resonate loudly inside the Manse, like a fire alarm. Through a window to my right I saw for a moment in the shadows of the room a group of women in period costume chatting and laughing, among them was Judith sporting a fantastic wig.

The scene was thrilling yet strangely unsettling, like catching a glimpse of a haunting.

"Any joy?" shouted my wife from the path, "the play starts in five minutes."

"Maybe it's the wrong Manse," shouted another voice.

Again there were dark mutterings about the Minister's Rhodies but they were saved by the arrival of six more audience members.

"Do any of you need the toilet?" I asked, but they shook their heads sheepishly.

"We're all desperate," said my wife, "and we can't get in."

"Can't get in," repeated our son Adam for good measure.

Suddenly the door creaked opened and a tiny elderly lady appeared. Straight-backed, smiling faintly and beautifully pale she hovered ghost-like on the threshold. It was the Director.

"Please do come in," she said very formally, "we've been expecting you."

My wife was first through the door.

"Are there toilets?" she asked in a strangulated posh voice.

"Why, yes of course, do you have a ticket?" asked the Director looking as if she was trying to dodge a bullet.

"For the toilets?" asked my wife as she prowled the hallway.

"For the play dear, the play," replied the Director, her voice fading as she was swamped by her toilet focussed audience.

Someone asked if there was an interval and if the bar would be open, someone else wanted coffee, the clamour of voices quickly reaching fever pitch.

"Hold on everyone, hold on!" shouted the Director who was now struggling to stick to her script, "do you all have tickets?"

We did but Adam still had to collect his so he presented the Director with a ten-pound note for his £8.50 ticket.

"What am I meant to do with that?" she asked glaring at the tenner as if it was a dead Haddock.

"Put it in your purse?" suggested Adam.

"I'm sorry?" exclaimed the Director, possibly mishearing Adam.

"There are two toilets!" shouted my wife, eliciting a loud cheer, then adding grandly, "ones to the left, twos to the right!"

The Director was left staring at half her audience.

"Does anyone else need the toilet!" she asked wearily.

"I'll go if you need a volunteer," I said.

The Director slowly turned her steely gaze on me.

"You're that writing group, I've been warned about you," she began but was interrupted by my wife's critique of the beautifully appointed toilet.

"Fantastic," said the Director through gritted teeth, "I'm so pleased your impressed with the facilities, now can I remind you to switch your phones off, please!"

"Yes, switch your phones off!" repeated Adam loudly, then turning to the Director added, "I suppose that would be an anachronism if a mobile went off during a play about the Suffragettes."

The Director peered at Adam before moving him along the hallway with that same steely gaze. It could have been a superpower, some kind of mind control. Unfortunately it wasn't working on the rest of our party who were now laughing wildly at the end of the hallway, the front door wide open for air. Maybe it was mass toilet break hysteria.

The Director twitched again and glanced nervously at them, seeing perhaps one of the Witch scenes from Macbeth.

"Do you think they might be leaving?" she asked me hopefully.

Suddenly one of the nicely behaved audience members tapped the Director on the shoulder making her spin round.

"Excuse me," they asked, "is this the show?"

"It may well be!" replied the Director throwing her hands up.

"The show is not the show, but they that go," I said, then added, "Emily Dickinson."

"Is she the one who threw herself in front of a horse?" asked Adam, idly leafing through the programme.

"Yes that's right," said the Director smiling malevolently, "I might try it myself sometime."

"It's good isn't it!" enthused a woman standing opposite me, "you'd almost think it was real."

"Very realistic," replied her friend, popping a peppermint into her mouth.

Frightfest

I'm not normally given to sudden frights. What I get are secondary frights after my wife has been startled out of her wits by something inifintismal.

We were in the car on our way into town on Saturday when we shared our first sudden fright of the day. Right in the middle of a conversation my wife suddenly screamed because apparently there was a body in the middle of the road.

I braked hard and frantically searched for anything in the road resembling a body but all I could see was a patch of fresh black Tarmac where a big pothole had recently been filled.

"Oh, sorry," said my wife, "it's just some tar, what a fright I got."

By the time we reached the multi-story carpark I was just about back to normal. But as my wife stepped out of the car she screamed again because she thought she'd seen a rat. Not that we have much experience of rats but I suppose you can never be too careful.

"It's just a bag," I said picking up a brown paper bag.

"Are you sure?" asked my wife.

I held the bag out for inspection making my wife retreat nervously.

"Oh, hold on a minute," I said peering into the bag, "it does actually have a rat inside it." I added making my wife scream again and take off across the carpark.

I didn't think it was funny either. But to be fair I was aiming for a sort of weary, dry sarcasm not a belly laugh.

In a Florist shop calm and order was restored until we were leaving and just a couple of yards from the door my wife shrieked and pulled me towards her.

Apparently I really did jump out of my skin. According to the florist there was a split second where there were at least two versions of me about a yard apart.

"How did I look in the second version?" I asked.

"Much same as the first," replied the florist, "alarmed."

For some unknown reason a large tin vase of flowers had leapt from a nearby shelf and missed me by inches soaking the floor with water.

"Does that happen a lot?" I asked. The florist thought about it for a moment, "not really, mainly it's just strange noises."

This was scarier than the flying vase.

"I'm not surprised that florist is haunted," said my wife as we hurried from the shop, "all those orchids give me the creeps."

I was pondering the flying vase incident a few hours later in the gym as I walked down the long narrow corridor towards the changing rooms.

The corridor is lined with grey lockers one on top of the other and up ahead I could have sworn I saw a locker door tremble and open slightly.

'Trick of the light' I laughed to myself, or my imagination working double time having been thrown into fright mode.

I was about five or six feet from the door in question when it flew open. Heart in mouth, blood draining to my feet I think I may have had wobbled slightly, certainly everything blurred for a moment. I suspect this may have been the result of me jumping out of my skin.

In fact it's possible I experienced a bonafide out of body experience. Certainly by the time the ghostly face appeared from the locker I had left my body and was in someone else's.

It was interesting that I didn't think to run. Instead I just clung to the opposite wall as a tiny hand appeared at the side of the ghostly face and lifted it up.

Underneath it lay the cheeky face of a little boy.

"Sorry, I thought you we're my mum." He said.

I think he was about four years old.

"Do I look like your mum?" I asked shaking visibly.

"A little bit," he replied.

"Do you know what a CCTV camera is?" I asked pointing up at the camera above us.

"No," he said and then slowly disappeared back into the locker.

"You can't stay in there," I warned.

The boy blew a long raspberry in response, or at least I assumed it was a raspberry.

A few minutes later while I was changing I heard a woman's scream.

The boy was gone by the time I had changed but I thought I'd mention it to the guys on the reception desk. Small children hiding in footlockers sounded like something they should know about.

"Yes, we saw you on the monitor speaking to one of the lockers but we didn't see a little boy," said one of the trainers, glancing at his pal.

I was laughing but secretly the hairs were standing up on the back of my neck.

"Very funny!" I replied and we all laughed. Then I screamed when the lead from my headphones ran across my right arm.

Both the musclemen behind the desk visibly jumped. In fact one of them had to sit down and take deep breaths. Whatever it is my wife's got, it's obviously infectious.

House Training

While on a train last weekend my wife happened to sit opposite a mutual friend. Michael was with his wife whom neither of us have met. There was the usual chat about the weather, reasons for travelling etc until it occurred to Michael that my wife was travelling alone.

"So where's Roddy?" he asked.

"I've left him at home," replied my wife slightly anxiously, "to be honest I'm always nervous when he's alone in the house, you never know what he'll get up to, or how much mess he'll make. Especially in the kitchen."

"He can't be that bad!" laughed Michael, "surely he's fully house trained?"

"In theory," replied my wife making Michael's wife look concerned.

"How old is Roddy?" she asked.

"Almost sixty," replied my wife matter of factly.

"Almost sixty!" exclaimed Michael's wife, looking startled, "I thought you were speaking about a teenager!"

Meanwhile back at the ranch I was coming to terms with the practical side of my house training. I had been very careful not to come into contact with any of the serious electrical appliances that were out of bounds – the washing machine being the mysterious Turin Shroud of appliances.

I had also resisted interfering with anything that has been carefully arranged. I particularly hadn't touched cushions, flower arrangements, pictures, plants, rugs, blinds or stuff that is neatly stacked or lined up in order of height.

Stuff that my wife has taken an aesthetic fancy to, like records or books with interesting covers are also out of bounds. This is a tough one if it happens to be a book I'm reading. Apparently the military use the word 'contact' for a close encounter with the enemy. I bear this in mind when I'm tempted to move something to a more agreeable position.

You might think this would narrow my options, but you would be wrong. I can mess around in the loft to my heart's content because the loft contains a duplicate set of household stuff. Most of it is boxed or bagged from two or even three previous house moves, but at least I know it's there waiting for me if I ever feel the urge to plump a cushion or dust a picture.

However, there was no time for frivolity, while my wife was out I had a task to complete that was fraught with potential danger. Consequently I had been building up to it for the best part of an hour.

Thankfully my instructions were quite clear, change the bed linen. I've helped my wife change all this stuff many times but I've never gone solo. I was aware this could be a big step forward for me, either that or it was a trap. Possibly both. But if I made a good job of this who knew where it might lead? Eventually I might even be allowed to empty the dishwasher unsupervised.

"Are you absolutely sure about this?" I had asked suspiciously, "you're not thinking of anyone else?"

"Listen," Said my wife as she took my hand, "I trust you, I'm sure you'll do a great job."

There are moments in life you look back on and regard as seminal. Staring now at the pure off white bed linen I felt dizzy at the prospect of all the excitement that lay before me.

I started with the under sheet which because of its elasticity proved slightly unpredictable but eventually I got the measure of it.

Changing the pillowcases went relatively smoothly, although I had to do them twice because I forgot to take the old ones off first.

The duvet cover was the real test but the tutorial video I found on Youtube was very helpful. First I had to turn the duvet inside out and then just peel it over the duvet. I had the video playing on the iPad as I worked just to make sure.

After twenty minutes I was hot, demented and no further forward. I managed to shove the duvet into the cover but it lay on the bed in a huge unruly heap. I felt sure it was meant to be flat.

Logic finally took hold however, when I hit upon the idea of crawling into the duvet cover and dragging the duvet behind me. It was just like getting into a tent with a huge sleeping bag and although I came close to suffocating at one point it worked surprisingly well. It's just a pity I didn't think to video it for future reference.

Unfortunately as I squirmed backwards out of the duvet I banged into the bedside cabinet, which banged into the dressing table. Nothing was actually broken but it was a tragic ending to an otherwise fun packed afternoon.

"So this small earthquake," began my wife as she perused the bedroom, "was it very local?"

She told me what Michael's wife had said on the train and then asked why the duvet cover was inside out.

"I'm sure it was like that in the Youtube video," I replied.

My wife's face brightened.

"Is there a video about emptying the dishwasher?" she asked enthusiastically

Night at the Opera

I'm notorious for slipping into my theatre seat just seconds before curtain up and quite often I'll walk into a concert hall in tandem with the conductor.

Which is a fantastic feeling if you can time it just right because you get applauded to your seat and you can bet there will be at least a couple of dozen people in the audience who think it's you they're clapping.

One of the reasons for my timely arrival is that I can't stand hanging around waiting for a performance to start while I pretend to be immersed in the programme. Far better to leave it until the very last minute and then run through the streets like a fugitive and arrive sweating and panting.

The main reason I cut it so fine is because it's always later than I think. So last week I set the clock in the car ten minutes fast.

"That's fooling no one," said my wife, checking her watch against the car clock. But for once she was wrong because I arrived at the opera a full fifteen minutes before curtain up and didn't know what to do with myself.

Actually there wasn't a curtain at the venue so I could have just taken my seat and amused myself by studying the set for Bizet's Carmen. But I couldn't even do that because I had to hang around in the foyer waiting for my son Adam because I had the tickets.

There's only one thing worse than trying to stand out in a crowd so you won't be missed and that's being conspicuously stood up. I now realise this because several complete strangers sidled up to me and told me as much.

I just smiled back then looked suitably forlorn.

"Never mind," consoled one old gent, "I'm sure she's got a perfectly good excuse."

After that I decided Adam had missed his train so I joined the last trickle of people and went upstairs to find my balcony seat. As luck would have it I was on the wrong side of the Hall and by the time I was heading in the right direction the applause had started for the conductor. Perfect timing.

I took a bow and sat down. The moment I leaned back in my seat an elderly lady at the end of our short five-seat row stood bolt upright. For a moment I thought we were all on some kind of seesaw arrangement and I had sent her flying.

However, she sat down again after a brief but feverish exchange with an usherette. Then she was up again and peering at the stage, then she was back in her seat and squirming around - handbag up, handbag down.

I wasn't sure what was going on but it was fascinating stuff and I almost forgot about the overture, which was now in full swing.

Deciding I should keep one eye on the stage and the other on the elderly lady I angled myself round and draped an arm over Adam's empty seat. Unfortunately the young woman sitting in the next seat obviously thought I was about to get familiar so she leaned away from me as far as she could without falling into the lap of the woman next to her.

Then the jack-in-the-box lady was up on her feet again and everyone in the vicinity just carried on as if nothing was happening. Sometimes audiences can be very unforgiving, darting one another dark looks for breathing loudly but this one was very accommodating.

Just as well. Out of the corner of my eye I saw a large figure standing a few feet behind me laden with a jumble of bags and a violin case. Under the rim of a gigantic fur trimmed parka hood there was a familiar smiling face.

"Aha!" he declared, pointing at me with his violin case while tramping up and down on the spot.

Adam had made his grand entrance to the strains of the March of the Toreadors looking for all his might like a member of the North Pole Symphony Orchestra.

How he found me I have no idea. Maybe he had tracker dogs with him he certainly seemed to have everything else.

The trouble is you just can't hide someone like that. For a start the parka was big enough to fit a telephone box and since Adam had run all the way from the train station with half his worldly goods he looked as if he had been boiled in a bag.

An interesting contrast to the ladies and gentleman in the rest of the audience who had put a considerable effort into dressing for a dapper night at the opera.

Thankfully an usherette came to Adam's aid and laid his bags and violin safely out of harm's way, then Adam squeezed past me and filled his seat with parka.

With his enormous hood still up he must have been blocking the view of half the balcony.

So I recommended he put the hood down, but when he did it doubled in size like a giant Frilled Neck Lizard and poked the demur young woman next to him in the side of the head.

Incredibly she said nothing, but she screamed like a banshee a few seconds later when the jumping bean lady shot out of her seat again.

I had forgotten about her. But I was delighted to see her back in action

Adam also got the fright of his life and sympathised with the young woman who rather sweetly I thought, apologised for making such a noise.

She was fanning herself with her programme and affording Adam a welcome draft when the elderly lady's accomplice shot up out of her seat. Obviously they were now taking it in turns.

The young woman shrieked again but this time Adam just sighed and shook his great fur trimmed hood from side to side, the soldiers onstage meanwhile played cards self-consciously and sang about the midday heat.

Consequently the pop-up lady and her pal now swapped seats and took their coats off. So I told Adam to do the same. By this time the audience were past caring.

Adam's problem however, was finding somewhere to put the big parka, which was more like a sleeping bag. In the end we had to lay it across both of us like a quilt and after a few minutes I felt myself bobbing off.

At the interval Adam decided he would escape so I helped him out with his bags. He was apologising for creating a bigger spectacle than the opera but I reckoned he was upstaged by the antics at the end of our row.

Right on cue while I was carrying Adam's violin case through the crowded foyer someone behind me declared, "oh look, I told you it was bad, even the orchestra are leaving."

Jaws

I think if you've been forced awake at 4am by a nagging bladder you've probably earned the right to a decent yawn. It's one of life's great free pleasures, although it's not something I'd ever given much thought to. But then you shouldn't really have to think about yawning, it's like an extension of breathing.

It's also highly contagious unless of course you're a psychopath. I certainly looked like a psycho when I caught myself in the mirror after stumbling into the bathroom.

I also felt that yawn building towards its gloriously satisfying conclusion except there was no conclusion because my mouth wouldn't open. Not completely. It got about half way and went back to sleep. I tried again but it just wouldn't wake up. In the end I suppose I just absorbed the yawn. To be honest I was more concerned about my dozy mouth.

I tried looking in the mirror again while opening my mouth but it stuck again about half way. I'm not sure what difference staring at myself was going to make but at 4am it was the best I could come up with.

After doing my best goldfish impression in the mirror for several minutes it became clear that my mouth wouldn't open completely because my jaw was stuck. 'Problem solved!' I thought sleepily then ambled up the hallway and back to bed. Another yawn cropped up but then vanished mysteriously.

Curiously I could still speak, although in a sort of chewy grumble. I thought briefly about waking my wife and mumbling at her. She would probably have been quite pleased to hear I had at last been silenced or at least muffled. But I thought I'd surprise her with it in the morning.

A horrible ripple of panic ran through me as I thought about that. Surely I had just been lying on my jaw and it had gone numb? All I had to do was go back to sleep and let nature's healing hand take its gentle course. In the morning I'd be munching my way through my cereal as normal.

I was just about to roll under the duvet when the word 'lockjaw' suddenly came into focus. Still doing the goldfish impression it occurred to me that I might have contracted Tetanus while I was asleep and now my jaw was locked.

'More nonsense!' I thought and smirked to myself as I rolled into bed. Two fierce minutes later I was in the kitchen surfing the internet on my iPad.

Amazingly around half a million people have woken up in the past two years with their jaw stuck. Not all at 4.00am of course. But the main thing was it didn't look like it was Tetanus, probably more likely to be TMD or Temporomandibular Joint Dysfunction, which actually sounded far worse.

Teeth grinding and whiplash are the favoured causes and over use of laptops and iPads due to the constant lowered angled of the head.

"What!" I shouted and in an instant my jaw unlocked. Strangely, exclaiming loudly due to surprise wasn't one of the recommended cures. Facial exercises were though.

There were four basic moves to practice, all of which employed resistance in one direction or another. In the first you had to place your thumb under your chin and push gently upward while slowly opening and closing your mouth. The second was the same but pulling your chin downwards with your thumb. The third involved holding a pen between your teeth and moving your jaw from side to side.

The fourth was my favourite because it was basically the goldfish gawp but with your tongue stuck to the roof of your mouth. This was the kind of thing I could do anywhere, in the car, at the theatre, in shops. I went back to bed running through my facercise repertoire and fell asleep with my mouth wide open.

I think my wife was slightly miffed that she missed what was now known as The Lockjaw Incident.

"Why didn't you wake me?" she asked, "I would have paid good money to see that."

"How about this?" I asked and demonstrated my new repertoire of facercises, building up to the one where I had to keep my tongue stuck to the roof of my mouth.

"Is that instead of the lockjaw, or as well as?" asked my wife.

At the library on Saturday afternoon she got the chance to decide for herself. I had orders for a couple of large print titles from an elderly friend and my wife helped me find them. Up at the desk I decided to give my new jaw exercises a road test, but while my wife was pretending she wasn't with me, my jaw locked.

"Can I take your books Sir?" asked the librarian but all I could manage was a mangled mumble.

"Are these your large print books dear?" asked my wife loudly, over pronouncing every syllable.

"Hiss ov." I muttered back.

I have to say though large print books are a lot easier to read, particularly when you are gawping at one like a goldfish.

Through a Window Darkly

After an unusually warm Easter week spent mostly at the beach things seemed to have taken a decidedly gloomy turn back at Phillips Mansions, despite the fact that the sun was actually shining.

Unfortunately, it wasn't shining inside our house. For a moment I thought I'd forgotten to take my sunglasses off but it turned out the windows were opaque.

"I thought the window cleaner was meant to come last week," said my wife wiping the inside of the kitchen window with no effect.

"It was Passover last Monday," I said.

"Is the window cleaner Jewish?" asked my wife.

"No, but maybe there was a plague of locusts," I replied, "and they got stuck to the windows."

My wife grimaced at the darkened window before her.

"It looks more like mud to me," she said, "could be a plague of mud I suppose."

From the outside it looked like my wife was right, there had obviously been a plague of mud. Every window had been well and truly smothered.

"Maybe it hasn't rained all week!" I shouted through the kitchen window.

"I think the plague of locusts was more realistic," shouted my wife, "when is the window cleaner due?"

"I'll check the window cleaning schedule!" I shouted back.

My wife gave me the double thumbs up and looked impressed. Not half as much as I was. If I actually had a window-cleaning schedule I'd probably certify myself.

Instead I phoned Gary the window cleaner.

Gary doesn't clean windows any more, like me he pays other people to do it for him. So far this arrangement has worked out quite well for both of us.

Gary also has an actual window cleaning schedule and after consulting it he said someone was due round the following day. Which was great news.

"Did you tell him they were really bad?" asked my wife.

"I told him to bring a blowtorch," I replied, "and he said it might be better if we replaced the windows completely so his brother Steve the joiner's coming round to give us a quote."

The following afternoon while we were out one of Gary's crews turned up and cleaned half the windows, missing out the most important one in my wife's studio.

"Is this some kind of joke?" demanded my wife.

"I know," I said, "what a cheek, it's only me that's allowed to do half a job!"

We checked all the windows twice to make sure it was half a job.

Apparently they ran out of water. When I reminded Gary that we have an outdoor tap he sighed heavily.

"If only it was that easy," he said, "I'd love it if my guys could use customers' outdoor taps but their windows would be streaky, that's why we bring our own pure water with us and that's why you don't have streaks."

"When you actually clean our windows," I added.

"Pure water and no streaks," repeated Gary. I waited for him to start laughing but he didn't.

This was big news. "You mean like mineral water?" Asked my wife amazed, "can we have fizzy, I'd prefer fizzy."

The window cleaners were back the following day and again we were out. I reckoned they were parked at the end of the road waiting for us to clear off.

This time they cleaned all the windows and made a very fine job. Except of course my wife's studio window, which again had somehow managed to render itself invisible.

My wife laughed but in an evil way. It was frightening. I phoned Gary and told him. He was baffled because he'd never heard my wife's evil laugh.

Two days later apparently someone came back and cleaned the offending window but my wife didn't see them because she couldn't see through the window and it still wasn't clean and shiny with that streakless finish that you only get with pure water.

Gary and I were now growing quite close so I reminded him exactly where the dirty window lived and about my wife's evil laugh.

"Gary wondered if you'd cleaned your studio window lately on the inside," I said to my wife, "he also wondered if it could be a trick of the light."

I was on the other side of a closed door when I said this but it opened suddenly so I ran for it.

The next morning I had a meeting in the garden with Gary and the rest of the Marx brothers. Amazingly every one of them, Roberto, Bugs and Andy claimed to have cleaned the studio window, although when I pointed at it they seemed surprised.

"Oh, that window!" shouted Bugs, jumping with shock as if the window had just appeared from nowhere.

In silence we gazed at the dirty studio window, through which we could just make out the vague figure of my wife waving her fist.

"If you wait a minute you'll hear the evil laugh," I said.

"If you write about this," said Gary still staring at the dirty window, "can you put in my mobile number?"

Cue evil laugh.

Knock Knock

Sometimes I quite like the cold evening air wrapping around me, especially if I've just come from a stifling room that feels like a Pizza oven.

The writers' workshop room was a little too toasty last week so after I had set the timed exercise and served everyone their hot beverage of choice - 6 normal teas, 3 Lemon and Ginger teas, 1 hot chocolates, 1 black coffee and 1 plain hot water, I thought I'd award myself a five minute fresh air break and take the evening air, cold as it was.

I probably should have taken my jacket and the workshop door key because after ten minutes I was on the brink of hypothermia and I was locked out.

There's a hallway and another door between the writers' room and the front door of the workshop. Everyone always comments on how quiet and sound proofed the room is but it has never really been tested, until now.

A casual knock on the heavy front door brought no one to my aid. A series of sharp raps proved just as useless. The door was so thick it probably sounded like a bird trying to peck its way in. I knocked harder and waited, and waited.

There's a window in the door just about the size of my face and through it I could see along the hallway and into the warm glowing room I had so rashly left behind. At the end of the table of engrossed writers I could see Carolyn hard at work on her piece. I tried waving then knocking until at last she stopped writing and looked up.

'Thank goodness for that!' I thought, 'I'm in!'

Just as well, that refreshing, bracing cold air had now turned life threatening for a bloke in a thin shirt.

But now I was saved and smiling and waving madly across the little window, 'any moment now,' I thought, 'I'll be pouring myself a cup of hot tea, I might even go completely wild and have a ginger snap to celebrate'.

But Carolyn was still staring at me, more accurately she was staring blankly into space searching for the right word or phrase for her piece.

Suddenly I remembered I had my mobile in my pocket. But rather than phone Carolyn and disturb the entire workshop I thought I would try a more subtle, creative approach.

Opening messages on my phone I texted 'knock knock' to Carolyn and waited. A few seconds later she stopped writing and picked up her phone. She read the text, frowned and read it again. Then she showed it to Ellis who was sitting next to her busily tapping away on his laptop.

It hadn't occurred to me that Carolyn wouldn't have my name in her contact list so the text must have arrived from the great and mysterious Unknown.

Ellis paused mid-sentence, stared at Carolyn's phone and then looked baffled. Meanwhile I waved like an elated madman across the little window. An old lady passed with her dog and gazed at me with a sort of detached interest.

"It's my turn to be the peeping tom," I said and the old lady's dog barked at me.

Suddenly my phone warbled in my pocket. It was Carolyn replying to my text. 'Who's there?' she asked.

"What the what!" I exclaimed out loud.

I texted back 'it's me' and then added one of those smiley face things.

I watched Carolyn jump in her seat when she read the text. 'Now we'll get some action' I thought and we did. Carolyn promptly dropped her phone on the desk, then for some reason swivelled round and round scanning the room, which was lined with stacked chairs.

Ellis now picked up Carolyn's phone read the text, looked surprised then laughed nervously.

'Who's is this?' he texted back. By now several of the other writers were involved so I phoned Carolyn's mobile.

I think the whole room jumped when it started its piercing bird whistle. Ellis was elected to answer it.

"Hi Ellis," I said calmly making him sit bolt upright, "can you put Carolyn on please?"

Nervously Ellis handed Carolyn her mobile, I waited a moment until she had the whole room's attention.

"Carolyn?" I asked.

"Yes, speaking," she replied hesitantly.

"Knock knock," I said and then banged with my fist on the door.

Again the whole room jumped and again Carolyn dropped her phone.

Some people thought I'd gone too far but I was freezing and I couldn't help thinking I was being kept outside intentionally, possibly to give the writers more time to finish their exercise.

"Actually I did hear knocking," declared one of the writers.

"So did I," said another, "but I just thought it was someone outside."

"That's right," agreed a third, "it was like someone knocking outside."

"Possibly at a door?" I added.

"Wait a minute was that part of the exercise?" asked Carolyn.

"Absolutely!" I said, "next week I'll be up on the roof in my pyjamas!"

"We could definitely write about that!" chorused everyone.

Now I have to buy a ladder.

The Memory Mattress

We were meant to pass like ships in the night that was the deal. Five minutes tops in the bedding department or I would turn back into a pumpkin.

There is no mystery to mattresses that I can see, no documentaries about the secret abuse of mattresses in care homes or articles in the National Geographic predicting the great mattress extinction in the Amazon basin.

Mattresses are simple, straightforward things. In fact they're like dogs, they either take to you or they don't, but according to my wife this was all wishful thinking because apparently a mattress is a dual purchase.

I got the wrong 'dual' at first and thought we were going to have fight for it. At least it would have been all over in an instant, with me on the losing side of course. So we made the ships passing in the night deal.

In reality our ships were taking a long time to pass and after just ten minutes in the bedding department doldrums and they had already come close to a life threatening collision.

After half an hour floating from one mattress to the next my ship finally sank without trace and I resigned myself to the life of a person who stares at mattresses in department stores for a hobby.

The problem was my wife said she couldn't remember what type of mattress she wanted. She had read about it in a newspaper or a magazine and tried to describe it by conjuring up a picture of a hippo and a chick sharing a bed. But this was just a pictorial metaphor she hastened to add and not the actual mattress made by the company that used a hippo and a chick as marketing devices.

Nor was it a direct visual reference to us, which I was glad to hear after checking myself in a wardrobe mirror.

In the reflection I saw the assistant demonstrate yet another mattress by bouncing up and down on the end of a bed. It must have been the sixth or seventh time she had done this and her hair was beginning to regret it.

"What a great job you've got," I said.

"Tell me!" she replied, "I used to be in shoes."

I raised my eyebrows for more detail.

"Murder," she whispered glancing round the department.

"I can imagine," I agreed, "I don't fancy handling other people's feet, I couldn't be a reflexologist."

"Fancy being a mattress buyer?" interjected my wife suddenly.

"Well this one looks great in a similar way to all the others we've looked at let's buy this one!" I announced making myself comfortable on the nearest bed.

My wife joined me and agreed it was very comfortable, not exactly what she was looking for but very supportive none the less and giving where it mattered.

"It's great," I said lying back and staring at the air conditioning pipes above me, "but you don't think it's a bit squeaky, maybe a touch slippery?

"The polythene comes off," replied my wife flatly, "unless you want to keep it on for emergencies," she added loudly.

"What kind of emergencies?" I asked out of the corner of my mouth.

"The kind you need polythene on your mattress for!" declared my wife loudly.

The assistant had by this time found something absolutely fascinating about a point of sale card and I'm sure I caught her giving a secret SOS signal to another assistant. She must have done because a smart young bloke in a suit appeared from nowhere with a tired little painted-on smile and asked her a made-up question so she could leave.

But then right on cue just as they were making a getaway for the curtain department my wife remembered the type of mattress she was looking for.

"A memory mattress!" she shouted, "excuse me it's a memory mattress we're looking for!"

The assistant made her excuses about the fictitious problem that the young bloke wanted help with and returned full of enthusiasm to our cause.

"No problem," she said, "they're over here, if I remember correctly," she added smiling away to herself at her joke, so we joined in and had a right old laugh.

"So this memory mattress, does it just remember it's a mattress or does it remember other things, like the order of playing cards, or capital cities of Central America?" I asked staring at yet another apparently identical mattress.

"It remembers your shape," replied my wife prodding this magical mattress.

"What, like a plaster cast remembers shape?" I asked and we both looked at the assistant.

"I mean you could you use it as a mould and make a full-sized sculpture of yourself?" I continued.

The assistant moved her neck slowly to one side and it made a distinct cracking noise.

"Surely if you move around a lot when you sleep it would just remember a big messy shape?" asked my wife.

The assistant picked up the brochure that was lying on the memory mattress and began to read it.

"Would it remember if anyone else had been on the mattress apart from us?" I asked.

"Like who?" asked my wife sharply, "Goldilocks!"

"That would be a false memory syndrome mattress," I quipped.

"Sorry to interrupt but it says here that the type of memory mattress you need is determined by how much you weigh," announced the assistant reading from the brochure.

"But that would mean we'd need two, in the hippos and chicks scheme of things," said my wife staring at me blankly for inspiration.

"I see you can buy a memory pillow," I began, picking one up, "if you smothered someone with it, would it remember?"

Suddenly my wife was off, pointing enthusiastically.

"Look, memory mattress foam toppers!" she shouted, rubbing her hands together with what can only be described as unfettered glee, "they're singles so we could have one each!"

The assistant glanced at me and pointed to an exit that would apparently lead me to a place of greater sanity.

The worrying thing is unlike the memory mattress my wife didn't realise I had gone.

Vacuum Packed

I was in the gym when I saw it. I can say that with some certainty because the gym is the only place I watch trashy TV. It's a guilty pleasure assuaged by the fact that I'm normally in pain and sweating myself out in buckets.

As I strode my way to nowhere on the cross-country trainer my trashy TV viewing took a particularly surreal twist. Channel hopping I stumbled upon a programme featuring a family of couch potatoes watching trashy TV. In fact they were watching a programme about people who go to the gym just to watch TV. Or at least that's what it looked like. Basically it was TV mating with itself.

Nervously I glanced up at the nearest security camera but thankfully it was pointing in the other direction. You can't be too careful these days with wall-to-wall reality TV programmes.

Suddenly there was high drama as one of the couch dwellers changed position slightly and spilled a huge bowl of snacks over the floor. Much consternation ensued which boiled quickly over into an argument about who would get the vacuum. You could almost hear the programme makers rubbing their hands with glee.

Amazingly everyone wanted to get the vacuum. Eventually after standing her ground the Mum won, apparently it was her turn. She knew that, because she'd made a note. There was something gravely wrong with this arrangement, unless of course they were all playing up for the cameras.

I was hoping my wife was watching, but peering over at her on the treadmill I could see she was glued to Lambing Live.

Meanwhile the couch potato Mum was back with what appeared to be a vacuum from the Starship Enterprise.

It was white, silver and skinny. It was also cordless and appeared to be as light as a feather. At one point it took off across the living room on its own, guzzling the stray snacks in its path.

It was so impressive the couch potatoes became unstuck from the TV screen and gazed at it lovingly. It made me slow my pace just so I could see it in action, but when the Mum plugged the vacuum into an iPad I really wanted one.

"That's seven calories I've just burned!" she announced and made a fist of triumph. Her family were impressed.

"Who needs an expensive gym?" said the Dad, then added pointing under a stool, "you missed a bit dear."

I mentioned all this after our workout to my wife, but she just looked at me strangely.

"It was a vacuum right, and you want to buy one?" she asked, then put a hand on my forehead, "you are quite hot, but then you should be. Are you sure it wasn't just a long TV commercial you were watching?"

She had a point, but either way for some weird reason I was hooked on the sleek space age vacuum.

Obviously we have a vacuum but it's so bulky and cantankerous it takes a planning meeting and both of us just to negotiate the thing out of the hallway cupboard. It's a workout in itself just heaving it from room to room. Not that I use it that often, my job is purely transportation and waste disposal. It's also vintage, 1980's and probably highly collectable, but you can't plug it into a computer.

An executive decision was made, it was time to go digital in the vacuum department.

"There's something not quite right about this," said my wife suspiciously, "am I missing something?"

"It looked like fun to me," I replied and immediately wondered who had said that.

"Oh my God, you'll be dusting next!" said my wife backing nervously away from me, "it's like the body snatchers, or the Stepford Wives, you've been replaced by some weird housekeeping robot. I love it, I think."

We decided one of our sons would fall heir to the old antidiluvian vacuum. When the new one arrived in its tasteful box I unwrapped it like some priceless artefact. My wife gazed at it open mouthed.

"It's beautiful," she said slowly, then picking it up burst out laughing, "it's so light, you can pick it up with one finger. That's why the couch potato family liked it of course, but who cares it's amazing."

It came pre-charged and so for the next half hour we tussled and squabbled over it. At one point it broke free and vacuumed the hallway all by itself.

"Well someone's burned 4 calories using it," I announced after connecting it to my laptop.

"Great!" said my wife, "we'll only have to spend an extra half an hour in the gym tonight."

We were out when our son Adam came to collect the old vacuum. He sent a text thanking us, saying how much he appreciated it and wasn't it amazing. That last word concerned us and our suspicions were confirmed when he texted again saying he had just burned 9 calories vacuuming his flat.

We had it back and the battery charging within twenty minutes. Then we toddled off to the gym.

The Yellow Car

Apparently my wife doesn't have a natural gift for navigation; I just have no sense of direction.

Last Monday evening I found our friend Ellis' house without my wife saying a word.

I was quite pleased with myself, it was dark and there was a slight mist but we were a few minutes early. However, as we waited for Ellis' to make an appearance it occurred to me that his house had doubled in size since I had last seen it.

I looked at my wife. She was reading so she just shook her head.

"Next street up," she said.

We were on our way to our Monday evening Creative Writing Workshop in Lewes and picking up a couple of friends on the way seemed like a perfect plan. Next on our passenger list was Katy who I reckoned lived about a couple of miles or so from Ellis.

Even though none of us have ever been to Katy's house I wasn't too concerned. She'd given us the address and my own living Satnav woman was switched on and raring to go. Just one turn off the main road and she roared into action.

"I don't think this is the right way," said my wife.

"I think you're right," I said peering into the gathering mist, "this road looks deserted to me."

"That's because it is," replied my wife.

She had a point. There were no houses to be seen, so I turned back onto the main road and took the next left.

"This is more like it," announced my wife confidently, even though neither of us had ever been on that particular road.

The meeting started in half an hour in a village hall 12 miles away, but we still had plenty of time. I also had an ace up my sleeve in the form of Katy's car, which she said would be sitting outside her house. The car was bright yellow.

"I don't think you can put 'Katy's yellow car' into a Satnav," said Ellis from the back seat. He was tapping away on his phone but the signal was fading.

"Hold on, I've got a signal!" he declared, "no its gone, oh wait it's back, what was the address again?" he continued, "no it doesn't like it, oh hold on, you're on the right road, yes keep going, no problem, we're very close, there's a junction coming up any second and you need to take the left turn, yes left turn."

My wife said nothing. A mile or so later the junction still hadn't appeared so I turned around and my wife told me to take the next right. Two minutes later we passed the junction so I turned back again and took the left turn.

"Actually it might have been the right turn," said Ellis, quietly.

Maybe it was just me but I could sense the tension mounting as the darkness and the mist tightened around us. More to the point we now seemed to be going round in circles because we were back at that same junction.

"Good," said my wife, "now take the right turn and carry straight on."

Suddenly in the gloom my headlights caught a very light coloured stationary vehicle.

"It's Katy's car!" I announced as I pulled up behind it. Strangely there was no sign of a house but there was a gate. I got out for a closer look and next to the gate found a large sign warning me that I was in grave danger of electrocuting myself.

"So Katy lives in some kind of electricity substation?" said Ellis when I got back into the car.

"Yes she does," I said, "but she's too charged up at the moment to join us."

It may not have been Katy's house but it was definitely her car because I recognised the dents. There was talk of phoning Katy but we didn't have her number or a signal for that matter.

"What about the police?" asked my wife.

"I don't think they'll have Katy's number," said Ellis.

I wasn't so sure.

I got out of the car again. It was hard to tell the parked car's actual colour, maybe it wasn't yellow, it could have been a creamy white. More to the point if it was Katy's car why was it parked outside an electricity substation?

"Maybe her Dad works there and they have a cottage at the back," suggested my wife.

Determined to find Katy I set off in the wrong direction and immediately got us completely lost. Two minutes later we were back at the yellow/white car.

By this time I was almost losing the will to drive. Reluctantly we abandoned poor Katy and my wife sagely guided me like a demented robot through 12 miles of dark misty lanes.

"This must be what it's like being in Top Gear," mused Ellis at one point his teeth rattling.

In the end we were only twenty minutes late for the workshop. Unfortunately I had lost the power of speech.

"If it had been daylight," said Ellis as we walked in, "that would actually have been quite a nice run. It's a shame Katy missed it."

The Phantom Raspberry Blower

I heard it from the bedroom so it must have been pretty loud.

"That sounded painful!" shouted my wife.

"It did sound painful, but it wasn't me," I replied.

"I wonder what it was?" said my wife as she appeared in the bedroom doorway.

"Terrible wind?" I suggested.

"Hmm could be, it is a bit windy outside," she said sounded unconvinced.

Seconds later another loud raspberry noise ripped through the hallway.

"Blimey, that was a bit unlady-like!" I said.

"I'm sorry!" declared my wife, "that wasn't me, that was you!" she added, then another long, loud raspberry blew itself up the hallway, ricocheting off the pictures and making the rubber plant quiver with fear.

We looked at one another in silence until another raspberry, much lower and more sinister than the others growled towards us. Now we were getting scared.

"We're being haunted by a flatulent ghost," I whispered making my wife hurry into the bedroom.

"I hate it when that happens," she said clinging on to me.

We had just returned home and I had been changing into something more comfortable as they say. My wife still had her coat on and now looked as if she was ready to make a run for it any minute.

"I'm not hanging around if there's a farting ghost in the house," she whispered, wide-eyed as another noisy fart broke the silence. She jumped then told me stop it.

"I'm not doing anything," I insisted, "I'm certainly not breaking wind by proxy!"

Right on cue there was another raspberry. This time it was a funny one, like a Panto trumper and we both laughed.

"It's like having a surrogate wind breaker," said my wife.

"Saves you the bother and the inconvenient aftermath," I added.

Unless we were going to spend the rest of our lives in the bedroom it was time to get to the bottom of the phantom raspberry blower.

"You realise we're in a vintage comedy sketch?" I said as we crept down the hallway. My wife looked none the wiser.

I went on to remind her about the The Phantom Raspberry Blower of Old London Town, a recurring sketch in The Two Ronnies show. It featured a Jack the Ripper style madman stalking the streets of Victorian London, who killed or stunned his victims by blowing them a raspberry.

Another prize raspberry roared out from the living room making us jump.

"That's him at it again," I muttered grimly.

In the living room the phantom raspberry blower seemed to be hovering outside our windows. A fierce wind had got up outside, we could see trees bending and waving around like mad things in the moonlight.

"If he's out there, he won't last long," said my wife as another loud fart blew across the room.

I reckoned I had the culprit. We've had windy days before and I hadn't noticed a farting sound effect, but now of course we had new venetian blinds. Somehow the wind was getting in and playing the blinds like a giant wind instrument.

"We're not taking the blinds down because you think they're making an annoying noise!" declared my wife, "you can forget that!"

We have three windows in the living room. The raspberry was only being blown by the middle set of blinds, so I suggested at least pulling them up to see if it made a difference.

"No way!" said my wife, "it took me ages to get them all level!"

I crossed my heart and promised to put them back exactly where they were but my wife just laughed darkly.

An hour later with the farting noise driving me to distraction I was ready to pull the blinds down and throw them out the window.

"We mustn't let it get into our heads," soothed my wife, "it's only a noise and quiet a natural one at that. It's a little weird, but it won't be here tomorrow, we should be enjoying it while it lasts."

'It was an interesting theory', I thought as I dragged out the toolbox.

As a compromise I was allowed to pull the centre blinds up. It made absolutely no difference. I tried half closing them, tilting them down, then up, then fully open. But the phantom raspberry blower prevailed.

The farting noise was now accompanied by a moaning high-pitched whine. It was like being in an episode of The Clangers where they've all had beans for tea.

"Do you think we'll have to call in an expert?" asked my wife.

"You mean like a comedy noise eradicator?" I asked.

As an experiment I decided to open the middle window. We braced ourselves for the penetrating gale and sure enough it did its best to force its way in and wreak havoc, but the farting Clangers stopped.

I quickly closed the window and they returned, like a flatulent Recorder group.

"Phew, that was close!" said my wife, "for a moment there I thought we'd lost them."

We had lots of fun and games that night until the wind dropped. I suppose that's what people did before TV.

Blue is the Colour

When we arrived at the restaurant on Saturday evening it was already running at nursing home temperature then someone must have turned the heating up. It was packed so everyone started to stick together, literally.

"It's just to make us drink more," observed a friend.

"That'll work for me!" I said filling up a glass with water.

After the main course I was so hot I had to stand outside with the Vapers. I was tempted to conduct them because they looked like a band of street musicians all blowing into little wind instruments.

Back in the restaurant toilet I thought I looked a bit off-colour around the gills. I'd undone an extra button on my shirt for ventilation and now I looked slightly blue around the top of my chest. I was wearing a new blue shirt so it could have been some sort of strange reflection. I reckoned it was nothing to worry about.

While I was taking my pulse a bloke turned up and gave me a wary look.

"Just checking to see if I'm still here," I said making the bloke force a brief smile, "yup, not dead yet!" I added.

I was however done to a turn. Back at the table my wife had a very healthy pink glow and was fanning herself with a menu.

"Are you OK?" she asked adjusting my shirt collar, "your neck's gone a strange bluey colour."

"I wonder if it was the fumes from those electric fags?" I said nodding at the crowd vaporising outside on the pavement.

My wife felt my cheeks and my forehead. I was still very hot and my face was apparently quite flushed, but my neck and chest definitely had a slightly blue tinge. A friend was asked for a second opinion.

"Oh yes I see what you mean," they said dramatically, adding that it was hard to tell in the light but there was certainly something creepy going on.

Our friend took a photo of me with her phone and ten seconds later I was on the internet looking quietly bewildered. Another friend sitting next to me showed me the picture on their phone. Then they took a photo of us both and posted it online. I think that was my first double selfie.

Meanwhile my wife began inspecting my chest again, then she rolled up my shirt sleeves. We stared at my forearms for a moment.

"Are they... blue?" asked my wife squinting at my arms.

They looked blue to me but again I was hoping it was the light. Within seconds my blue tinted forearms had been snapped and were hurtling towards the ether for world wide entertainment.

I was about to become the centrepiece for the evening's entertainment when my wife suggested we find out why I was turning blue. At the bottom of the stairs next to the toilets my wife started unbuttoning my shirt. Right on cue a young woman emerged from the Ladies, looked disgusted and told us to get a room.

But my wife was more interested in my back, which apparently was even bluer than my front.

"This is really weird!" she said, so off I went to the Gents to see how weird it really was.

In fact weird didn't really cover it. My entire torso including my arms had turned a sort of dingy grey blue. Even though I now had my shirt off I looked as if I was still wearing it.

Suddenly the door sprang open and my wife's head popped in.

"It's the dye from your shirt!" she announced, "you've sweated it out."

Then she was gone, but suddenly she was back again.

"Probably be hard to wash off," she said and left me staring at my blueness.

She was right of course it wouldn't wash off. After ten minutes of determined soapy scrubbing my chest looked as if it had a huge uninteresting tattoo that had run in the rain.

I'd only bought the shirt that day, it was only fiver so perhaps that explained it. Then I remembered my wife was wearing a new top she'd bought from the same store. It was dark pink and my guess was – she was also dark pink.

The Gents door flew open again and my wife showed me her pink arms.

"I'm all pink!" she shouted and laughed, slightly hysterically I thought.

I could hear my Mother's prophetic words ringing in my ears, "Buy cheap and you buy dear!"

At the time I never really understood that maxim. Now faced with a blue dyed version of myself I could see her point.

"Maybe it's your genetic Woad seeping to the surface brought on by all this talk of Independence," suggested an American friend.

"Or, it could be you're a natural true blue Tory!" said another making the table roar with laughter. My wife meanwhile kept her Labour party leanings to herself.

In the shop I had a choice between the blue shirt and a tan one. I'm going back for the tan one.

Neckless

I was standing outside a shop last week discussing the weather with one of our local GPs, actually I was trying to work the conversation round to the funny twinge I've been getting on my left side, when my wife appeared and suddenly seemed very alarmed by the fact that my head wasn't jammed straight onto my chest.

"Oh hello," she said smiling to the GP, then turning to me and looking alarmed she added, "oh my God you've got a neck!"

"You'd better cover it up," she continued, adjusting my scarf.

The doctor who has no doubt seen it all at least twice looked surprised and was about to say something but my wife hurried off into the shop.

"Actually I did notice your neck myself," said the Doctor, "but not in a bad way, don't worry," He added laughing at my alarmed look, "anyway must dash."

I was vaguely perplexed but didn't give it too much thought. As far as I was concerned I'd always had a neck of sorts, my wife and the doc just thought it was a good idea if I covered it up during the winter months. The chilly wind was blowing up inside my jacket for some reason so I headed quickly back to the car.

Later that afternoon I caught up with my wife at the hairdresser where we had a double appointment. We hadn't deliberately planned this, it just sort of happened because of the availability of appointments but we ended up sitting next to one another.

Oddly enough we always seem to sit together in the same position, with me in the driving seat so to speak and the hairdresser's was no different.

Coral the salon owner seemed to be genuinely fascinated by this curious anomaly when my wife interrupted and started telling everyone about my neck. I was about to take my jacket off and let Coral wrap me in one of her anti-static gowns when she stopped and peered at me in the mirror.

"Oh yeah, I see what you mean," she said looking absolutely fascinated, "that's amazing," she continued, "look at that!"

I looked up at her in silence as she called one of her juniors over for a second opinion.

"Pull your scarf down!" ordered my wife.

"Oh yeah..." said Jools the Junior, mimicking Coral, "I see what you mean, that's amazing!"

Now I was getting genuinely scared.

"Excuse me," I said indignantly standing up and removing my scarf and jacket, "I did have a neck before you know, in fact I think I've always had a neck!"

"Of course you have dear," comforted Coral, "its just that we couldn't see it before. Now then where were we?"

I sat back down and Coral draped the gown over me tucking it in to the back of my neck and smoothing it over my shoulders.

"Uh oh! She exclaimed, "he's got shoulders!"

My wife reached out from her seat and tried to touch my left shoulder but I was too far away, in fact I may have moved slightly to avoid her grasp. Deciding this was far more important than getting her hair done she stood up, taking Jasmine her hairdresser with her.

"Shut the front door!" she shouted as she groped first my left then my right shoulder, "I hadn't noticed that!"

"You're getting a new man!" declared Coral. Then Jasmine had a go. I was actually starting to enjoy this.

"Now I've got a neck maybe you could give it a quick massage?" I suggested and was promptly slapped.

Feeling my left shoulder and then my right I was amazed to find they were curiously bony. Then in the mirror I saw the neck. Somehow it looked much thinner than I remembered so I started looking for the rest of it.

"What's happened to my neck?" I asked more to myself than anyone else.

"Show's you how often he looks in the mirror." Laughed my wife.

"It's that gym." Said Coral, "you want to watch that, you'll gym yourself away to nothing."

"From the neck down?" I asked.

Apparently that's how it works and because my shoulders were trimmer my jacket wasn't fitting properly and the wind was blowing up it. The last thing I wanted was a spindly neck and narrow shoulders, I was going to the gym to man up.

I was still perturbed about my neck and how it had managed to appear like some miraculous visitation that actually stopped people in the street. But my main concern was what had been there previously.

"Are we talking Jabba the Hut here?" I asked but only my wife was familiar with the huge slug-like neckless alien from Return of the Jedi and she was visibly thinking it over.

Within seconds Jools the Junior had Jabba up on her iPad.

"Actually there is a resemblance around the eyes," said my wife as she was handed the iPad.

"He doesn't have such a slim neck as you though." Said Coral.

And my wife wonders why I try not to surprise myself in the mirror.

De-throned

I don't think I've ever had an accident in the toilet. Which is surprising when you consider the potential dangers such an environment presents - sharp, slippery surfaces, steam, hot water, and of course the most dangerous of all, those horrible unexpected encounters in the mirror.

The trouble is bad stuff normally happens when you least expect it, so when I sat down on the loo I didn't expect the earth to move beneath me. It's just not something you're prepared for so I think I may have screamed or maybe shouted but I was alone in the house so I'm not sure who I was shouting for.

I had been reaching for my current book of choice when I was suddenly pulled over to my right in a casual crumple, meanwhile the toilet seat slid away to my left. Another inch or two and I would have caught my head on the edge of the sink, instead I put my hand out and smashed it into the end of the toilet brush, splitting my trousers as I went over.

Dazed and slightly confused I pulled myself up and stared at the poor broken brush, the innocent white ceramic toilet bowl and the evil pine seat lying on the floor like a wooden noose. Technically I suppose you could say I had been dethroned.

All I could think was, 'oh my God I've broken the toilet seat and all because I wanted to read a book!'

Obviously I was now on death row and unless I could fix the seat or replace it before my wife came home there was little hope of a reprieve. I might as well start planning my last meal.

A closer inspection of the seat revealed one of the hinges had sheared right through. After some ingenious negotiation I managed to fit the seat back on and was quite pleased with myself. I just held it in place while I got back to the business in hand, without the book of the month.

While I was checking local DIY stores online for toilet seats my wife came home and went straight to the toilet. "Sorry, I'm desperate!" she shouted.

"No problem," I shouted back, then sat straight up because of course there was a problem.

Hurrying to the toilet I waited for the scream but there was nothing. Perhaps I'd made a better job of putting the seat back on than I had first thought.

"Are you OK?" I asked outside the door.

"Yes why?" asked my wife, "I see you put the seat back on, isn't that a pest?"

This was one of those moments when I turn and look at the audience.

"Yes, it is a pest," I replied, "and flipping dangerous!"

"Dangerous?" asked my wife as she opened the door suddenly making me step back.

"I fell off it," I said, "and nearly split my skull on the sink, I could have fallen into the bath and drowned!"

"Were you having a bath?" asked my wife perplexed, "anyway I told you about it this morning and I left a note on top of the cistern," she continued, turning and pointing at a small piece of paper on top of the cistern.

Personally when you leave a note that is essentially a Health and Safety warning its not a good idea to write it on the back of a till receipt, even if it is the only piece of paper you can find and in you're in a hurry.

'Remember the seat is broken' it said in dark brown eye-liner pencil.

Selecting the new seat was easy. At the local DIY store I just pointed at every seat on display until my wife said 'yes that's the one!' even though it was a different coloured wood from the existing one.

"Time for a change," said my wife as paid for it, "this one will match the floor."

Actually the last one went with the floor because that's where it ended up.

"I'll fit it in a couple of minutes tops!" I announced as I grabbed some tools and headed for the toilet.

Two hours later my back and my neck were about to give up hope as I lay curled up on the floor under the toilet bowl. The nuts on the bolts that held on the hinges of the old seat refused to budge so I had decided to saw through the bolts. The first one had taken about half an hour and most of my sanity, the second one had turned me into a desperate man.

"Nothing's going to get in my way now!" I muttered through gritted teeth as the sweat spilled from my forehead and made my eyes sting.

Once I'd fitted the seat I enjoyed a thrilling wave of satisfaction.

"Well, it almost killed me but it was worth it!" I declared opening the bathroom door with a dramatic "Ta-ra!"

My wife looked at the seat in silence.

"Do you know what would look great?" she said, "a black one!"

Again, that's me staring at the audience.

Not Dead Yet

You really shouldn't stare into people's houses at night when they've left their curtains wide open and their lights are full on. At least that's what I keep saying when my wife and I are out patrolling the policies of an evening. But then again sometimes it's hard to resist the odd glance into a stranger's living room.

Last Sunday evening there was nothing out of the ordinary to report until we saw some Christmas lights twinkling in the distance.

"They're a bit early with the Christmas lights," I said.

"Maybe they keep them on all year round," said my wife, "it's not uncommon for people to get addicted to Christmas."

I was still trying to imagine what that might be like as we passed the house. There was a large twinkling Christmas tree on the far side of the room. On the mantelpiece I saw a little illuminated snowman frozen in mid-wave and from the ceiling slightly tired looking paper decorations hanging limply.

There was also a very old man sitting in an easy chair in front of the TV. His head was right back and his mouth was wide open. In fact just glancing at him made me yawn.

"Come on!" said my wife, "you can sleep later."

As we walked up the road we wondered about the Christmas decorations. The old man didn't look strong enough to put them up never mind take them down.

"Maybe he just really likes them," I said, "probably cheers him up."

An hour or so later after visiting the local shop we headed home.

"Let's pass that old man's house again and see if he's taken his decorations down," I said.

Approaching from the other end of the street the lights appeared to have vanished and we assumed they had been turned off but they were still twinkling away and the little frosty snowman was still frozen in mid-wave. The old man also looked like a permanent fixture. It was probably my imagination but he also looked a lot paler.

"Do you think he's all right?" asked my wife peering into the living room.

"He does look a bit pale doesn't he?" I replied.

"For all we know he could have had a heart attack." Said my wife.

"For all we know he could have had a heart attack on Boxing Day!" I said.

For some reason we glanced around and then up and down the street. Maybe we were looking for an answer or perhaps an ambulance. But there was nothing. Every house had their blinds or curtains drawn. Ironically only the old man's house showed any signs of life.

"I think the lights are on but its possible there's no one in," I said.

We seemed to stand for a long time staring at the old man, long enough in fact to notice any obvious signs of life.

"He's not moving is he?" said my wife. I shook my head slowly.

"Maybe we should knock on his door?" continued my wife looking for the front door. She found it round the side of the bungalow, then came back.

"Any sign of life?" she asked, but I shook my head again.

"What do you think?" continued my wife.

"Well what happens if he answers the door?" I asked.

My wife frowned at me.

"Well that's good news isn't it?" she said.

"Absolutely!" I said, "but what will you say to him?" I continued, "oh hello, I just happened to be passing and thought you might be dead?"

My wife stared at me in silence for a moment and then headed back to the front door.

"Ask him if he wants a hand taking down his Christmas decorations!" I shouted.

Suddenly my wife was back again. It was freezing and I was really starting to feel it.

"Sorry am I holding you up?" she asked sharply, "you realise we might have to break his door down?"

"You realise we're missing the Bake Off?" I said.

"We don't watch the Bake Off," replied my wife, "do you think we should call someone?" she continued.

"What, like an undertaker?" I said.

My wife took a deep breath and checked the old man again, this time from quite close to his window. If he'd looked out at this point I think questions might have been asked, but there was still no sign of movement.

"It doesn't look good to me. Phone an ambulance, I'll go in and give him CPR," she said purposefully then disappeared again round the side of the house.

I was wondering how my wife was going to break down a heavy front door when a woman appeared with a small dog.

For some reason I couldn't bring myself to tell her why I was standing outside the house. I said hello as I hovered near the gate but she just walked on.

Suddenly I saw the old man's collar twitch.

"He's moving!" I shouted, "he's moving!"

My wife stuck her head round the corner of the house.

"Yes!" she whispered making a fist, "we have lift off!"

"I wonder how much a portable defibrillator would be?" she asked as we walked home.

Blowin in the Wind

I don't think I've ever had to ask my wife what she would like for her birthday. Things just come up and if I'm paying attention, which of course I am, I'll take a mental note of those things.

For instance a couple of weeks ago we passed a young girl busking with a guitar in a shopping centre. I thought she was rather good, probably because she quite attractive, but my wife decided she could do better and I wasn't about to stop her.

The girl had a hat brimming with money and as I said it looked like a lucrative and fun activity. My wife could also combine her interests in music, shops and hats.

When I first met my wife about forty years ago we went to a party and I found a guitar to pick at in an enigmatic manner. A few minutes into my meanderings my wife took the guitar from me and immediately launched into a rousing performance of the Bob Dylan song 'Blowin' in the Wind'.

When she finished everyone applauded and I was duly presented with the guitar. That laid a pattern for my wife's relationship with the instrument that lasted until her birthday last week.

Just a few minutes after hearing that busker we were in a music shop looking at guitar songbooks.

"Oh these are easy!" declared my wife, "anyone could play these."

"That's a Ukelele songbook," I said.

"What's the difference?" asked my wife and I pointed at the little Ukeleles on the shop wall behind her.

My wife shuddered and decided she would stick with a guitar songbook for now.

I think it was called 101 Busker Songs. Whether or not that was 101 different songs or arrangements for 101 buskers I wasn't sure, but it was a big songbook, with clearly marked out chords that you could see if you were busking in the rain.

We also bought half a dozen plectrums based purely on their colour and patterns even though my wife said she didn't believe in them.

"Does Joan Baez use a plectrum?" she asked the young disinterested sales assistant. The girl had a bolt through the end of her tongue so it was hard to tell.

Meanwhile I was busy trying to work out where this was going. I have an very old, very interesting guitar, which I play and polish occasionally. In between our sessions it waits patiently for me on its own special stand in my study. It's a thing of fascinating beauty and if I'm in the right frame of mind can sound rather magical.

As far as I know this is not the family guitar. Many people have tried to engage with it but none have succeeded. Now my wife was leaving a music shop with a guitar songbook and a bag of full of pink and purple plectrums. It may have been panic but I took the hint.

"You'll need a birthday guitar if you're going to start busking!" I said.

My wife stopped in her tracks and looked genuinely surprised then ceremoniously handed me the music shop bag.

"Great!" she said, "I can't wait!"

A week later on the big day I was rather pleased with myself. Not only had I bought my wife a guitar I'd actually bought her three different types.

When I told her this she looked concerned and said something about the expense.

"I mean, I probably won't actually go busking," she added.

"Don't worry about that!" I said and opened her iPad on the kitchen worktop in front of her, "they're digital guitars!"

There were three to choose from, a nylon string, a metal string and a 12 string all with authentic sound and to change chords you just pressed a button.

I brought up the metal string acoustic and strummed the strings then played some chords. My wife was astonished. When she ran her thumb over the screen and the strings rang out it was as if she had discovered fire.

"That's amazing!" she said, "it sounds so real and I don't even have to tune it."

"Exactly and you can plug these in," I said, producing a pair of headphones.

"So cheap as well," added my wife as she left with her iPad and songbook under her arm.

I was a genius for almost fifteen minutes until my wife discovered that you can't actually play an iPad guitar with a pink plectrum. Also the sound of her singing with no accompaniment was a situation I hadn't bargained for.

Having said that when she sang 'Bridge Over Troubled Waters' accompanying herself on the iPad I thought it was fantastic and of course the iPad would be ideal for busking, very neat and light.

When she closed the iPad her silence and look of resignation spoke volumes. A minute later I was handing her my cherished guitar.

"Just a joke," I said, "this is for you, I'm sorry its not wrapped up."

She took the guitar with appropriate reverence and then two seconds later she was banging out 'Blowin' in the Wind' with impressive gusto.

Dylan also said the times they are a changing but sometimes I wonder.

Finger Jam

I was at the cinema when my finger jammed. Apart from being engrossed in the classic Frank Capra film 'It's a Wonderful Life' I wasn't engaged in anything particularly demanding. Unlike the rest of the cinemagoers around me I wasn't eating a kilo of popcorn or scoofing a litre of coca-cola.

I think James Stewart's brother was about to go off to fight the Nazis. I was minding James Stewart's business when the forefinger of my right hand just sort of stuck in a bent position.

I tried to open it - gently at first but it wouldn't take me on. So I attempted a little force and the pain made me jump, which in turn made my wife and our son Adam jump.

"Are you OK?" they whispered.

"I'm fine but my finger's stuck," I replied.

"In what?" asked my wife still watching the film.

I held the crooked forefinger up and she glanced at it.

"Do you want me to go somewhere with you?" she asked and someone behind us said 'shush!" loudly, so someone else further back said 'shush!' even louder.

I hunkered down and got back to James Stewart's wonderful life and tried not to think about my not so wonderful curly finger. Every so often I couldn't resist trying to open it but the pain soon put a stop to that.

A strange thing happened at the end of the film. The audience actually applauded, or at least everyone did apart from me. I tried my best but it's hard to clap when you have a finger in the way.

"Didn't you enjoy it?" asked my wife, wiping her moist eyes.

I held up the curly finger.

"Still stuck?" she asked looking closely at it.

I gave it a little persuasion and winced at the sharp hot pain.

"Well that's much good is it?" said my wife.

"Do you think you'll be able to drive?" asked our son Adam.

"It's a good job its not stuck in a perpendicular position!" I said displaying the curly finger.

"It could be handy like that though," said my wife, "look on the bright side, you could make the OK gesture without hardly moving a muscle."

Adam was on his phone, for a moment I thought he was going to call for a taxi.

"I'm just looking it up on the internet," he muttered.

Meanwhile my wife examined the finger. It didn't appear to be swollen and prior to it being stuck and refusing to straighten there had been no pain or any sign of unwillingness to work. I had to admit I was beginning to panic slightly, the finger had been frozen in a hook for over half an hour and had thwarted all my attempts to straighten it out. What if it was permanent?

A long list of things ran through my mind that I would have difficulty doing which I started spouting.

"Why are you panicking?" asked my wife, "You've probably just damaged a ligament or maybe the joint is dislocated."

I held it up and gazed at it again. It looked perfectly normal, just curly.

"Can you remember what you were doing when it stuck?" asked my wife, "I hope your weren't picking your nose, what do you think Adam?"

"I don't think picking your nose would do that," said Adam, still engrossed in his phone, "but I'll tell you one thing, you can't make the OK gesture in Brazil, Germany or Russia, because it's considered a supreme insult and in France, its used to tell someone they're a dope!"

Adam looked up from his phone for a reaction, "Amazing eh?" he said, then continued reading from the screen, "in Spain, Eastern Europe, and in some parts of Latin America, the OK hand gesture is also considered extremely rude."

"Fascinating!" I shouted, then thought about it, "actually I think I've made that gesture to waiters in French restaurants."

"So nothing there about sticky fingers?" asked my wife. Adam shook his head.

In fact driving wasn't tricky at all and by the time we reached home the finger was straightening out, but it was throbbing and still painful.

Time to consult Dr Google I thought. Needless to say I couldn't type with my forefinger, which should have been a clue. I managed to search for 'finger won't straighten out' and up came a condition known as 'Mallet' finger.

"So did you hit your finger with a mallet or a hammer?" asked my wife peering over my shoulder at the screen.

A few clicks later I reckon I found the culprit – 'iPhone finger' a close friend of 'iPad finger' caused by swiping the screens of said gadgets'.

When I thought back to the cinema I had in fact remembered my phone was still on so I dug it out of my coat pocket and turned it off with a determined swipe. That's when my finger must have jammed.

"Well that's easy," said my wife, "just get rid of your iPhone and iPad. Case closed!"

I have a stiff curly finger, I'm not mad, not completely anyway.

No Right Turn

"So why did auntie Madge give us a tin opener for Christmas?" I asked, I wasn't being facetious, I was actually genuinely interested, "it seems a bit random to me although I suppose it's a very practical gift and there's nothing wrong with giving someone a practical gift."

I was trying to picture my wife's face if I had given her a tin opener for Christmas. "But it's a very practical gift." I was saying. Then I pictured my face as I tried to dodge the flying tin opener.

"Actually, it's a very expensive tin opener," said my wife, "and as gifts go its perfect because our tin opener is on its last legs, in fact I've binned it."

I was mystified as to how auntie Madge – who is an honorary aunt and won't mind me saying that, knew our tin opener was on its way to the bin. She is reckoned to have psychic powers and once found the neighbour's missing cat, although, having said that, it was sleeping in a cupboard in her house. But if her powers extended to kitchen utensils then she should be putting them to better use, like world peace for instance.

I had a close look at the tin opener and had to agree it looked expensive and slightly complicated.

"It's state of the art apparently," said my wife as I peered at the mechanism, "and Madge thought you would really appreciate it."

"I would really appreciate it?" I said, trying to remember when I became a tin opener aficionado.

I haven't seen many state of the art tin openers, but I took Madge's word for it.

It did look rather sleek but the problem wasn't its looks, it was its attitude. Basically it didn't want to work, it just wanted to lie about the kitchen drawer looking well designed and smug.

For the past quarter of an hour my wife had been trying to persuade it to open a tin of garden peas and her patience had now come to a bitter end. While I was examining the beautifully designed non-functioning tin opener my wife started rummaging in the bin for the old one.

She found it and held it up by one leg at arm's length.

"I might have to sterilise it first," she announced.

I wasn't that desperate for garden peas but I can't resist a challenge so I rolled my sleeves up and got to grips with Mr state of the art. The first problem was how to fix it to the tin.

"So how does this work?" I asked my wife, but she just shrugged.

"That's the problem, remember?" she replied folding her arms and taking a deep intake of breath.

After much persuasion and creative manipulation I managed to attach the opener to the lip of the tin and then I started turning the knob. I assumed the tin would just turn and simultaneously open like it was supposed to, but instead the tin opener turned and kept on turning and turning.

After ten minutes of this I was ready to jump into the bin myself along with the tin opener.

"So much for Auntie Madge's practical tin opener!" I shouted.

"What about Google?" asked my wife.

"It doesn't open tins," I said grumpily and was duly smacked.

Who could have predicted that there would be a video tutorial on the internet demonstrating how to use our new state of the art tin opener? Apart from my wife.

We stared at the video and played it back three times. Then stared at the tin opener. It looked so simple on the video but there was obviously something we were missing.

"Maybe we're trying to open the wrong type of tin," I suggested.

We both thought about this for a moment and had to shake ourselves back to reality. This tin opener was beginning to exert a strange power over us, which was about all it could do.

"Maybe it's some kind of weird IQ test thing," said my wife, "which we've failed miserably."

Looking at the tutorial video again it suddenly occurred to me that the cutting bits on our opener were on a different side.

"It's upside down!" I declared, "the cutting bits on our opener are on the wrong side, it's a factory reject!"

"Thank God for that!" said my wife.

Refusing to be beaten I tried the opener one last time and for some reason I turned the knob anti-clockwise. The cutter bit straight into the tin and opened it in about three seconds flat. My wife was speechless.

"It's a left handed tin opener," she muttered.

I stood over the open tin smirking. 'So this is what Sherlock feels like', I thought.

"Elementary!" I declared.

But the question remained as to why auntie Madge would send us a left-handed tin opener that I would really appreciate. Suddenly my wife's face lit up.

"She must have read your column about you straining your right arm," she said.

Next week I'll be writing about my wife's sciatica and how we really need a luxury cruise.

Doddery

The big topic of conversation around the charity shop counter was the internet and how it had been designed to bring the world to a standstill, possibly even to its ultimate extinction. Two assistants - a bearded young man and a middle-aged woman and a customer – an elderly gentleman were locked in the debate.

The conversation had sprung from the old chap's request for an executive summary on the interweb as he called it. He'd been to a class at the local community centre but was unimpressed.

"All people want to do is buy stuff or find distant relatives they'll never meet, load of nonsense if you ask me." He had declared.

"The real problem," announced the male assistant stroking his beard, "isn't the internet, its people."

His colleague and the old chap nodded gloomily.

"Once we get rid of people," continued the male assistant, "everything will be fine."

"Absolutely," agreed the customer, then after a moment's thought he added, "bit radical though, couldn't we keep a couple of people?"

"What about the shop Gordon?" asked the female assistant, a nervous lady with thick lensed glasses and a hankie permanently in her left hand, "we wouldn't have any customers."

"Exactly!" declared Gordon waving his hands in the air, "Halle-flippin-luya!"

There was an awkward silence.

My wife appeared for the third time and started browsing amongst the scented candles.

"Still here?" she asked quietly, "there are other nuthouses, I mean charity shops you know."

I had been leafing through records and browsing books for about twenty minutes, a long time in charity shop world. I had tried to leave twice but then the conversation at the counter would take an even more bizarre turn and I would be glued again to the spot.

So far we had covered flesh-eating bugs, benefit cheats, the madness of Brexit, the obvious link between extreme weather and aliens and now we were onto the global conspiracy that is the interweb. And I hadn't said a word.

At one point when the trio started whispering about someone they knew who worked at the BBC in the sixties with Jimmy Savile I had to pretend to be fascinated by some glass paperweights just so I get closer to the counter.

"Why don't you just buy a copy of The Daily Mail and be done with it," said my wife.

Suddenly there was a fourth member of the brains' trust, a bloke I had seen earlier talking to himself at the DVD section joined the group.

Earlier at the DVDs I thought he was speaking to me so I had smiled and agreed with him thinking he was probably commenting on the range of films. But then he carried on the conversation without me.

Now he was talking to himself up at the counter and the trio were standing listening. Every time someone tried to answer the bloke he butted in and answered himself.

My wife had seen enough – "I'll have to go somewhere less random," she said but then she was distracted by a red spotty top – she has a thing about red and white spots.

Suddenly I spotted a rack of old records on the floor near the counter so I went over for a rummage just in time for the bloke who was speaking to himself to announce his departure.

"Righto, see you tomorrow!" he said, "absolutely, see you tomorrow," he replied to himself leaving the counter in a state of mild bewilderment.

I was kneeling on the floor going through the records when my wife approached and without looking up I showed her a Ken Dodd LP.

"Can I buy you this as a secret birthday present?" I asked but there was no response, so I persisted with my best Ken Dodd impression.

Laughing away to myself I continued to leaf through the records but every single one of them was by Ken Dodd.

"How bizarre!" I said, touching my wife's booted leg to get her attention, but she jumped back.

"Honestly check this one out, it's absolutely brilliant, I mean just look at the size of that tickling stick!" I announced standing up and presenting my wife with the LP.

Only it wasn't my wife. It was a horrified woman I had never seen before in my life.

In my defence she was the same build as my wife and was wearing a very similar coat and almost identical boots. Glancing at Ken's tickling stick she forced a wary weak smile.

"Sorry!" I said, "I thought you were my wife."

"I don't think we've even met," replied the woman looking at the assistants and the elderly gentleman who were now transfixed.

"No, I meant, I mistook you for my wife, she was in the shop earlier," I explained.

All four of them gazed at me in silence, beardy man stroked his beard, his colleague dabbed her mouth with her hankie and the old chap glowered darkly.

"I think I've gone a bit doddery," I laughed, holding up the record, "personally I blame the interweb"

"I rest my case!" said beardy banging the counter.

The Unpromotion

The bloke seemed to hover towards us through the busy shop as if he had been parachuted into the crowd. We weren't even shopping. It was freezing outside and the rain was turning to sleet so we had dived into the store for cover. Although a shortcut through a department during a January Sale isn't really a shortcut, more of a cosy detour.

Then the bloke was hovering next to my wife and following us as we walked.

"Have you heard the good news?" he said in a drab monotonous voice.

"Sorry what did you say?" asked my wife, looking concerned and thinking the bloke needed assistance.

"He asked if we had heard the good news," I said.

"Is the good news about you?" asked my wife.

The bloke looked baffled so we stopped for a moment while he collected himself. Meanwhile shoppers swam around us blindly on both sides. We had created an obstacle but nothing would stem the tide of bargain hunters.

The bloke had some leaflets in his hands, which he checked from time to time, possibly just to make sure they were still there. He was in his late thirties and casually dressed in a shirt and trousers, so he obviously hadn't been outside lately.

"Have you heard the good news?" he said again in a slightly less monotonous voice.

"You've done that bit," I said and was summarily poked by my wife.

"Never mind him," she said, "tell us the good news."

I think at this juncture we both assumed our friend was some kind of evangelist bringing the good news that God was among us and consequently we had been saved from buying pointless stuff just because it was half price.

"Is it about God?" continued my wife, sensing the bloke was having a problem conveying his good news, "because if it is, that's not a problem."

The bloke laughed, more to himself really, which was slightly creepy.

This was certainly a unique strategy for getting people's attention. I've developed a friendly but dismissive smile that is perfect for warding off free range sales people but I hadn't had time to deploy it and worse still my wife was genuinely interested.

I explained how we weren't actually shopping and that we were taking a shortcut through the store because it was freezing outside and the rain had turned to sleet.

"It's not about God," replied the bloke, "its about..." he looked at one of his leaflets, "sorry about this," he continued, "I'm new to this, I'm meant to be folding T-shirts in menswear, but we're short staffed." Suddenly the bloke looked crestfallen and he started shaking his head.

If he was selling by disinterest or default it wasn't working for me and I tried to leave but my wife stopped me. Worryingly she had that sympathetic look.

"Don't worry," she said angling her head in an attempt to read one of the leaflets, "is it an instore promotion?" she asked.

"Yes!" declared the bloke cheering up, "its some kind of new store card...I think."

"You think?" I said laughing and tried again unsuccessfully to make my escape.

"Why is it new?" asked my wife, "can you tell us how its different from the old one?"

But the bloke couldn't tell us, instead he started reading the leaflet again so my wife stopped him.

"I hope you don't mind me saying but you're terrible at this," she smiled, "anyway the good news is we won't be getting some kind of new store card, but thanks for the offer."

"But I haven't done my complete presentation yet," said the bloke perking up.

We both laughed.

"You can't practice on real potential customers," I said, "haven't you been trained?"

"The training girl's got that Norovirus thing," replied the bloke, "half the shop's off with it."

"Let me see the leaflet," said my wife taking one of them and scanning it.

The promotion, or 'the good news' was a £100 to spend in the store, the catch of course was the bank account bursting store card.

"Right," said my wife looking around the crowded store for potential victims. Two unsuspecting women approached and my wife pounced, immediately engaging them.

"Hello, how would you like a hundred pounds each to spend in the store today?" she asked showing the women the leaflet. Within seconds they were old pals and laughing away.

The bloke looked on amazed and then back at me.

"I don't think this is allowed," he said anxiously.

"Its good news though, for you," I replied.

My wife handed the two women over to the bloke.

"That's how its done," she said, "training day over."

But then stopping in her tracks she turned back and took the women aside.

"Actually the apr rate on the store card is enormous," she said, "so I would avoid it if I were you."

We smiled and waved at the bloke as he was sucked into the crowd of half crazed, half dazed shoppers.

"Have you heard the good news?" asked my wife.

"Is it about me?" I asked hopefully.

The Hot Ticket

We booked our cinema tickets online, mainly because its cheaper but also because I thought there might be a bit of a rush. A freezing Saturday evening in February seemed the perfect time to head off to the cinema to watch a new much raved about creepy movie.

Needless to say we were running late. But at least we had our tickets so our seats were safe. Unfortunately they weren't numbered so we would have to make do with was left.

As I suspected the cinema was packed and we had to battle our way through the crowd just to get to the automatic ticket machines, both of which were out of order.

I joined the ticket desk queue while my wife debated about visiting the loo, which also had a queue outside the door. After investigating the queue in close-up she decided she would wait until we were seated and then go to the toilet.

"I'll be happier once I know we've got decent seats," she explained.

"So you'll squeeze past lots of people, sit down for two seconds, get up, squeeze past them again, go to the loo and when you come back disturb them all again?" I said.

"Hopefully," said my wife, "if we get good seats in the middle."

We assumed we'd missed the start of the film but the girl who took the tickets assured us the trailers were still running.

"Thank goodness for that!" I said as we hurried along the corridor towards Screen 2.

"Calm down, its not life or death," said my wife and then bolted past me.

By the time I caught up with her she was standing silhouetted against five giant versions of the actor Kevin Bacon. For that moment she looked like his little pet doll.

I assumed she was scanning the cinema for two decent empty seats.

"It's going to be tough!" she shouted, making me jump.

For a few moments we both stared in disbelief at the empty cinema until it occurred to us we were in the wrong screen. The tickets however, confirmed it was screen 2.

"This must be a terrible film," said my wife as we took our time choosing the best empty seats in the best empty row.

Its a strangely unsettling experience sitting in an empty cinema. For a start it seemed huge, which was unnerving, but at the same time it felt exclusive, which in a very literal way it was.

But it lacked atmosphere, watching a film in a cinema should be a collective experience even when someone's kicking the back of your seat and the bloke with the big bag of crisps sitting next to you smells of rotten turnips.

There was also an annoying emergency exit that was far too bright so I went off to investigate closing it. Since we were alone anything was possible.

The exit turned out to be doorless and the light was coming from a corridor so there was nothing I could do about that. However, I did manage to cover the bright emergency exit sign with my scarf.

On the way back to my seat I started dancing while my wife sang along to the onscreen trailer. Suddenly we felt totally liberated, we could make any noise or commotion we could think of, so being completely mature adults, we did.

We began singing loudly again and because we were drinking coke we were free with our exhalations, if not downright impressively noisy. My mobile rang – appropriately my current ringtone is the Dance of the Marrionettes, the theme music to the TV series The Alfred Hitchcock Hour.

The film was starting so I kept my phone conversation short. A few minutes later some email came in so we discussed them and I replied to them, then I had to phone someone else.

Meanwhile the film unfolded and turned out to be more of a silly, creepy fairytale that was alternately daft and scary. During the daft bits we booed and shouted abuse at the onscreen antics and whenever we got a fright we jumped out of our seats. My wife screamed so loud at one point I may have permanent ear damage.

We only moved three times and always during boring bits of the film. Eventually we sprawled out with our legs over the seats in front. Just for the hell of it I went and bought the noisiest bags of sweets I could find and we ate them without restraint.

"I could get used to this," announced my wife, and then repeated herself at maximum volume.

"So could I!" I shouted and then screamed because my wife stroked the back of my neck.

We also jumped at the end of the movie when a shadowy form assembled from one of the front row seats and rose up stretching out its dark spindly arms. My wife threw herself at me as the figure moved slowly along the row of seats and began making its way up the aisle.

I saw him briefly as he passed.

"Don't forget your scarf mate!" he shouted.

The Two-Minute Warning

There is normally a nugget of truth in your average cliché but watching paint dry isn't as boring as its cracked up to be. My wife had painted sample colour boards and it was hard to decide between them while they were wet so as we waited for them to dry the tension was mounting.

My money was on a dull sage-like green but my wife was recommending we go warm with a deep and dusty plum. Two natural colours, although not the sort of thing you would normally see on a bookcase, even if it was vintage.

Thirty odd years ago when someone paid a month's salary for the oak grain effect Schreiber bookcase the last thing they would have done is slap a layer of paint over it.

Curiously this is probably why we haven't painted it yet. It cost all of fifteen quid and it's a retro classic that looks great in our living room, the niggle is, it could look magnificent if it was painted or in contemporary parlance, 'upscaled'.

The make-over, we have decided would add an element of irony to the bookcase and it wouldn't look as if we still owned it from the first time round.

"It has to look vintage ironic," declared my wife.

I was more concerned about how I was going to paint the two sliding doors at the bottom. They wouldn't come out without taking the entire bookcase apart so after much deliberation we decided it would be even more ironic if we left them in. This apparently would keep us in touch with the bookcase's heritage.

Even though we have never owned an oak grain effect Schreiber bookcase it still qualifies as a piece of nostalgia. Not only are we turning into our parents we're now buying their furniture and their bric-a-brac. I suspect the reason we feel we have to paint the bookcase is because we're partly in denial. We want our youth back but not at the cost of our house looking naff.

It was a tough call on the colours so in the end we went for both. The outside of the bookcase would be sage green and the inside a dusty plum. As I surveyed the various planes of the bookcase I was already looking forward to my brush skills being tested to the limit.

"Actually I quite like it the way it is," I said lying.

But my wife just laughed. In fact she was still laughing in the DIY store as we hunted for the paint mixing section.

"It's a design classic," I said in my defence, "and we're going to deface it."

"You're a classic!" replied my wife.

The paint mixing section was unmanned but I found an assistant nearby studying a bottle of thinners.

"Just press the big button Sir and someone will be with you within two minutes," he said.

"Within two minutes?" I asked and he nodded. I took this surprisingly exact time back to my wife.

"Why two minutes?" she pondered, "that's unusually precise."

Behind her I spotted a large button ringed by small red lights, which said:

'Press the button and if an assistant hasn't arrived within two minutes we'll give you 10% discount'

We both worked that out at £2.19.

There was no one in sight, but I checked round the corner in case there was a sneaky assistant lurking. I then checked the other end of the aisle and then gave my wife the all clear.

The big button was duly pressed with a certain amount of pomp and my wife checked her watch. She wasn't taking any chances.

Two minutes is a surprisingly long time in 10% discount world. As the seconds went by the little red lights illuminated just to crank up the tension.

This was ingenious stuff. With one simple button, the store had cleverly reversed what normally happens. Instead of wishing an assistant would hurry up we were now hoping they would take their time.

"I wonder how this works?" said my wife biting her nails as she stared at the button.

"There must be a designated paint mixing assistant who has some kind of pager," I replied and right on cue she appeared at the end of the aisle.

"Blast!" muttered my wife, but just as all was lost an elderly gent accosted the assistant with an enquiry and they disappeared.

The excitement was now killing us as the red lights slowly came to life and the £2.19 discount loomed ever closer.

"If she appears again," whispered my wife, "you walk up and distract her and then I'll deal with the paint, she'll never know we're connected."

It was a plan, but as it turned out it was never put into action. The two minutes passed and we danced with unfettered joy. Then we waited another five minutes for an assistant to turn up and when she did the scanner didn't work.

"That's OK, we'll come back tomorrow!" announced my wife.

It was the most fun we've had buying paint, even more exciting than watching it dry.

Counter Management

It was certainly the biggest crowd I had ever seen in a post office and it was a big post office. I joined the overspill at the door and tried to peer in over the shoulders of a leatherclad biker.

"Is it a party?" asked a tiny old lady beside me.

I was about to answer but her tall friend beat me to it.

"Don't think so, everyone looks too grumpy," she said. Then they left looking grumpy.

I couldn't blame them. I had only had a couple of cheques to pay in and a few things to post. In my head I had decided that would take five minutes at the most, but now it looked like it was going to take five minutes just to get into the post office.

A sweaty bloke in his shirtsleeves appeared in the doorway huddle and told us about some industrial action that was taking place.

"Its business as usual though!" he declared his face reddening by the second, "the management team have stepped in and are doing a wonderful job!"

He then handed everyone a little ticket with a number on it, mine was 145. I stopped him before he disappeared back into the throng and asked for an approximate waiting time.

I held up my ticket for him to peer at it and he blew out a long breath as he tried to work it out.

"Half an hour maybe," he said, "40 minutes tops." Then he apologised again and vanished as if he had been hoovered up.

"Well I'm not waiting half an hour!" declared the woman next to me and handed me her ticket.

There were some books waiting to be browsed in a nearby bookshop so I decided I would wait there. This could work out rather well I thought smugly and made a mental note to keep an eye on the time.

Three quarters of an hour and several books later the tiny thing that had been moaning at the back of my mind finally summoned enough grey matter to help it spell out 'Post Office!'

I was there in minutes but I just missed my number because 145 was already on the screen. A woman with a shopping bag full of parcels bustled past me holding up the number like a winning ticket.

The place was still as busy. There were six counters being manned by management staff all in the early stages of a nervous breakdown, the cracks were definitely showing but they were still refusing to crumble.

I was about to leave when I remembered I had another ticket. I drew it slowly from my pocket and it turned out to be half a cinema ticket from the night before. I tried the other pocket and there it was, number 153 and it was about to be called. I don't think I've ever been so excited in a post office.

The bloke behind my counter had obviously gone round the bend a long time ago and probably felt a lot better for it. In the morning I imagine he embraced the forthcoming challenges of the day with a mixture of trepidation and enthusiasm. All of which had now been replaced by a fixed, unearthly grin and a prominent twitch in his left eye.

The four small parcels went through no problem at all, although at one point 'Geoff' - big improvised name badge - did shake one of them a little too vigorously for comfort.

"Value over ten pounds?" he asked twitching.

"Not now," I said flatly.

It was the envelope with the cheques that stumped Geoff. He peered at the orange envelope from all angles, including side on.

"So how does this work?" he asked, his smile flickering on and off.

I explained the concept of banking cheques at a post office and how he had to type in the sort code etc and give me a receipt. I was assuring him how easy it was when he grabbed a passing colleague, but Derek didn't like the envelope either.

Derek was busy sweating so he stopped Susan, she was sniffing a lot and looked as if she was being pulled in several directions at once. She gazed at the envelope for a moment and then at Geoff's screen.

"Oh, I know!" she shouted and everyone looked relieved, Geoff smiled warily at me, but then Susan froze and added, "no, sorry, just ignore me!"

"Have you seen this done before?" asked Derek leaning across the counter.

"Not like this," I replied.

"Why can't you take the cheques to your bank?" asked Susan edgily.

I explained the nearest branch was about 50 miles away in London but this didn't seem to wash. Meanwhile the crowd behind me began to thin, it was possible some of them had died of old age.

Suddenly a smart looking woman bustled up, took my envelope and dealt with it in five seconds.

"How do you spell resignation again?" asked Geoff, glancing round at his colleagues.

"Just type it in, stamp it and remember to get a receipt," I said.

Beating the System

I had two large takeaway black coffees when I left the café in the supermarket. Thirty seconds later when I reached the car I had one. Hardly a mystery of Poirot proportions but baffling nonetheless so for a moment I actually wondered if the assistant had poured two cups in the first place.

I could easily have carried two cups but the girl put them in one of those cardboard double cup holders so off I went rejoicing with my dainty cardboard handbag. I don't think these cardboard carriers inspire much confidence. I'm always waiting for the cups to slip through and crash to the ground, showering me with hot coffee.

In fact it was one of the cups that let me down, or rather, let the coffee down. Thanks to a tiny hole in the bottom of the cup I'd left a dark telltale dribble trail right through the store and out into the carpark. In the supermarket a vigilant assistant was already hot on the trail and it was literally vanishing before me.

There was no problem getting a replacement coffee, but I don't think the assistant grasped the consequences of gravity.

"So what happened to the coffee?" she asked as she held up the cup to inspect the hole.

"What do you mean?" I asked, "It just dribbled out onto the ground."

"Oh that's a shame," she said.

I thought my wife would be back at the car by the time I returned, but there was no sign of her.

"You get the coffees," she had said, "and I'll just get a few things."

The few things had obviously turned into many things. I now needed the loo so I went back into the store.

This is a familiar pattern these days. Once we're more than a mile from home its really just a case of looking for the nearest toilet. If the toilet is in a supermarket even better and if there is a café in the supermarket we're made. So basically we're always just travelling between toilets.

As luck would have it I bumped into my wife as I came out of the loo.

"Oh there you are, where have you been, did you get the coffees?" she asked, "never mind, I've forgotten the mayonnaise, I'll have to go and get it."

There was no time to explain about the coffee fiasco instead I was despatched to checkout number 22 where the shopping was waiting to be packed. Some of the checkouts had charity packers at the end of them. Number 22 had a rather elegant looking lady standing at attention waiting to do the needful.

She looked very efficient but my wife isn't wild about strangers packing our shopping, particularly if they stuff things in upside down or throw a bag of apples on top of the yoghurts.

I've been properly trained in grocery management, its taken about thirty years but I think I'm now almost fully accredited. My wife still double-checks everything I've packed of course, 'just to be on the safe side'.

The check-out girl was about to start so I thanked the charity packing lady and told her I would take over.

"I'll make a donation though," I said smiling. The lady smiled back but I could sense she was slightly put out.

By the look of the items I had obviously been behaving myself because there were some unexpected treats amongst the usual low fat, no taste, frugal offerings. My wife had even thought to buy me my favourite expensive brand of Vodka and it wasn't even my birthday.

Then I remembered my wife was having some of her friends round later in the week so I reckoned most of the shopping was probably for them.

"You can tell I've done this before," I said to the charity lady, who was now standing with her arms folded, keeping a keen eye on my progress.

"You're doing very well," she said, "I'm impressed."

"It's a system my wife and I have," I continued, "better safe than sorry."

"Oh, I couldn't agree more," replied the woman watching me closely.

I packed the lot as neatly as I could and pulled out my debit card but then hesitated when I remembered my wife was due back with the low fat, no taste, no point mayo lite.

"Oh, are you going to pay for it as well?" asked the charity woman, "is that what you meant by making a donation?"

As I stared at her I saw my wife hurrying down behind the checkouts with our tasteless Mayo, in her other hand she had one of those cardboard double-cup holders.

"I've already got the coffee," I said, "twice!"

"What about our shopping?" asked my wife pointing behind me, "you've brought the check-out to a standstill!"

As I surveyed the disgruntled queue and the anxious nail-biting checkout assistant the charity woman leaned over and smartly paid for her shopping.

"Thank you so much," she said to me with a big smile, then turning to my wife added, "he's very good but I think you need a better system."

The Beach

Ideally you want to be teleported to a Buddhist meditation class. One shout of 'beam me up Scotty' and the next thing you know you're arriving at the class in a transcendental pillar of sparkling light.

"That's how you should leave the class," corrected my wife, "people go because they are stressed, they don't de-stress before going to the class. That's like cleaning your house before the cleaner arrives."

Which my wife has actually done.

I do wonder if some people work themselves up into a lather prior to the class just so they can get their money's worth. Personally I'd rather be chauffer driven there like our friend Sylvia, then I wouldn't have to get myself wound up battling through heavy traffic and hunting for a parking space.

Not to mention worrying about the car, which recently seems to have contracted a mechanical form of Chronic Fatigue Syndrome.

"More like chronic depression," suggested my wife on our way to collect Sylvia.

"Hardly surprising considering all the stress and potholes it has to go through," I said, "In fact its probably got post traumatic stress syndrome as well."

"Which doesn't mean to say you've got it," replied my wife.

This of course is one of the basics of Buddhist teachings. When the car's broken it doesn't mean you have to be broken up about it. Our attachment to the car is nothing more than a delusion.

I quite like being attached to my car even if it is a delusion and said as much but my wife had spotted Sylvia standing at the end of her road. This was very thoughtful of her because her road has the sea lying at the other end and it's hard to turn. I was going to say our car doesn't like it but that would be a delusion.

I've collected Sylvia before but I still had the Satnav on. I find the Satnav woman's voice a comfort. True she's led me astray on several occasions, in fact she even advised me to drive off Beachy Head once but mostly she's got me where I am today. In fact I've grown rather attached to her.

"Another delusion!" said my wife when I refused to turn Satnav woman off.

"Don't worry," said Sylvia from the back seat, "I know a great short cut."

This is how people got lost in the old days. I've been taken on many a shortcut and I don't think any of them lived up to my expectations. Sylvia certainly had us going in the right direction, in fact her shortcut turned out to be pretty much as the crow flies. Rather than nip back out onto the main road we would follow the coastline to Bexhill. It was easy, Sylvia told us, all we had to do was keep the sea on our right hand side.

"Is that your right or mine?" asked my wife and confused all three of us.

But apparently Sylvia knew this route like the back of her right hand, she had taken it countless times so there was no need to fret, even though the class started in 20 minutes and we were still 10 miles away.

As the road began to narrow Sylvia told us about her beach hut.

"You'll see it in a few minutes," she said, "its white, actually they're all white, ours is probably more grey though because it could do with a lick of paint."

Suddenly Satnav woman chipped in and told us in no uncertain term to turn the car around.

"What did she say?" asked Sylvia.

"Turn around when possible!" repeated Satnav woman.

"Oh, just ignore her!" said Sylvia, "who does she think she is interrupting people like that. Just carry on!"

So we did until the road turned into a rough track and the car began to lurch from side to side and creak like an old boat.

"The car doesn't like this one bit," I warned.

"It's depressed," explained my wife.

"The sea air should do it good then," said Sylvia.

"Stop the car immediately and turn around!" declared Satnav woman.

Suddenly we broke free of the rough track and could see a line of white beach huts with a grey one right at the end. My wife was enthusing about Sylvia's beach hut but I was more concerned about the pebble beach we were now driving across.

"Isn't that the sea?" I asked, nodding nervously at the waves crashing about twenty yards away.

"Yes, isn't lovely!" said Sylvia, "I think the tide's in."

There was a house up ahead but still no sign of a road. Past the house there was no road at all. A bloke at the door of the house stared at us as we crunched passed.

"So you drive this way all the time?" I asked Sylvia.

"Actually," said Sylvia thoughtfully, "now I come to think of it, we only ever walk this way."

"Stop the car immediately and turn around!" announced Satnav woman.

I wasn't bothered. It was the car that was on the beach, just yards from the incoming tide, not us.

The Double

One of the unexpected side-effects of having our children in our early twenties is that while they grew up we pretty much stayed the same mental age. Consequently we now think we're younger than our sons who are in their thirties.

Mostly we like to think that age is an attitude, a state of mind until of course something else drops off or falls out and then suddenly we see ourselves being fitted for matching Zimmers.

We were in a sprightly frame of mind earlier this week, however when we arrived at the pub where we hold one of our writers' workshops. We had been rained on quite severely and we had managed to make a decent run for it, so the Zimmers could wait.

Dripping wet on our way through to the function room at the back of the pub, Rachel the owner stopped us. She was very excited.

"Oh my God!" she began, "something really weird just happened, about half an hour ago we had your double in."

I stopped her dead in her tracks.

"Not again!" declared my wife.

Rachel swallowed her words and looked alarmed.

"Every full moon my mad twin brother escapes and wreaks havoc through the town," I explained, "eventually villagers with torches and pitchforks track him down and bring him to justice."

Rachel was about to interrupt with her version of my doppleganger story but my wife interjected.

"Roddy's been haunted by a double for years, the length and breadth of the country," said my wife, "some people might say that he has a very common face, but it may be the case that his Dad was just very sociable during his younger years in the navy, if you know what I mean."

This was too much detail for Rachel who was now rattling her head in an effort to regain some sensibility.

"Well, the guy we had in earlier," she began.

"Did he ask for a double?" I interrupted again and my wife and I laughed.

I then regaled Rachel and the barmaid who had just joined us with strange tales of my doppleganger.

How for instance a woman I had never seen before in my life approached me in a Glasgow art gallery and informed me in no uncertain terms that she had stopped speaking to me.

"Sorry to hear that," I said, "especially since we've only just met, I'm sure we would have had a lot to talk about."

The woman had smirked grandly.

"Don't bother calling me because I won't answer the phone," she continued, her tone taking a distinctly dark turn. I laughed nervously and explained how I wasn't the person she thought I was.

"No you're not," she had snarled back, "and that's the problem in a nutshell!"

My wife turned up at this point and asked if everything was OK. The woman stared at her and then back me.

"A little bit of advice," said the woman, "I'd keep a close eye on him if I were you."

"I'll bear that in mind," replied my wife looking baffled.

The woman gave her a forced smile and left. Just as well because I was about to make a run for it.

That was more than twenty years ago. Since then there have been regular strange incidents of a doppleganger nature.

Rachel and the barmaid listened intently as I told them about the bloke dressed completely in black leather who sidled up to me in a park in Amsterdam and said he would meet me with the package just after midnight.

"A few years later in Harrogate two blondes in an open top sports car stopped at the side of the road and told Roddy they'd see him on Sunday at the barbecue!" said my wife.

"How weird!" said Rachel.

"Yes, that's bonkers!" agreed the barmaid.

"I'll say," I replied, "I never know what I've been up to and isn't it odd how I'm ageing at the same rate as my doppelgangers."

Everyone had to think about that one, even me.

Meanwhile Rachel was eager to clear up the identity of her mystery customer.

"To be honest, we actually thought it might be one of your sons," she began, "he really was your double, with grey longish hair and a little white beard."

I thought about that for a moment.

"Neither of our sons has a little white beard," I said shaking my head, "but if he comes in again tell him about our writers' workshop, I could do with some help and two heads are always better than one."

We all laughed, but on the way into the function room my wife grabbed my arm.

"How old does Rachel think we are?" she said through gritted teeth, "we'd have to be in our mid seventies at least to have a son with grey hair and a little white beard!"

Suddenly the years piled up behind me like an avalanche, a great white beard of an avalanche.

"But I'm only 22," I said weakly.

"That's your story," replied my wife under her breath, "and if Rachel asks, I'm your third, much younger wife!"

The Horn of Plenty

At first we assumed the tent was the toilet, so there was a certain amount of excitement tinged with the prospect of relief.

When you're traversing the countryside, bona fide toilets become a sort of primitive reward system and as toilets go this one was rather sweet, more like a miniature big top really.

There was a large crowd outside it, some of whom were seated, which wasn't a good sign.

"Looks like everyone's going before the performance starts," said my wife, "I wonder if there's another toilet?"

"There must be more than one toilet," said Jill anxiously from the backseat.

"Not everyone needs the toilet all the time," I said, but I don't think anyone believed me.

"You don't think that could be the stage?" asked my wife and everyone laughed although I had my suspicions. There was no sign of an actual stage but it looked the sort of tent a travelling theatre company might use if they were on tour with a pocket-sized Shakespeare production.

Pitched in the sweeping lawn of a grand old castle the charming candy striped tent looked very picturesque, if slightly nervous. It was either trembling in the breeze or people inside fighting.

"If it is the stage then I'm not staying," declared my wife. There was silence from the back seat. We had all bought tickets to see the performance in the setting of the grand old castle and the consensus of opinion was that the size of the stage was irrelevant.

Unfortunately my wife has an uncanny gift for correctly judging a film's quality by its opening titles. She can also judge a Shakespeare production by its tent.

In fact it was the stage and we did stay. Mostly I think because we were all at bladder tipping point and the toilet turned out to be some distance away in a tearoom and gift shop surrounded by beautiful ancient gardens.

By fluke I had managed to find a parking space just across the little road from the lawn and the expectant crowd. I think that was the first time I have ever parked my car watched by 500 wine drinking picnic nibbling spectators.

It was a tight space and it was touch and go whether or not we would make it.
"You're just dragging this out for an encore," said Dave from the back.

Probably because there was nothing else to look at hundreds of faces gazed at us as we quickly unpacked the car. I took a bow and was dragged off by my wife in search of the toilets.

On the way back my wife accused me of having delusions of grandeur.

"Let's hope the audience has delusions of grandeur!" I replied as a busty blonde woman in a top hat and tails appeared from the tent banging a big drum, she was followed by a sailor playing an accordion. All we needed was a trombonist I thought and out he came right on cue dressed as a clown.

This I assumed was the opening storm. It must have been because the performers started rolling from side to side and another bloke dressed as a sea captain turned up with a pair of cymbals

My wife shot me her 'told you so' glance and we heaved a despondent sigh. The audience however were captivated probably because there was at last something to watch apart from latecomers parking their cars.

Our companions were also thrilled even though we had to sit right at the back on a grassy knoll, a spot reserved for people with Marvel comic hearing.

My wife and I spent twenty minutes lip reading before we gave up, but our friends were riveted, even Dave who admitted the last live theatre he had seen was a wrestling match.

"Really Dave?" I asked and a couple in front turned sharply round and told us to be quiet.

But Dave was transfixed, no doubt by the busty blonde with the drum, but I may have been wrong.

We took the hint and set off for what we reckoned would be a two-hour walk.

"I'll just walk home," said my wife flatly.

At least it wasn't raining, in fact the sun was struggling to come out, either that or the theatre company had a really big light with them. It was however, starting to get nippy so we went to the car for our jackets and our comfort brolly.

As usual, I had forgotten about my car alarm problem. If I don't put the key immediately in the ignition the car horn starts blaring and it did with a vengeance, but this time it wouldn't stop. While 300 people stared at us and the performance came to an abrupt halt I fiddled with the key until eventually I gave up.

Our friends didn't believe us of course even though the horn was blaring all the way out of the castle grounds to the main road where for some reason it stopped.

"What a relief!" said my wife, "right, nearest toilet Jeeves!"

Posie

I have an informal but highly effective bedtime routine, which basically involves falling asleep while pretending to read a book. Because I'm lying on my side at the time I have to choose the book very carefully. If it's too heavy and it hits me on the face as I drop off it can be counter productive, so lightweight is always best and obviously nothing too interesting.

One night last week while lying in bed I could sense my book slipping through someone else's fingers when suddenly a strange smell crept into the story.

Up until then it had been a background element but now it was all about the smell. It was ancient, mildly exotic and curiously compelling, something that had risen perhaps from the dry, dusty floor of a Pharaoh's tomb.

More to the point, I was awake thinking about the smell. Turning round I spotted the culprit on the dressing table, a small vase of flowers that appeared to be past their smell by date.

Dragging myself out of bed like a lead weight I escorted the vase quietly through to my wife's studio. Strange smell dealt with, studio door firmly shut and back in bed I tried not to focus too much on my book, but the smell had followed me. In fact it was bigger and stranger than ever. So I rolled out of bed again and threw the window wide just as my wife came into the room.

"Too warm for you?" she asked.

"Too smelly!" I replied.

My wife frowned and sniffed.

"All I can smell is that lovely new perfume you bought me," she said.

"That's it?" I asked, my face screwed up, "that's the horrible smell that woke me up?"

After a painful visit to the dentist the previous week I had decided my wife needed to get her smile back, so I suggested buying the new perfume she had talked about. It was sitting on the dressing table looking very innocent but one quick sniff and the back of my head promptly blew off decorating the wall behind me. That was the one.

"Isn't it fab?" said my wife as she climbed into bed, "I love it, I might get the room spray and the body lotion. It's quite dreamy, in fact it's meant to help you sleep, that's why I sprayed some on our pillows"

Squinting blearily at the bottle I saw the words 'Night Garden' and thought 'that's exactly where it's heading, along with the pillowcases!'

"What the hell's in it, or should I say, which part of hell is in it?" I asked wafting the air with a T-shirt.

My wife laughed and suggested I was being weird, apparently she loved it so much the perfume would now be her signature scent.

"I've still got the receipt," I said hopefully.

I found it hard to define this perfume. Over the next few days it came at me from many different directions, most of which originated underground. Ambiguity was it's key strength, for a few seconds it could be friendly, but mostly it was just peculiar and disturbing.

My wife however, seemed to be bewitched by it and I just had what they call in the business an undeveloped nose. So for a fresh set of creative opinions I gave the smell to my writers' workshop as an exercise and asked them to write about it.

"What a great idea!" enthused my wife as she picked up her scented strip of paper.

At first the writers had stared in a state of bemusement at the blank strips of paper, but then a latecomer arrived with a screwed up face.

"Blimey!" said Bill, "I'm having a bad smell day!"

A collective lightbulb switched on and everyone started sniffing their strips of paper. Most recoiled in alarm, someone started coughing, another had to blow their nose, then we had to open a window.

My wife now had the bravest fixed smile I've ever seen.

"It's not that bad," I said and everyone laughed.

"What skip did you find this in?" demanded Alan.

"Is it toxic?" asked Wendy holding it at an arm's length.

"Actually I quite like it," said my wife meekly, "in an odd sort of way."

The results were extraordinary to say the least, consistently dark, comic and strange.

Smell is our most evocative sense. It's linked to the Limbic System, the part of the brain associated with memory, but I don't think any of the writers conjured up anything that had actually happened to them. Apart from Jenny who wrote about how she had fallen into a sewer when she was a little girl and had to be rescued by a sniffer dog who later had to be revived.

"What is it anyway?" asked Sue as I handed over the bottle at the end of the exercise.

"Posie of Night Garden," she announced and then turning the bottle upside read the acronym that was printed in tiny letters underneath, "PONG!"

"Where on earth did you get that?" asked my wife, "the perfume joke factory?"

Case closed.

Shopping with Intent

There is something very liberating about driving the wrong way across an empty carpark. Contrary to its 'Open 24 Hours' promise the supermarket was disappointingly closed and it was only 11.30pm. After crossing the carpark as the crow flies I drove right up to the door to check. The lights were on but apparently there was no one in.

"I think they're just hiding until we go away," said my wife, peering into the store, "I'm sure I saw someone move just now."

There had been a mass exodus from the carpark as we arrived. A stream of boy and girl racers had roared past us in their little customised cars, like a caravan of mobile discos, their various beats at windscreen splitting volume.

"I always thought mobile discos were disappointing," reflected my wife, "I mean it's not as if you could actually dance in them."

Suddenly as I drove away from the supermarket entrance one of the mobile discos loomed into my rear view mirror.

"I wonder where they came from?" said my wife looking over her shoulder.

I was thinking the same thing because the car had materialised out of thin air.
Considering they had a huge empty carpark to choose from it seemed odd that they should roar up directly behind us, particularly since we were driving diagonally across the parking spaces.

Undaunted I continued our unorthodox route, taking in the disabled and mother and child spaces, a loading bay and the bus stop. The little black car followed in hot pursuit, so I began zig-zagging my way to the exit.

"They're definitely following us," said my wife checking in her wing mirror.

I started widening my zig-zag and then turned back towards the store entrance thinking that our pal would have tired of his little game and drive straight on out of the carpark, but they didn't.

I had to admit it was more than a little threatening and quite unnerving, particularly since the car's windows were so dark and I couldn't see the driver, if indeed there was a driver at all. For all we knew it could have been a remote controlled car.

"Maybe it's someone we know," suggested my wife hopefully.

I reckoned it was time to leave so turning round I put my foot down. The little black car stuck to us like an ominous shadow.

"This is getting scary!" said my wife.

I was about to put my foot down even more when I changed my mind and slowed down to a crawl. It was stupid but I had risen to the challenge and wasn't about to be chased out of an empty supermarket carpark by a bunch of kids, even if it was pitch dark and there wasn't a living soul in sight.

I'd seen the slowing down tactic in a Tom cruise film. While he was being chased by the police, he turned down a busy street and slowed down his car enough to step out of the moving vehicle and then quickly blend into a nearby bus queue. The car meanwhile carried on without him, crashing into an oncoming police car and creating a chaotic diversion while Tom boarded a bus.

I explained all this to my wife but she wasn't impressed.

"The black car's still there," she said, and I don't see a bus queue we can blend into or a police car for that matter."

She was right about the bus queue, but not about the police car. The blue lights had probably been flashing in the black car's grill for some time before I noticed them.

"Thank goodness for that!" said my wife, "it's the police."

I duly stopped and the black car pulled up alongside.

"It's not an offence to drive around an empty carpark like a weirdo is it?" asked my wife.

I wasn't sure, but I had a feeling I was about to find out.

A young jolly policeman stepped out of the black car, in the dark he seemed to be wearing some kind of partial uniform, maybe it was the casual unmarked look.

"Good evening folks," he said brightly.

"Boy are we pleased to see you!" replied my wife, "we thought we were being followed."

"Oh, who by?" asked the policeman looking round the carpark.

"You as it happens," I said, and we all laughed, but not really.

"Sorry if I caused any concern," said the policeman, "have you had any alcohol this evening?"

I was slightly taken aback by this and shook my head dumbly.

"He often drives around empty carparks at night like a twit!" interjected my wife.

The policeman was now close enough to appreciate I hadn't been drinking. I told him we had assumed the 24 hour supermarket would be open but that it seemed to be closed for some reason.

"Maybe it's being robbed while all the staff are held hostage," I added, "could be your big break!"

Again we all laughed, but not really.

"He was very good looking," said my wife, as she fastened her seatbelt.

"Well that's the main thing," I replied.

Skylight-Walker

It seemed impossible but it sounded as if someone was on our roof.

"But there can't be someone on the roof," I said as we stared up at the skylight directly above my wife's easel.

Suddenly I could see a vague form clumping diagonally across the semi-opaque skylight and then onto the roof.

"Oh my God, there's someone on the roof!" I exclaimed.

"I know!" shouted my wife, "I told you that half an hour ago."

Disturbed and distracted by the continuous noise above her as she tried to focus on her painting my wife had come to me for a second opinion and I had fobbed her off with tales of strong winds and broken branches.

It was possible one of the branches had got stuck on the roof and was flapping around. There was some history of broken branch activity on our roof.

"That was in our last house, 800 miles away and there's not a breath of wind outside!" said my wife glancing out of the window.

She was right. The wind had dropped completely, so I went through to her studio to investigate and at first heard nothing. But now we had a rooftop interloper staggering around above us.

"We're not expecting anyone are we?" asked my wife.

"If we were, I think they'd come to the front door wouldn't they?" I replied, "very few people would go straight to the roof."

"I'll bet it's Alan checking up on things," said my wife staring up at the skylight.

It could have been Alan, I thought, back for one his random sorties. Alan had made a remarkably thorough job of finding and repairing the mysterious and highly annoying leak in our roof. It was meant to be a two-day job but Alan had been back and forth for weeks until he was satisfied the leak was well and truly fixed.

I decided to phone Alan to find out if he was on our roof but as it turned out he was laid up with a septic hand and couldn't work. "I wish was up on your roof mate," he said.

"Alan's got a septic hand," I told my wife, "he has to get an emergency operation."

"Oh that's terrible," said my wife, "well, he definitely shouldn't be on our roof."

Suddenly the clumping noise above us stopped and my wife grabbed my arm.

"I hope he hasn't fallen off," she said, then shouted, "Alan, Alan are you all right?"

I set the record straight about Alan and we lived with the mystery of the phantom roof walker for a couple of days. On Monday he was back with a couple of pals.

My wife's studio roof is almost flat and unless you have a scaffold tower or a fire engine ladder you can only access it through a hatch in the pitched section of the roof and you'd have to get inside the house and the loft for that.

"This is getting creepy," said my wife as we stared up at the skylight walkers, "Oi!" she shouted at the top of her voice making me jump a foot in the air, "get off our roof!"

Then she hurried off and returned a few seconds later with a long handled brush and began poking the skylight. It made no difference. There was nothing else for it, I would have to go through the hatch, or at least my head would.

Ten minutes later after doing a highly uncomfortable commando crawl along the tight loft space I reached the hatch and battled with it until it fell in on top of me. This I suspect is a design fault but it's better than the hatch falling out onto the roof, because then I would be forced to squeeze through the 18 inch wide opening and retrieve it.

Crawling forward I stuck my head out but the skylight was clear and there was nothing untoward on the roof, apart from my head.

"What was it like up there?" asked my wife.

"Lonely," I replied.

I reckoned it was birds, possibly very large birds.

"Wearing big boots?" said my wife.

"How about aliens wearing big boots?" I asked.

The following day we decided it was too warm to eat lunch inside. My wife made my favourite toasted sandwich - a giant cheese, ham and mustard on wholemeal bread. I was rubbing my hands as I sized it up.

"You'd better eat that before it goes cold," said my wife sitting down at the table with her own lunch.

I was perusing the toastie, thinking it might be a good idea to cut it in half when something white flashed in front of me. Apart from a light draught that's pretty much all I can report. In the blink of an eye I was sitting empty handed, sandwichless and speechless.

Meanwhile a huge gull stared down at us from the flat roof, my entire toasted sandwich in its beak. Turning grandly it began slowly clumping its way towards my wife's studio skylight.

"I wonder if he wants a drink with that?" I said.

Poleaxed

First there was a dull clang and then for a moment I thought I could hear the sound of distant laughing, like a cinema or theatre audience but very far away. My wife maintains that no one laughed but I have my doubts because I would have laughed.

Walking down a quiet street on our way into the town centre a friend turned up in his car quite by chance and parked beside us. We gave Tom a double take and he followed suit. He put his window down and said he was just about to call me.

"How strange!" we chorused.

Tom was picking up a friend and as it turned out we just happened to be standing outside their house wondering why the street was so empty.

"New parking restrictions," said Tom, "it's made quite a difference."

It sure had. Normally cars and vans would have been nose to tail the length of the street, but now you could actually see the road and the gutters, which were in need of repair. Tom and I discussed this for a few minutes until my wife decided our conversation was so fascinating she wouldn't be able to handle much more.

We laughed and bade Tom a fond farewell. I must have been waving back at Tom as I headed off down the pavement, I'm not sure because the world stopped shortly afterwards and the laughing started.

The pavement is probably about six feet wide and the metal pole I'd walked into is five inches across so in theory, that gave me approximately five and a half feet of space to play with. Or as my wife put it enough room to drive a small car through.

In my defence the pole holding the parking restriction notice wasn't there last week and it's a pale silvery colour so on a dull day it doesn't exactly jump out at you. Although this one certainly seemed to.

My wife said later that it wasn't so much the impact that alarmed her which was impressive, it was the fact that I didn't bounce off. When Mr Bean walks into an immovable object he bounces back, possibly even falls over for maximum comedy effect. But when I walked face first straight into the pole I stuck to it. There was also no noise, no sound effect.

"These are normally added on later," I said, but my wife wasn't convinced.

"It was actually quite creepy," she replied, "one minute you were laughing away and the next you were stuck to a pole, silently stuck to a pole."

I think this was probably because I had knocked myself out for a few seconds.

"To be honest, we wondered what was going on." Continued my wife.

Apart from me being poleaxed there really wasn't much else happening. After the impact my face froze to the pole until eventually I began to slither down it, then I came to myself and heard that distant laughing.

My wife caught hold of me and for a few seconds I was reluctant to pull my face off the metal in case half of it stuck. In fact I think I was very lucky. Apart from a four inch wide red stripe right down my face there didn't seem to be much visible damage.

To my amazement there was also no pain, just a curious throbbing numbness about four inches wide, which slightly limited my ability to speak properly or change the facial expression I had when I hit the pole.

My wife said I looked permanently dismayed, so in fact there was very little change.

Once I'd reassured everyone I was still in one piece we set off again, but I think a vital part of me was still attached to that pole. Twenty minutes later I was examining my new face in the mirror of a department store toilet. I thought I looked like the ugly half of Beauty and the Beast. My nose and forehead had mutated into one insistent red lump and my chin was at least twice the size.

My wife had been nagging me to tie my shoelaces in case I performed another silent movie stunt so after sorting them out I stood up directly under the hand dryer. This time I bounced back then sat down on the floor in time to catch the dryer's plastic cover as it fell into my lap. Again I could have sworn I heard distant laughter.

The girl at Customer Services looked very concerned when I told her how I had head butted the hand dryer in the Gents. I could see her trying to picture it for a moment then she asked if I required first aid.

"Your face does look a bit sore," she added.

"I beg your pardon!" I bridled, "there's nothing wrong with my face, I hit the dryer with my head."

The girl blushed and smiled, but apparently I wasn't thinking straight.

"We could have sued them for millions," said my wife, "instead you went for the laugh."

Actually I went to Casualty for an X-ray.

Phone Farce

People talk about turning into their parents as they grow older, but I think I'm turning into my father-in-law. In coffee shops for instance he would have raised an eyebrow at the list of exotic beverages on offer and then asked for a cup of coffee.

In the coffee shop on Sunday afternoon, the girl behind the counter smiled at me for a moment before helpfully running through the mind-boggling options.

I politely considered them for a moment.

"Just an ordinary cup of coffee please," I replied.

She was probably used to this type of thing. I can't be the only person who goes into coffee shops and asks for an ordinary cup of coffee without cinnamon, foam, chocolate, marshmallows, sprinkles or oat milk and who doesn't want to be bothered about the size of the cup, or whether the milk should be hot, cold or indifferent.

There was one free table covered with Sunday papers, which was a bonus. I could read them while I waited for my wife and friends to turn up.

After ten minutes I called my wife but unsurprisingly her phone was off. In fact it was probably sitting in a drawer in our house. There was one day a couple of years ago when my wife actually answered her phone so there's always a slim chance she might accidentally do it again.

A minute or so later to my amazement my phone started vibrating on the table in front of me. This explained why I hadn't heard from anyone, I'd obviously inadvertently put my phone on mute.

There was no caller ID and normally I'm reluctant to answer calls like that because it normally turns out to be a robotic voice trying to sell me something.

The caller turned out to be an elderly woman who wanted to speak to Julie. I explained that I wasn't Julie but she wasn't convinced.

"Sorry, but you must have the wrong number," I added.

There was a long silence.

"Hello, I'm afraid you have the wrong number," I repeated and was about to hang up when I heard the woman telling someone beside her that I wasn't Julie.

"Are you sure?" she said, "I'm her aunt Doreen."

"I'm really not Julie," I replied and said goodbye, then turned the volume up on the ringer.

Just as I laid the phone back on the table it rang. It was the woman again wanting to speak to Julie.

"Same wrong number again I'm afraid." I said.

"Really, oh dear, are you absolutely sure?" asked the woman, 'I'm looking for Julie Robertson, it's her aunt Doreen, are you the new boyfriend?"

I explained to aunt Doreen how I had never heard of Julie Robertson, but if she turned up I would tell her to call her. Doreen liked the sound of this and thanked me.

Two minutes later Julie's friend Susan was on the phone looking for her.

"I've just had her auntie Doreen on," I said, "there must be something wrong with Julie's number because it looks like her calls are being forwarded to my phone."

I wasn't even sure this was possible, but Susan laughed. She called back ten seconds later just to make sure.

"Hello Metropolitan Police, how may I help you?" I said with some authority.

This flummoxed her and she was about to hang up when I came clean.

"Still not Julie though," I added.

By this time I was beginning to wonder why Julie was so popular. No one had called or texted me all day.

The next caller was Julie's father. He was quite dad-like and official sounding. He gave me the aunt Doreen background story and I added her friend Susan for good measure. This was going well at first but then Julie's dad got down to business.

"Well, as you can imagine I'm very keen to know why you have my daughter's phone," he said, "particularly if she's not with you. Did you find it somewhere, it's an i-phone I believe and she'll be lost without it."

I could see his point. If a stranger was answering my daughter's i-phone I'd want to know what was going on.

"I'm afraid this is my phone," I said and then gave him my theory about the calls being forwarded or crossed satellite dish signals or something, but he wasn't impressed.

"So it's your phone now is it?" he said darkly, "don't you think you should hand it in to the police?"

Suddenly it crossed my mind that I was the victim of a practical joke. I stood up hoping to see either my wife or one of our friends in the coffee shop stifling laughter but all the customers were busy chatting or reading papers.

Just then a harassed young woman appeared and asked if I'd seen her i-phone.

"I've been looking for it everywhere!" she said scanning the table.

I felt for mine in my coat pocket and found it.

"It's for you Julie," I said holding out her phone, "it's your dad, he sounds nice."

Laughing nervously she took the phone while I went off to hide in the Gents.

Sleepless

It's a slippery customer sleep. Just when you think you've got it squarely in your sights it evaporates as if it never existed. In fact sometimes you begin to wonder if it ever did.

The strange thing is when you need to stay awake and pretend you're seriously fascinated by some mind-numbingly boring conversation up pops sleep with a rescue plan and you have to fight it off.

Then of course it takes a sulk because the next time you're lying awake at night for no good reason, you can't even imagine what it's like to be asleep.

The trouble is I don't think I've properly recovered from the clocks going forward a few months ago. I often get ambushed early evening and carted off to nap land when I should be doing all manner of creative things. Twenty minutes later I wake up looking like Rip Van Winkle and wonder why I'm dribbling out of the corner of my mouth.

Then my wife says, "you won't sleep tonight you know," and I scoff at such an unlikely outcome, thinking to myself, 'that will be right'.

Up until a few nights ago I was getting away with it, but then I made another big deposit at the bank of naps and the whole lot finally caught up with me.

Once in bed I settle down for my usual ten-minute read during which my book normally begins to melt before my eyes in a most satisfying manner. This I always take to be the secret doors to the kingdom of Morpheus opening. I slip inside and then three hours later I nip back out again for a comfort break, while hoping that I'll get back in again.

The other night my book had actually fallen out of my hands without me realising it, so for a few minutes I'd been in free improvisation mode with my eyes shut.

Obviously I was already half way towards sinking into a deep sleep but for some reason the usual process began to reverse itself. Instead of falling asleep I steadily woke up until after about half an hour I was raring to go.

Baffled I tried not to think about it and ended up thinking about it in great depth. The trouble is, you can't lie back, relax and say to yourself, 'right, I'm going to fall asleep'. Nonsense of a mildly diverting and often troublesome nature keeps getting in the way. As a distraction I began playing the piano in my head, thinking I could probably come up with a lullaby that would send me to sleep. Actually I came up with a rather interesting tune around which I began to construct a lovely set of variations.

I could have been in for a few hours of amazing virtual music making but instead I decided to try a method of self-hypnosis I once read about. I didn't read the whole book - it was in a bookshop, and I wasn't that keen on the idea of permanently hypnotising myself, but the section on curing insomnia sounded handy.

The trick was to lie on your back with your palms flat on the bed, then chant the word 'the' to yourself while trying to imagine a large eyelid in front of you that was so heavy you just couldn't lift it no matter how hard you tried. I was in the middle of this routine when my wife's disembodied voice broke the spell and I jumped about a foot off the bed when she spoke literally out of the dark blue.

"That's a great name for a driving school," she said, laughing to herself.

My wife doesn't like sleeping, she thinks it's a waste of time, a necessary evil, like Mono-unsaturated fats – handy in small doses but there's no need to make a meal of it.

"Go on then, let's hear it," I said into the dark and my wife started laughing again but then there was silence so I ended up making up my own.

My first and rather feeble attempt was 'The L-Passo School of Motoring' then I remembered a driving school in Glasgow, called 'Crashcourses'. That made me smile. Then the one in Aberdeen called, 'Accidont' and the one in Cambridgeshire called 'Steer We Go."

Laughter might be the best medicine but it's not the first thing that springs to mind when you can't get to sleep.

However, shortly afterwards I was ambushed by a surprise sleep attack and sucked away on a strangely vibrant dream about a never-ending driving lesson on an enormous roundabout. The instructor was a piano playing, chanting lunatic, who for some reason kept falling asleep.

The Stash

I've often fantasised about finding a massive stash of cash and then battling courageously with the moral dilemma of whether to hand it in to the police or keep it and go slowly crazy worrying about the money's nasty owner tracking us down.

I think it probably depends on the amount of cash. If it was millions and we kept it my wife and I would have to go into luxuriously appointed hiding, change our identities, undergo plastic surgery, obviously an improvement for me, then we'd have a strange but exciting, tension filled new life until one hot night in the Caribbean a menacing shadow would slip silently into our fabulous beach house.

"Probably just give it to charity," I said out loud, surprising myself as much as my wife.

She was squinting at me from the other side of our recycling bin.

"Keep it down Sundance," she whispered, "I said I've found some money."

"I know," I replied, "I was already fantasising about being murdered in my sleep by its owner, in the Caribbean."

"The Caribbean sounds nice," said my wife, "what happens to me?"

"I don't know, it was too scary so I gave the money away to the PDSA. How much have you found?" I asked, "if its millions we're in big trouble."

"I'm not sure," she replied glancing nervously up and down the garden while holding the bin firmly shut.

A neighbour passed with her dog and we both smiled and managed to look very suspicious loitering around our own bins.

"Everything OK?" she asked, her dog barking in chorus.

"Yes fine thanks," I shouted, "just checking up on our bins."

This wasn't too far from the truth. A few months ago our recycling bin was stolen in broad daylight, stuffed to the brim with recyclable stuff. Now some cash had appeared in the new bin. I could already see some kind of pattern forming.

The neighbour was still staring at us.

"You can come and check mine if you like," she said knowingly, "its full of fascinating stuff."

We laughed nervously and waved her off.

"She meant her bins right?" I asked.

"Never mind that, let's see how much we've won," said my wife slowly lifting the bin lid, her eyes widening. I could barely handle the suspense and to be honest I was slightly relieved when my wife produced a single ten-pound note.

"Thank goodness for that!" I said.

My wife was baffled. Apparently when she first spotted the tenner it looked like it was sitting on a big pile of tenners. Undeterred she scrambled down into the mini-mountain of soggy cardboard, smelly cans and plastic containers, but all she could produce was a pile of receipts and old money-off vouchers that were just pretending to be tenners.

"Actually I think its mine," I said, "I must have thrown it out with those receipts when I cleaned out the car yesterday."

"Please don't tell me you're going to start recycling money, I don't think that you're that daft yet," said my wife, looking through the receipts, "anyway there's a receipt here from Domino's pizza that's not yours either."

"No, probably not," I lied.

Obviously my wife had forgotten about the substantial cheque I flushed down the toilet just a few days earlier.

I'd only had it for thirty seconds, that must be a record. I'd folded it and put it in the top pocket of my shirt before going to the loo. Just before I hit the flush I dropped my phone, but I managed to catch it before it fell into the bowl. That's when the cheque must have slipped out from my pocket.

I hunted for hours for that cheque until I was back in the toilet where the flushing scenario occurred to me. I re-enacted the whole thing with a folded piece of paper and bingo! down it went.

I was going to remind my wife about the vanishing cheque but for some reason she had decided the tenner belonged to our neighbour Grant.

"I wouldn't want to spend it accidentally," she said as she climbed the stairs to Grant's flat.

Unfortunately Grant was in. At first I think he was quite pleased to see my wife.

"Hi Grant, sorry to bother you," began my wife, "I just wondered if you might have accidentally thrown something into the recycling bin?"

Grant considered this for a moment and then asked my wife to repeat the question, which she did word for word.

"I thought that was what you said, is it a trick question?" asked Grant.

"No," laughed my wife, "I found some money in the recycling bin and I wondered if it was yours, Roddy says its his, but I don't think he's stupid enough to throw money away, not that I'm suggesting you are either of course by any means, but anyway have you lost some money?"

"I don't think so," said Grant, "how much is it?" he added hedging his bets.

My wife held up the tenner for inspection.

Grant stroked his beard, "to be honest its hard to say, they all look the same to me. Tell you what, lets split it."

"That's very generous of you," replied my wife smiling broadly, "why don't I buy something nice for you worth five pounds."

"Perfect!" said Grant.

I think they actually shook on it. Which is just the kind of thing that puts you off recycling.

Armchair Theatre

I've discovered a secret path inside our house. It's basically an escape route for stuff we've deemed misfits. Before working its way out to the nearest charity shop or recycling centre the path starts in the living room and then continues to the kitchen dining room before heading up to the loft.

I think there's some sort of cul-de-sac up there because the path continues back out of the loft, into our bedroom, then on to the hallway. There's a brief diversion into my wife's studio and then it's back up into the loft.

If it ended there the loft floor would have collapsed on us with the weight of unwanted stuff a long time ago. Fortunately there's also a handy shortcut straight into the bike shed where the misfits moulder before making the final slog to oblivion.

Unlike all the other stuff that didn't quite hit the mark the old upholstered armchair we've lugged from house to house over the past 15 years never made it up into the loft. It moved along the secret path from room to room then just lingered, basically because it wouldn't fit through the loft hatch.

Over the years a long list of people have eyed it up and were often begged to take it home with them, but for one reason or another the armchair stayed put until it ended up in the bike shed. Meanwhile our bikes hovered anxiously in the hallway.

Or at least they did until last weekend when I had a purge and filled the car to bursting point. I was convinced the chair wouldn't make it but sheer determination persuaded it into the back of the car along with half a dozen boxes of books and DVDs.

My wife came along to supervise but once outside the charity shop she decided she couldn't part with the armchair.

"Just give it one more chance," she pleaded.

"Sweetheart," I said, holding her hands, "it's time to set the chair free, it needs to make its own way in the world, it'll be fine, you'll see."

Apparently I'm heartless so my wife went off to Marks & Spencer in search of sanity and solace.

The books and DVDs went down well in the charity shop and the manageress actually clapped her hands when I mentioned the armchair.

"Bring it in!" she said enthusiastically, "it sounds lovely!"

This was the sort of response I was hoping for. Now I could tell my wife the armchair went to a good home, albeit a temporary one, but at least it was appreciated.

Getting it out of the car however, was even harder than it had been getting it in. Somehow it had made friends with the back seat and was now perfectly at home.

A male assistant called Malcolm came out to help, but he was beaten quite early on after one tug at the chair when his back made a strange noise. Another assistant called Elspeth was next on the scene.

Elspeth apparently had some experience extracting awkward pieces of furniture from cars and immediately took control of the operation. After a few minutes things were looking up when Elspeth suddenly stepped back from the fray for a breather.

"How on earth did you get it in there?" she demanded, "or did you build the car around it?"

A traffic warden appeared and surveyed the problem. He had to remove his cap for a think.

"Why don't you just keep it in the back of the car?" he suggested then said he would be back in ten minutes. That was the tipping point. Opening the other passenger door I launched myself at the chair and shoved it until it start rolling out and Malcolm caught it.

Once inside the shop the armchair was a big hit. Everyone took turns sitting in it until the Manageress leapt up suddenly and declared that it would have to go.

"What did it do?" I asked, "I'm really sorry I thought it was house trained."

"It's not fire retardant." She Intoned making her staff members step cautiously back.

"Really?" I asked, already picturing myself forcing the chair back into the car before driving ten miles to the nearest recycling centre.

"Would go up like a torch." Said Malcolm with great seriousness.

"Be good for bonfire night though!" Chimed Elspeth.

"Good idea!" declared the Manageress, "Save it for November the fifth and put the Guy on it."

"Brilliant!" shouted Malcolm, who wanted to try the armchair once more before it went up in smoke.

"So that's it?" I asked, "we can't spray it with something?"

"Like what?" asked Malcolm, "Petrol?"

At least they helped me force it back into the car. Half way in I could have sworn I heard the car moan.

My wife turned up a few yards in front of the traffic warden.

"You kept it, hooray!" She shouted, her face brightening with joy.

"I see you took my advice Sir," said the traffic warden leaning into the open car window.

"What a lovely man," said my wife and blew him a kiss.

All done, until the next volume...

35494121R00214

Printed in Poland
by Amazon Fulfillment
Poland Sp. z o.o., Wrocław